KNACK™
MAKE IT EASY

FISHING
FOR EVERYONE

FISHING
FOR EVERYONE
The Complete Illustrated Guide

SCOTT BOWEN

PRINCIPAL PHOTOGRAPHY BY DAVID E. DIRKS

KNACK™
MAKE IT EASY

Guilford, Connecticut
An imprint of The Globe Pequot Press

Copyright © 2009 by Morris Book Publishing, LLC

Editor-in-Chief: Maureen Graney
Editor: Katie Benoit
Cover Design: Paul Beatrice, Bret Kerr
Text Design: Paul Beatrice
Layout: Kevin Mak
Cover photos (left to right) by Allison Achauer/shutterstock, © Dewitt | Dreamstime.com, David Dirks, David Dirks

All interior photos by David Dirks with the exception of credits on page 239.

Library of Congress Cataloging-in-Publication Data

Bowen, Scott.
  Fishing for everyone : a complete illustrated guide / Scott Bowen ; principal photography by David E. Dirks.
    p. cm.
  Includes bibliographical references and index.
  ISBN 978-1-59921-399-6 (alk. paper)
  1. Fishing--Miscellanea. I. Title.
  SH441.B624 2009
  799.1--dc22

                    2008042723

The following manufacturers/names appearing in *Knack Fishing for Everyone* are trademarks:
Mylar®, Styrofoam®, Teflon®

Printed in China

10 9 8 7 6 5 4 3 2

Acknowledgments

My thanks to Jerry Gibbs, Phil Monahan, and Dave Klaust-meyer for their help along the way.

CONTENTS

INTRODUCTION
Starting with Rod and Reel

Here's a step-by-step guide for becoming a successful angler

People with a good deal of fishing experience will be the first to tell you that casting a line is not always easy—although they often make it look easy—but it is always fun. Fishing with rod and line is a very old sport—the technique goes back to various methods developed in ancient Rome, China, Egypt, and Greece—that offers multiple pleasures: wonderful natural environments in which to go fishing; the camaraderie of fishing friends and fellow anglers; the beauty, vigor, and wiliness of many different species of gamefish; and the lasting satisfaction of a successful day on the water.

This book is designed to guide you, step by step, in becoming a capable and knowledgeable angler—one who, with a set of basic skills, starts catching fish and continues to do so, refining your techniques as you go. The term "angling" derives from the development of the sport in England: The V-shape made by the rod and the cast line led to rods sometimes being referred to as "angles," and their use as "angling." Since the early twentieth century, basic angling concepts and the hardware used for fishing have been largely consistent: rods fling line and lures, reels wrap line around spools, and lures have to imitate the appearance and motion of the prey of gamefish. The materials that go into the making of tackle are what have evolved the most, as the science behind fishing devises newer and better ways to design and manufacture rods, reels, lines, and lures.

This book is the *how* about the *what*—how to identify the right stuff and put it to use, whether you want to fish for farm-pond sunfish and catfish, or trout in rivers, or off the beach for whatever fish are cruising by in the surf. There's also a good deal of information in here about minimizing trouble and maximizing enjoyment, such as how to wade properly, how to take great photos of your catch, and how to prepare fish for the table.

For freshwater fishing, the main choices discussed in this book are bait-casting tackle, spinning and spin-casting tackle, and fly-casting tackle. For saltwater fishing, the book addresses mainly surf-casting tackle and conventional tackle for inshore fishing. Innovative anglers can easily break strict rules about fishing tackle—the minute someone says, "You can't catch a big salmon with a bait-casting outfit," someone will do just so—but the type of lure or bait that you want to use, as determined by the species of fish you're chasing, influences your choice of tackle, and sometimes a particular kind of rod and reel is just right for a certain lure or bait. You have to ask: How heavy is the lure or bait rig I want to cast? How deep am I fishing it, in what kind of water? How big might the fish be? How far might I have to cast this lure, or bait?

For instance, largemouth bass often readily take a lure called a "crankbait"—an oblong plastic lure that mimics a baitfish. These lures tend to cause a good bit of resistance against the water when retrieved, and bigger largemouth are hard-fighting fish, so many anglers will choose a bait-casting reel because of its cranking power that helps bat-

tle bass, and pair this with a bait-casting rod stiff enough for use with crankbaits

In another situation, an angler casting bait to medium-sized catfish in a large pond could go with a number of choices: spin-casting, spinning, or bait-casting tackle, as long as the rod has sufficient stiffness to handle the weight of any sinkers, and the reel is powerful enough to haul in any fish you might hook.

A quality fishing reel these days is quite a good piece of equipment, especially when compared to the so-so reels American anglers had to use back in the mid-twentieth century, before the great innovations in tackle technology that occurred in the 1970s and 80s. In general, you can get away with using a slightly smaller reel than you might think for most freshwater applications, as long as it holds enough line. Using too big a reel just adds unnecessary weight.

Knowing how to set up and organize your tackle is central to success and enjoyment, and a number of chapters and spreads discuss how to do this the right way, because the alternatives—broken rods, clumps of tangled lures, and tackle boxes that offer little but mysteries—can often end your willing participation. What you spend on tackle depends, of course, on every angler's personal budget. Some brand-new high-quality tackle can be wildly expensive; its saving graces are usually its superior performance and ability to out-last everything else. Before buying new gear retail, scour various Internet outlets for quality used tackle and equipment, and also look for close-out sales from retailers that sell online. Various nationwide fishing shows provide opportunities to buy cut-price tackle and gear. And you never know what you might find at a flea market or garage sale.

As for the quarry themselves, most of the fish discussed in this book are classified as "gamefish," a term used loosely, but which usually means those fish that can be pursued with legal sporting methods by individual anglers. Not all gamefish are good eating, while others, such as salmon, comprise major commercial fisheries. Having official gamefish status protects some species in a number of states, while some states do not classify catfish and various panfish species as gamefish, but anglers pursue those fish just the same. In some jurisdictions or states, the lawful status of a gamefish often helps to promote the conservation of sport fisheries; a 2007 Presidential decision to classify striped bass as a protected gamefish prohibits the commercial sale of striper caught in certain East Coast waters and encourages eastern states to similarly declare the striper a protected gamefish under state law.

In a number of places in this book, you'll see mention of conservation of fisheries. As an angler, you have many avenues to make your opinion known about how we can ensure that your children, grandchildren, and generations to come will have as many—if not more—fishing opportunities as you do. There are a number of fishing groups and associations that you can join or support for the sake of the future of the sport.

Once you start fishing, you'll learn things from all directions—from other anglers, from real-time online fishing reports, from the water and the environment, and from the fish themselves. But you'll be able to turn back to this book again and again as you expand your endeavors, catch different kinds of fish, and develop new tackle needs.

Good luck, be safe, and put back more fish than you keep.

ORIGINAL PART: THE HOOK

There's a specific hook to choose for each and every fishing technique

The hook is the oldest item of fishing tackle, with the first hooks fashioned from bone roughly 9,000 years ago. The earliest written notation of a fish hook made from steel needles dates to 1496, after the development of fish hook materials evolved from bone to bronze to iron over thousands of years. There is now a great variety of fish hooks, depending upon their application; most are made from high-carbon steel, while others are made from stainless steel or alloys.

Single hooks (single point) and treble hooks (three points) are the most frequently employed types of hooks. Single hooks are almost universally used with bait or soft plastics (artificial worms and the like), while treble hooks are found on artificial

Diagram of a Hook

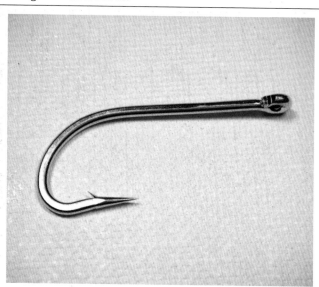

- The hook point penetrates, and the barb secures it. Various point-and-barb configurations can maximize penetration and holding ability.

- Sportfishing hooks usually have conical (rounded), curved (bent inward), spear, or knife points (a spear point is a heavy-bodied point section, and a knife point is a slightly concave spear-style point).

- Barb size depends on the fish species pursued, with larger, stronger, tough-mouthed fish calling for full-size barbs.

Smaller-Size Hooks

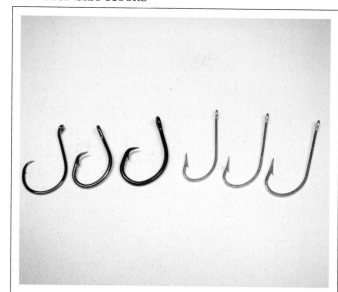

- Some hooks have an offset bend, left or right, to prevent the hook from spinning when fished with bait in current.

- Most hook types are named: Sproat (straight point), Aberdeen (round bend, light wire), salmon egg (very short shank), and claw (bait hook with offset point curved inward).

- The Limerick has a wide bend with a long shank.

- Long-shank hooks are often needed with artificial soft baits to be able to position the point midway down the lure body.

lures, such as plugs and crankbaits, and are not often used with bait. Some hooks are given a corrosive-resistant finish or a colored one, such as red, to play a part in the color scheme of a lure. Numerous hook styles have a bright brassy finish.

Hook size depends on the diameter, or gauge, of the wire used to make it. Fine wire makes small, light hooks for lighter game such as panfish and works best for dry flies that must float. Medium-gauge wire produces hooks for a variety of gamefish, from little bass up to smaller saltwater species. Heavy-gauge wire is used for the biggest species.

Large-Size Hooks

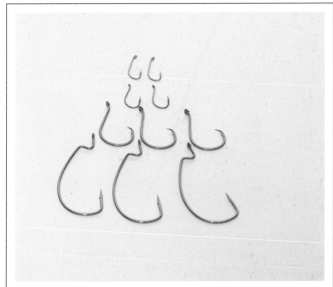

- The hook gap determines the numerical hook size.

- The largest hooks are measured from 1/0 ("one aught") to 19/0, getting larger as the first number goes up; these are almost all saltwater hooks.

- General freshwater hooks range from size 1 to 12, with fly hooks going as high as 24—the higher the number, the smaller the hook.

- Hooks do flex, but moderately. Too much flex and hook-sets are lost; too rigid and the hook can break.

Treble Hooks

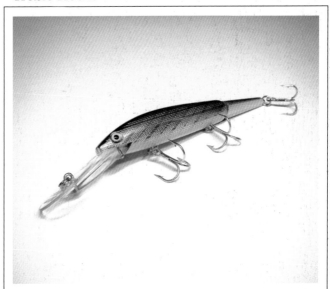

- Many manufacturers use acids to make hook points very strong and sharp, in a process called "chemical sharpening."

- Treble hooks tend to be particularly strong, as they are often employed on lures bitten hard by big fish.

- Nickel, nickel-Teflon, and zinc-oxide-nickel finishes are commonly used to prevent corrosion and abrasion on freshwater hooks.

- Saltwater hooks endure a terrifically corrosive environment and are often given cadmium-tin or chrome-zinc coatings.

REACHING OUT: LINES & LEADERS

The technology built into modern fishing lines gives anglers significant advantages

A look at any fishing-gear retail catalog reveals a near-confusing array of fishing lines. How do you figure out what you need? That depends on the type of fishing you're doing, the type of reel that you use, and what you want to spend.

Monofilament continues to be the most popular fishing line. You can use it most anywhere for anything, and it con-

sistently works very well with all kinds of fishing reels. In general, monofilament (nylon) tends to be the least expensive line. After that, there are fluorocarbon lines. This kind of line has extremely low visibility in water—some manufacturers will say it's invisible. If you fish very clear water, or for very spooky wild fish, it might be a key choice.

Monofilament and Fluorocarbon Lines

- Monofilament will stretch, which absorbs some hook-setting shock but also affects the sensitivity of the line.

- Monofilament also suffers from "line memory," which is coiling in the shape of the spool.

- Both monofilament and fluorocarbon come in a variety of low-visibility colors, but fluorocarbon is less visible in the water.

- Fluorocarbon lines sink faster than monofilament and have less stretch.

Braided Lines

- Braided lines are much more limp than monofilament and have minimal stretch, offering higher sensitivity to lure movement and strikes.

- Braided lines often have a smooth coating and are highly abrasion-resistant.

- Improvements over time have made braided lines usable with any conventional reel, and have ensured consistent knot strength.

- Line colors range from shades easily seen by the angler to colors that fool fish.

Then there are the superlines—braided lines that are fused or spun together using very thin synthetic fibers. These very small-diameter lines offer strength equal to or greater than their monofilament counterparts. They also tend to be more expensive than monofilament.

As for the terminal section of your line, the leader, you don't need to get into heavier stuff until you fish for sizable game or around rough structure. In light freshwater situations, a 10-inch section of monofilament with slightly greater breaking strength (meaning it will hold a greater load) than the main line is fine. Super-low-visibility fluorocarbon leaders come into play with very careful freshwater fish like trout.

When you fish for big bass, pike, muskie, large catfish, Great Lakes salmon, and saltwater species, consider using a leader section that can stand up against hard strikes, toothy mouths, rough scales, and sharp fins. Several different kinds of pre-rigged leaders can also be bought retail. Heavier monofilament and fluorocarbon—from 15- to 100-pound test or higher—nylon-coated steel, titanium, or wire cable form the strong, abrasion-resistant leaders that are necessary for big fish.

Leaders

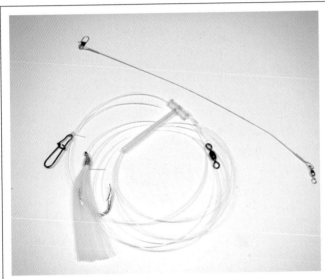

- Fluorocarbon leaders reach 80-pound strength and are tough enough for muskie and pike.

- Most light leaders are rigged with a ball-bearing swivel at one end and a snap at the other for connecting to the lure.

- Titanium leaders can be as flexible as monofilament leaders and range from 15- to 75-pound strength.

- Hand-wound (crimpless) wire leaders are sometimes necessary with certain lures that need exact balance.

Heavy-Duty Leaders

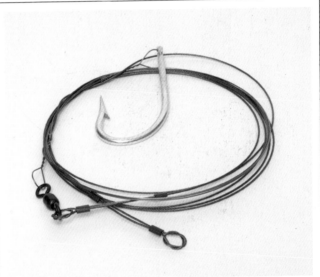

- Heavy monofilament comes in spools from 20- to 400-pound test.

- Big-game leaders for marlin, sailfish, and sharks are often made of very strong wire or cable.

- Most professional big-game anglers make their own leaders so that they know their exact strength.

- Heavy-duty big-game leaders range in length from 10 to 28 feet.

FINDING DEPTH: SINKERS & FLOATS
Success means putting and keeping bait in the fish's feeding zone

Fish can be found anywhere in the water column. They can feed inches below the surface, or they can hug the bottom. They might work the edges of fast, deep water, or glide along a slow, shallow eddy. Getting bait to the right depth for those fish calls for smart use of sinkers and floats.

Sinkers have been around for almost as long as hooks and come in many different forms. Some sinkers are designed to hold bottom, while others allow the line to have some freedom of movement. Some are designed specifically for trolling. Sinkers are also convenient to use, as most are easy to add to or remove from the line. They come in so many gradations of weight that you can carefully fine-tune the amount necessary to find the right depth without negatively affecting the performance of the line or rig.

Freshwater Sinkers

- Most still-water situations in freshwater call for several split shot or a small dipsey sinker (sometimes called a "bass-casting sinker").

- Deep freshwater situations might require ¼ to ½ ounce of weight, depending upon current.

- Heavy current, especially in deeper water, might necessitate 2 to 3 ounces of weight, with a sinker that sticks to the bottom.

- Egg sinkers and dipsey sinkers with snap-lock rings allow the line to move, and thus fish feel little resistance when they strike.

Special-Purpose Freshwater Sinkers

- A number of sinkers can be used with soft-plastic worms, such as screw-in bullet weights and Carolina rigs, which make worms swim and dive.

- Trolling for walleye often calls for sinkers that bounce along the bottom but keep the lure or bait free of snags, such as a Lindy Rig.

- In-line weights are weighted, flexible sections of cord that form a section of the main line or leader.

- Streamlined "flippin' weights" help draw soft plastics through heavy vegetation and timber.

More and more sinkers are now made from steel, tungsten, bismuth, or brass, insead of lead. These materials are slightly more expensive than lead.

Floats are made from hollow plastic or very light wood and are often referred to as "bobbers." Fishing with a round bobber puts the most resistance on a bait. This can work with fish that are hungry and grabbing the bait hard, but with much more wary fish, a slimmer-profile float is the right choice. Floats can be rigged as fixed floats (no line movement) or slip floats that allow some line movement.

YELLOW ● LIGHT

A number of states, including New York, New Hampshire, and Vermont, have banned sinkers and lures that contain lead. Research has shown that waterfowl will ingest bits of lead as they feed in lakes and ponds, often resulting in poisoning and death. Many anglers are avoiding lead altogether in freshwater, and this will be easier as more alternative metals are used in sinkers.

Big-Water/Saltwater Sinkers

- The design of the age-old pyramid sinker lets it punch into sand or mud and hold fast.

- The squared edges of a bank sinker keep it from rolling down an incline, thus making it highly useful along holes and drop-offs.

- The rounded sides of disc sinkers avoid snags in fast currents or tides.

- The heaviest saltwater sinkers range from 16 to 48 ounces apiece and are used to take big baits down to depths of 200 feet, as in halibut fishing.

Bobbers and Floats

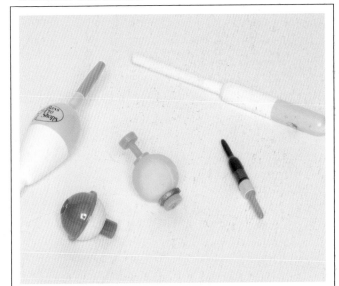

- Slim-bodied floats matched with one or two split shot on the line below do best to detect light bites in still or slow water.

- Split shot help put a slim float at its correct depth; a rising float indicates an upward strike by a fish.

- Cast a float rig upward, in a smooth lob, and not with any kind of snap of the rod.

- In current, use a float that rides higher on the surface so that the bait stays at the right depth but the float isn't pulled under easily by the current.

CONNECTORS: SWIVELS & SNAPS

These joints absorb pressure, reduce line stress, and help construct various rigs

While many times the best way to connect sections of line or to tie leaders to lures is to tie good knots (see Chapter 19), there are a number of instances in which a quality swivel, snap, or the combination snap-swivel can be highly useful. Swivels do just that—each ring end turns on a vertical axis. This is useful for situations in which the action of a lure or baited hook, or the pull of a sinker, might create twist in the line. The swivel serves as an intermediate connector, often between the leader and main line, that absorbs the torque created by fishing action.

Swivels need to be matched to the kind of fishing being done. A swivel that is weaker than the strength of the line is

Swivels

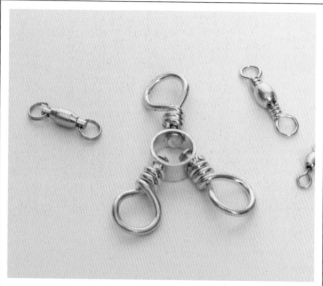

- There are two kinds of swivels: slide-bearing swivels and ball-bearing swivels.

- Most people use barrel swivels, which are technically slide-bearing swivels: The central wire strand that forms the rings and the rounded barrel body slide against each other.

- Ball-bearing swivels are superior to barrel swivels, especially those with solid rings instead of split rings, but are slightly pricier than barrel swivels.

- Quality swivels of both kinds are made of nickel and steel, and are corrosion-resistant.

Snaps

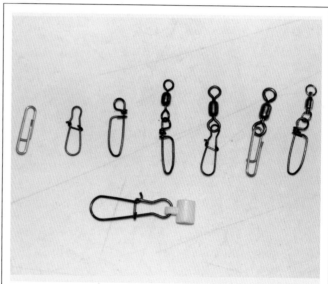

- The effectiveness of a snap depends on the quality of its metal and how well it locks and holds.

- Be sure the snap you use is rated to at least the breaking strength of your line.

- Duolock and crosslock snaps are probably the most effective at staying locked.

- For saltwater or big-fish use, choose McMahon or coastlock snaps.

no good—you need swivels that can handle as much, if not more, tension than the line can. Cheap swivels break, as do those that are corroded or bent.

A metal snap is a wire connector shaped like a safety pin. In lieu of a knot, it allows for quick lure changes, and works well in conjunction with heavier leaders and bigger lures cast to tough-mouthed fish. Snaps come in a number of configurations, so always choose one that has a quality finish, exceeds the leader's breaking strength (see page 3), and snaps shut securely.

The combination snap-swivel can be used to attach to leaders those lures that have an active swimming action that could put a twist in the leader. A twisted leader can throw off the action of the lure. You find this mainly with larger spinners, or when fishing big lures in heavy current. The snap-swivel isn't necessary for most smaller- to medium-size lures. A snap-swivel might also be used to connect heavy sinkers to the main line.

Using the Right Snap

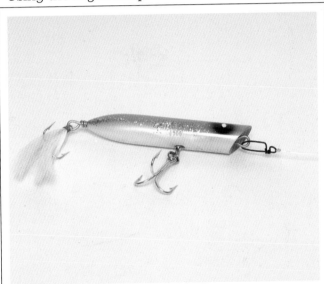

- The more round the bend of the snap, the more action a lure will have.

- Using snaps in lieu of knots is easier with lines that are difficult to tie, such as heavier monofilament lines and microfilament lines.

- Don't use snaps that are too light for the line and lures that you're using.

- You can use a snap with a wire leader, but be sure it is one of matching or surpassing strength.

Three-Way Swivels

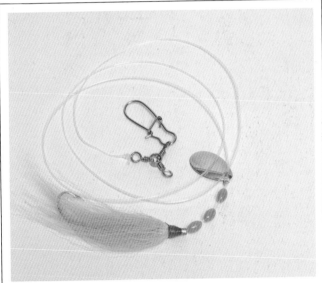

- Swivels and snaps for saltwater use must have a strong corrosion resistance, such as stainless steel, or will need to be replaced frequently.

- Big fish can bend lesser three-way swivels, so match quality and strength to both the quarry and heaviness of the rig.

- The classic fish-finder rig hinges upon a three-way swivel, from which you can rig one or two hooks.

- A snap can be added to a three-way swivel for quick sinker changes.

TERMINAL ACCESSORIES

Adding just a bit of color, flash, or flutter to a rig or bait can turn a fish's head

Given the amount of terminal tackle (tackle used at the end of a standing line) that comes ready-made from many manufacturers, you might not realize all the things that you can do with various lures and baits to create exactly the kind of style, coloration, and performance you want. The materials discussed here don't work with all gear, but are important to

know about because of their usefulness in some situations.

If you have a bit of mechanical know-how, you can customize any number of store-bought lures, switching spinner blades, skirts, and jig heads. Such alterations can and probably should be made when you find out through experimentation that fish go after a lure much more actively because of a color change or

Jig Heads

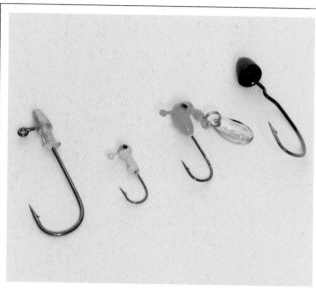

- The shape of the jig head determines if the jig will sink quickly, flutter, or sink downward at an angle.

- Numerous jig heads are fitted with a small spinner blade that aids its swimming motion or acts as an attractor.

- Jig heads designed to hook to tube baits are meant to fit inside the tube.

- You can use fluorescent paints and stick-on prismatic eyes to heighten a jig head's visibility.

Terminal Blades

- Add small spinner blades to natural-bait rigs, especially minnows, to give additional flash and vibration.

- Blade size and shape— round, long, or V-shape— affects the retrieval speed and the lure's vibration.

- Trolling rigs and bait harnesses are often assemblies of spinner blades separated by beads, which the angler makes to order.

- Spinner rigs are "in-line"— all the pieces attach to the leader or to a central wire, with clevises (small clips) securing the spinner blades.

reconfiguration that you created yourself. Changing the size and color of spinner blades on spinnerbaits can make them noisier and more visible, traits that under certain conditions (such as murky water or night fishing) can increase your odds. Adding a soft-plastic bait—a worm or a crayfish—to a heavy bass jig might give it that extra enticement to make a fish strike.

Even small touches, like the use of various beads as attractors on the line, aid in attracting fish and maximizing the performance of tackle. Live-bait anglers frequently place a colored bead just above a baited hook.

ZOOM

Some artificial lures can be tipped with a natural bait. Skirted jigs can often take a small minnow, grub, or waxworm, while a simple jig head can be hooked to a night crawler or minnow. A spinnerbait can be tipped with a piece of pork rind.

Skirts

- Changing skirts on spinnerbaits or buzzbaits is relatively easy, as the skirts are secured with a rubber cuff around the jig head.

- Skirts often match the overall color scheme, but you can switch both blades and skirts for any combination.

- Trim or adjust a skirt as necessary to get as much or as little pulsation as needed.

- Instead of a skirt, you can add a soft-plastic lure (see page 87) to the spinnerbait hook.

Beads

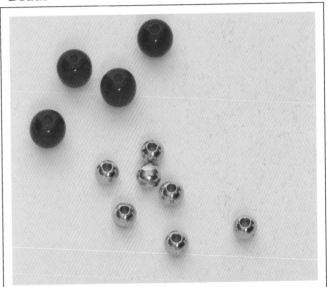

- Beads can be used as spacers for placing spinner blades along a rig for trolling.

- The body section of a spinner-bladed lure can be made out of stacked plastic and/or metal beads.

- Put one or two beads on the leader of a plastic-worm rig as attractors or as spacers for a spinner blade.

- Use beads to prevent plastic cuffs (which allow the main line to slide past the sinker, such as on a fishfinder rig) from fouling on leader knots or swivels.

ESSENTIAL HARDWARE
Fishing can be a lot easier with the right implement at the right moment

After all the hooks, sinkers, snaps, and line, there are a few other basic but crucial items that the angler needs before getting into lure or reel selections. These items are the tools that are required for successful fishing: hook-removal implements, a variety of knives, and fish-cleaning tools.

An effective hook remover is a must-have. Most likely, you'll release more fish than you ever keep, and noninjurious release is important to conservation efforts and the future of fishing. Select a hook remover that is matched to the kind of fish that you're after, and learn to use it efficiently. You'll probably need a couple different kinds, given the various sizes and mouth shapes of the fish you'll catch.

Hook Removers

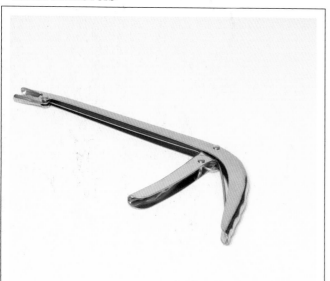

- Smaller fish, such as panfish and trout, can be easily unhooked using forceps.

- Various hook-removal tools slip over the leader and let the angler put downward pressure on the hook bend.

- Spring-grip hook removers work well with fish that have big mouths and wide gullets, like big bass or pike.

- Have on hand wire cutters or pliers that can cut wire, in case you cannot remove an embedded treble hook but are able to reach in and cut the shank or bend.

Fisherman's Knife

- The traditional freshwater "fisherman's knife" is usually a folding knife with a longer penknife blade and a fish scaler/disgorger (hook remover).

- A light fixed-blade knife with a penknife-type blade will also work well to gut fish.

- Gutting smaller fish calls for a 4-inch blade; medium-size fish take a 6-inch blade.

- Larger species and saltwater fish call for longer, heavier blades, up to 8 inches.

10

When you keep some fish for the grill or fryer, you'll need proper knives: one for gutting and cleaning, and another for filleting. You'll also want a general-purpose utility knife for cutting line or cord, and perhaps a Boy Scout–style pocket-knife for opening cans or bottles.

Beyond that, there are implements for cleaning fish—scalers, cleaning boards, and brushes—that make life a lot easier. The quality of your meal begins with the proper use of these tools and correct preparation of fillets and dressed-out fish.

YELLOW ● LIGHT

Most people cut themselves when the knife they are using isn't sharp enough to deal with the task, and they end up forcing the blade and making a mistake. A knife that's kept properly sharp cuts easily and smoothly and lets you get the job done. Anytime you use a knife, take care to cut away from your body and don't cut toward your other hand or fingers.

Fillet Knife

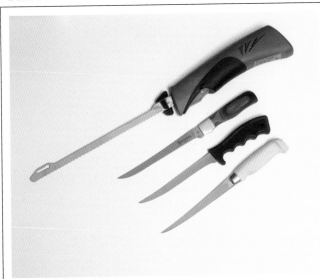

- A good fillet knife is flexible enough to bend slightly but the blade retains its shape.

- Choose a fillet knife that has a handle long enough for your hand.

- Select a knife with a blade long enough to cut across the fish's entire width with one stroke.

- The fillet cut requires a cut through the ribs, so on heavier fish, use a heavier-bladed fillet knife to make this cut.

Fish-Cleaning Tools

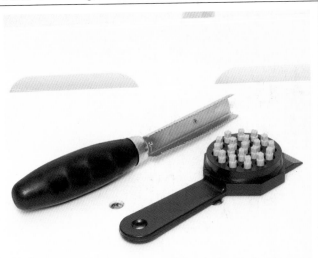

- You can use a knife blade to scale fish, but the numerous scalers available today make the job easier and quicker.

- Various wire-bristle brushes are highly useful for removing bits of blood and entrails from the body cavity or fillets.

- A proper cleaning board has a clamp to hold the fish so you can clean it without the fish's body spinning and sliding.

- There are specially designed pliers to grip a fish's head to remove it along with the skin.

LURE STORAGE: BOXES & BAGS

You can't put a handful of lures in your pocket and expect fun times

You will quickly find that fishing is a sport of stuff. If you're serious about it, you're going to come to possess a lot of hardware that doesn't help you do much else except fish. But that's the beauty of it.

Before you start shopping for lures, you ought to have a place to put them. You will find that eventually you will fill one, then two, and then easily three tackle boxes of some kind once you start fishing regularly. Fortunately, there is now such an effective variety of tackle storage that you can carefully select what best fits your needs and ways of fishing, whether you're simply out for panfish on the local pond or want to have an answer for everything any major gamefish would eat.

Tackle Boxes & Trays

- The classic small tackle box is still in use, though not often, due to space constraints.

- Something small is perfect for kids just starting out—they can easily carry it and keep track of its contents.

- A smaller box is also right for a small pond or creek that doesn't call for a wide variety of lures or baits.

- A divided tackle tray that can be slipped into a cargo pocket might also suffice for small water.

Tackle Boxes & Trays, Continued

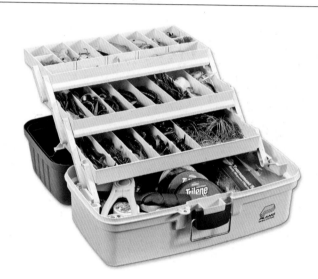

- Be sure to open your tackle box in a stable place, as its one drawback is that it dumps all of your lures if you knock it over.

- Tackle trays are designed for specific contents, to help organize sinkers, soft plastics, and hard-bodied lures.

- Use the bottom area for larger items, such as spools of line.

- Take care that your tackle box, especially the bottom section, doesn't become a mess of lines and hooks.

As you start out, you should probably get two tackle boxes—one that's the right size to take with you wherever you fish, and a larger one for storing lures at home. You can select lures from the bigger box and put them in your carry box before you go. The big box should be a bit larger than you think you need, because you will find that you will eventually fill it, and need another.

Tackle Bags

- Chests with large, stacked tackle trays can accommodate the most tackle, maximizing the angler's lure selection.

- Adjustable dividers in the lure trays allow for storage of small, medium, and large lures in a variety of designs.

- Most tackle bags are built for durability and are water-resistant, if not waterproof.

- Some storage systems allow for hanging lures by their hooks rather than lying flat, but always dry a lure before returning it to a tray or bin.

Equipment Bags

- Safe storage of reels and other gear in protective bags is crucial on a boat so that items are out of the way.

- Traveling anglers should use hard-sided cases to protect reels and gear on airlines or on the road.

- Numerous manufacturers make gear bags with wheels for easier movement through airports or in the marina.

- Boaters should consider having at least one "dry bag"—a watertight gear bag for wallets, keys, cell phones, and other electronics.

GOING MOBILE: VESTS & PACKS

Walking and wading with just a rod in your hand lets you cover a lot of water

Most anglers don't start out using vests or packs—they usually opt for a tackle box. They then set about fishing and learning about fishing. But the person who wants a certain kind of mobility, or has a sum of fishing experience and is looking for a more advanced system of carrying and accessing tackle, might want to use a fishing vest or pack.

While many people associate these vests or packs with fly fishing, they are in no way limited to that method. The bass angler, spin fisherman, or coastal angler can all make use of these wearable tackle systems. You can't store a huge amount of tackle, and you're not going to be able to carry many large-size lures, but what such systems allow you to

Standard Fishing Vest

- The abundance of pockets, most on the outside and a few on the inside, is what gives a fishing vest its functionality.

- Test the vest pockets before buying to be sure that you can fit the lure or fly boxes that you use, as well as other tackle and gear.

- Most vests have a zippered pouch on the back for holding larger items.

- Summertime vests often come with a mesh body for better breathability.

Heavy-Duty Vest

- Variations of the standard vest might be more comfortable for the way some people move and cast.

- Some better fly-fishing vests come with stiff pocket fronts that fold down flat to form a surface for fly selection or knot tying.

- A vest meant for fly fishing might, in fact, maximize the kind of pocket space a bass angler needs, so do some comparison shopping.

- Some vests come with adjustable straps, fitting them to most body sizes.

do is make exacting selections of what you want to take with you and then capitalize on your mobility.

Obviously, these items are made specifically for the angler who is on foot, doesn't want to lug a tackle box any distance, and might be doing some wading. Additionally, owing to a number of design variations, most anglers can find some kind of vest, pack, or satchel, or some combination thereof, that puts the right tackle at their fingertips while also being comfortable enough to wear for extended periods while casting.

Combo Packs

- Don't overestimate how much you can carry—always opt for less than more if you want to walk and cast all day.

- Carefully selected tackle and gear in a properly sized, comfortable pack work much better than too much stuff in too big a pack.

- Some fly-fishing combo packs come with a small chest pack for flies and leaders, and a waist pack for boxes and gear.

- Smaller waist packs can be matched with vests to carry extra gear and backup reels.

Saltwater Satchels

- Lure size is an issue with saltwater satchels, and most versions solve this problem with upright lure storage.

- Look for a satchel with a clip that attaches to your belt so the bag doesn't bang around when you cast.

- A good saltwater satchel will maximize storage surfaces, making for a lighter bag with a practical variety of lure selection.

- Fully loaded, the bag should offer quick access to pliers and not weigh so much that it pulls you off balance.

FOOTWEAR & WADERS

Your casting platform starts with your feet and the security of your stance

Proper, quality footwear can mean the difference between a successful outing and injury. When you fish, you're going to be crossing some slick, muddy, rocky, and uneven terrain. Sometimes you can get away with just sneakers, but if you plan on covering a lot of ground along a rocky shore or rough bank, and if you're wading, you're going to need a footwear upgrade.

Trail shoes of some kind can be a big plus. They perform better than tennis or running shoes, mainly in the support and stability they provide and in the construction of their soles that lets them grip uneven, mushy, or wet surfaces. There's a wide variety available, and they usually don't cost much more than a pair of quality basketball shoes.

Shoes

- Look for as light a shoe as will work well for you, without sacrificing performance.

- Waterproof shoes should be entirely so (they're usually Gore-Tex lined), while shoes that are supposed to drain water quickly should also dry quickly.

- Stretch-cord lacing systems or regular laces both work fine, but be sure you can tighten the shoe completely with either.

- Look for good arch support and cushioning combined with high uppers for ankle stability.

Hip and Chest Waders

- On small streams or ponds, hip waders might be all you need, but they're not enough for big rivers or surf casting.

- Hip waders secure to your belt and usually fit a little loosely, not like a sock.

- Most "hippers" are rubberized canvas, which is very durable, but some manufacturers offer them in breathable nylon.

- Some hip and chest waders come in elasticized nylon, making for a tighter fit that stretches.

Waders do double duty: They give you durable and stable footwear and keep you dry. In hot weather you can "wet wade"—use a pair of old trail shoes or wading boots without the waders—but when the water is cool enough to chill you, use waders. Many waders are "breathable" and let air circulate through the material, making for comfortable wear.

Boat shoes, or "mocs," are sneaker-like, waterproof footwear that aid stability on deck, especially in wet conditions. That's key when you're fighting a fish and don't want to worry about every step.

RED ● LIGHT

A very serious parasite that causes whirling disease in trout and salmon can sometimes be transferred by felt-soled waders. The parasite enters the fish as a spore, and those spores can be moved from river to river embedded in felt soles. If you still use felt soles, treat felt soles with a 10 percent chlorine-bleach-and-water solution for fifteen minutes and then rinse thoroughly with water, before you move from one stream or river system to another.

Boot-Foot & Stocking-Foot Waders

- Waders come in "boot foot" or "stocking foot" versions; boot foot has the boots attached, while stocking-foot waders allow you to select a separate wading shoe.

- Lighter nylon waders work fine in mild weather, In colder seasons, opt for thicker neoprene waders.

- The soles on wading shoes or boot-foot waders can be cleated, studded, or felt (sometimes combined with studs).

- You might need more than one kind of wading shoe to match the slipperiness or rockiness of where you fish.

Boat Shoes

- For dedicated boat shoes, look for something with light soles that won't mark a boat deck that's white fiberglass.

- Some kinds of boat shoes allow for complete immersion and double as wading shoes in sandy inshore waters.

- Mesh-bodied boat shoes should drain and dry quickly.

- Newer, slip-on booties can be used as both wading shoes and boat shoes, but some true flats boots are a bit too heavy to serve as boat shoes or can mar the deck.

PROTECTING YOURSELF

Sometimes you'll dress like you're going to the moon, but it'll be worth it

Once you develop a serious enthusiasm for fishing, you'll realize that you can't let difficult conditions stop you. That means two things: You're not going to sit at home when the rain comes down or when the sun is blazing, and you're also not going to suffer the ill effects of rain, wind, or sun while you're out catching fish. The same goes for bugs.

Dressing for fishing success means layering. In colder times, start with a thermal base layer and then add a heavier flannel or fleece shirt (enough layers to stay warm), topped by either a wind shell or rain gear. If the weather warms or the rain stops, you can always remove a layer. In direct, hot sun, wear a light layer of light-colored clothing on top of either a lot of

Rain Suits

- Rain suits are lighter waterproof outfits that work well in warmer conditions, when they can be used as the outer layer.

- In downpours or wind-driven rain, you can use a rain suit as extra protection under a rainproof shell.

- Most newer rain suits are made from breathable material; avoid rubberized clothes that don't allow much air circulation.

- Rain suits easily pack down into a small bundle, and can be carried in a fishing vest.

Rain Coats

- Better-made rain coats will have a windproof layer or a zip-in windproof jacket.

- Look for coats and parkas that are breathable but still 100 percent waterproof.

- Look for watertight cuffs that keep water from running up the sleeves and storm flaps that close tightly over the front zipper.

- Effective rain gear includes a coat hood big enough to fit over a cap, and rain pants with leg zippers that allow a quick, over-the-boot fit.

sunblock (UV rays can penetrate some clothing) or a white T-shirt. Wear socks to protect your ankles and a bandanna to protect your neck. In really sunny places, you might even want to wear gloves and something called a "buff," which is like a big bandanna that you can pull up around your face. Whenever you're in the sun, in warm or cold weather, always use lots of sunblock with a higher SPF than you think you need (at least 30), and always wear a hat—something to hold in heat in the cold, and to block the sun.

As for bugs, most people prefer to use some kind of repel-lant instead having to wear netting, but if you've ever been swarmed by blackflies or mosquitoes, you know that bug dope isn't perfect. Head nets, or even full jackets, might look a little strange, but they can save the day. Multiple bug bites will drive you crazy. So in buggy times and places, have some netting handy.

Bug-Proof Head Nets

- Get a head net big enough to use with a brimmed hat so the net hangs away from your face.

- Try to find a lighter, green-colored net, as black nets sometimes impede vision at low light, though in daylight they're fine.

- Be sure the bottom of the net tucks completely into your shirt or jacket top to seal out any bugs.

- In extremely buggy places full of no-see-ums (biting midges), a head net combined with a mesh jacket might be the only way to save yourself.

Sun Protection

- Warm-weather fishing clothes come in a variety of colors, but choose something in a lighter shade so it doesn't absorb the sun's rays.

- Good polarized sunglasses are a must—they might be pricey, but they will save your eyes and let you see fish.

- Pick a hat that covers both face and neck, or use a neck cover with a regular cap.

- Liberally and continually apply sunblock that's meant for your face and head, especially on your nose and ears.

LANDING FISH: CRITICAL TOOLS

Handling fish safely is an art within the sport, and usually doesn't work bare-handed

Stabilizing and unhooking a fish quickly, whether keeping or releasing it, is essential. In Chapter 1 we discussed dedicated hook-removal tools. Some of these, such as spring-grip hook removers, come in a variety of sizes and can be used for numerous fish. However, every angler should have at least one pair of quality pliers. They will prove invaluable for quick, easy hook releases, and also are necessary for helping with equipment repair, mashing down hook barbs, and numerous other important tasks in support of your angling.

Lip grips are very good for landing and securely holding bigger fish. They have a kind of metal pincer that grabs hold of a fish's lower jaw just like a thumb and index finger. You

Pliers

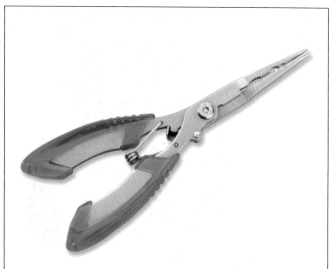

- Needle-nose pliers, or something close to that configuration, are most useful to anglers for hook removal.

- Premium-grade pliers are often made from titanium, but plated stainless steel will work fine.

- Select pliers with a built-in wire cutter, or keep a pair of cutting pliers in your tackle bag, too.

- A belt-sheath and lanyard for your pliers is the way to go—you can easily grab them, and if you drop them, you get them back.

Multi-tools

- Multi-tools can fulfill both the role of pliers and Boy Scout knife with their numerous applications.

- Multi-tool pliers often come in a needle-nose style and usually have wire-cutting blades set at the bottom of the shaft.

- Pocket-size multi-tools are fine for panfish and smaller trout.

- The largest multi-tools can work with big fish, but they cannot reach as deeply as a hook remover in big-mouthed fish hooked deep in the gullet.

can control the fish's head and most of its movement, and hold it still for hook removal or a quick photo.

A net is another highly effective way of stabilizing a fish for unhooking. There is now a wide variety of net designs, many with mesh that is nonabrasive or nonbinding to a fish's body, fins, and gills. Net depth will also vary, depending upon the size of the quarry and whether you intend a quick release without removing the fish from the water.

Grips

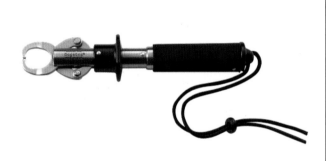

- Grips are for bigger, larger-mouthed, and toothy fish like pike, striped bass, big catfish, and numerous saltwater species.

- Grips open with either a hand-operated hinge action or with a cam system that opens when pushed against a fish's jaw.

- Most models allow for single-hand use, letting you keep the rod in the other hand.

- Many grips also have built-in analog or digital scales to weigh the catch while you hold it.

Nets

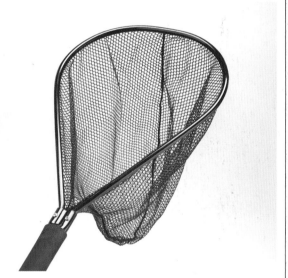

- Nets need to be species specific, to a general degree—the larger the fish, the deeper and wider the net.

- The mesh of many nets now comes with a smooth coating to prevent hook snags and tangles.

- Rubber-mesh nets, which are often flat-bottomed, protect a fish's slime coating, and the flat bottom allows quick access for unhooking.

- Very shallow, catch-and-release hand nets allow a netted fish to be kept in the water for unhooking and then quickly eased back into the stream.

PERSONAL WATERCRAFT

Easy enough for one-person transport, these vehicles take you where wading can't

The one-person watercraft available today for fishing has never been so varied or effective. Anglers who want a portable, quiet means to get to those fish that cannot be reached by wading can choose from a number of craft suiting their budget, ability, and angling destination.

Float tubes, once called "belly boats," and pontoon boats that ride on inflated cushions are comfortable and easy to use. They're stable, highly maneuverable, and easy to carry to the lake or stream.

A number of one-person canoes are now available. An individual with some experience can pilot a medium-size canoe, or even a big lake canoe, but that's a lot of hull to paddle around

KNACK FISHING FOR EVERYONE

Float Tubes

- Get a model with a high seat, one that isn't very low in the water or sits above water, so that you can see your casts clearly.

- Look for a model that has a rugged underside that resists tears and snags.

- You'll have to wear waders with these if the water is cold, and you maneuver using short swim fins on your feet.

- With some models you can run deeper creeks and smaller rivers with flat, moderate currents.

Pontoon Boats

- How high your seated profile is will affect wind drift, so consider that if you're going to use a pontoon boat mostly for lake fishing.

- Look for multichambered, tough-skinned pontoons that won't totally deflate with one puncture.

- Most models come with oar locks and an anchor system (get both), and some have a stand-up casting platform.

- Pontoon boats work well in both still water and in current, and larger models can handle some small rolls and fast, flat sections.

by yourself. One-person models offer just enough canoe for your gear and the stability needed for casting and landing fish, but one person can usually transport them short distances.

In the past ten years, a lot of design and technology has gone into making kayaks the right craft for anglers. Many of these are sit-on-top models with rod holders, storage bins, and mounts for depth-finders. Kayaks are now used extensively both in fresh and salt water to take a variety of species.

With all these craft, however, you should use a PFD (personal flotation device), or life vest.

Choosing self-propelled watercraft gives you a much more environmentally friendly experience on the water. There's no noise from an outboard motor, and there's no fuel emissions or leakage. You give yourself a workout and burn calories, while using a watercraft that lets you quietly get in close, at slower speeds, to carefully judge fishing spots and the distance for casting.

Canoes

- Solo canoeing can be made a lot easier using a double-bladed paddle, and a number of one-person fishing canoes are well suited to this approach.

- Be sure to get an anchor system that is easy to operate from the canoe seat.

- Several custom canoe makers can thoroughly outfit a fishing canoe to personal specs, but this will be significantly more pricey than retail models.

- You can attach an electric trolling motor to various models, on the stern or side.

Kayaks

- Both sit-on-top and in-hull-seat models are available—your choice depends on comfort, sense of stability, and how you cast.

- Look for a model with big-enough storage wells, a paddle holder, at least one rod holder, and adjustable foot-braces.

- There are a number of ocean-fishing kayaks big enough for larger quarry like snook, various bass species, and inshore sharks.

- Color choice is your preference—most anglers choose green or camo, but no one has yet proven fish react to boat color.

SUITING UP: VESTS & PACKS

Put everything at your fingertips, in the right place, so you can find it quickly

Using vests and packs to bolster your fishing success depends on how you set them up for your kind of fishing. When you're on the water, your vest or pack should, in a sense, act like a fishing buddy that hands you exactly what you need.

That convenience takes some thought beforehand. Sit down with your vest or pack and get a sense of its maximum capacity by testing what boxes and gear you can get inside it. But avoid maxing out the total weight, if you can, so you'll have an easier time moving around. Of course, most anglers fault on the side of having more tackle and gear than necessary.

Put your vest on and place everything you need in the

Organizing Vest Pockets

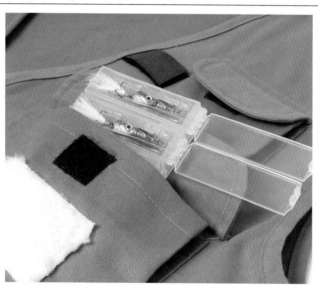

- Designate different pockets for various lure or fly boxes, such as plugs to the left, spoons and spinners to the right.

- Smaller front pockets shouldn't be so small that they're not practical for fitting packs of small sinkers or hooks.

- In larger inside pockets put items that will rest flush against your sides, like tippet or leader spools or a small, flat lure box.

- Upright large front pockets that zipper up and down work better for some anglers than horizontal pockets.

Fishing Vests

- A back-panel pocket should be large enough for a folded, light rain jacket, a first-aid kit, or lunch.

- Hot-weather vests often have a breathable mesh base but don't sacrifice pockets or necessary panels.

- Trout anglers often secure their nets over the back of their vest, using a lanyard with a magnetic connector for quick access.

- Extra spools of line and backup spools for fly or spinning reels usually fit most easily in the back pocket.

proper pockets. You'll need to figure out which lure or fly box should go in which pocket so that you can both remember its location easily and access it conveniently, without fumbling. Utilize the smaller pockets for small bags of split shot or other sinkers, hooks, and floats or strike indicators (small bits of foam used when fly fishing with nymph patterns). Figure out where your leader or tippet materials should go, and what fits easiest into the larger inside pockets or the back-panel pouch. You should be able to reach back, unzip the pouch, and get inside.

A fishing backpack can hold a lot of tackle and gear, but you'll have to slip it off to grab what you need from inside. You can sometimes lean over a shoulder to get into a fanny pack, or slide it around to your hip. The best system is to use a small chest pack in combination with a backpack or fanny pack. Put essentials in the chest pack—lures, flies, hooks, leader—and leave the rest in the backpack or fanny pack.

Packs

- Set up backpacks or fanny packs by arranging the contents evenly, centering the heaviest items in a higher compartment.

- Fanny packs often come with a tandem chest pack, but otherwise choose the smallest chest pack that gives you enough capacity for crucial tackle.

- Big backpacks with high capacity might be best left on the bank while you wade with just a chest pack or vest.

- If you trek a long way to fishable water, use a rod case that fits into your backpack.

Packs, Continued

- Vests or packs with fold-down front panels that serve as trays are a big help to fly fishers for selecting flies.

- Several pack systems are variable, with removable backpacks and waist packs that double as chest packs.

- Packs can be adjusted for a snug fit, letting the angler cast without packs shifting.

- Balance is the key issue when using a full pack system, so that front waist packs and backpacks stay in place.

FULL TRAYS: ARRANGING BOXES

Categorize your tackle boxes based on species, lure type, or body of water

As your fishing interests and experience expand, you'll better understand how a variety of lures work and how you plan to use them. Your storage and transport methods for various lures will follow suit as you start to focus on the specialties of your lures: you'll have your trout kits, your bass boxes, your catfish bag, your saltwater tackle boxes, etc.

The important thing in all of this is to know exactly what lure is where. Searching and fussing to find a lure is something you want to avoid. It does happen, given the somewhat chaotic nature of going fishing, but for the most part, when you select a specific tackle bag or box, you need to know what is in it, and where that particular lure or set of

Tackle Cases

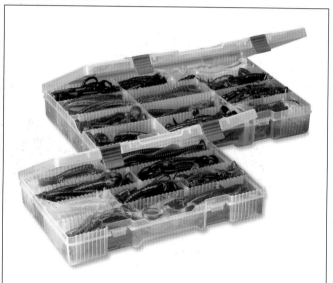

- When traveling light, various small trays and cases can fit in a cargo pocket or vest pocket.

- This system is best suited to smaller freshwater fish species—trout in streams, and panfish and bass in ponds or small lakes.

- Most trays don't anchor the lures, so you have to take care opening the box while wading or on a boat.

- Most types are see-through and let you find a specific lure without having to open the lid.

Tray Boxes

- Triple-tray boxes work well for medium-size lures, such as hard baits, spinners, spoons, jigs, and smaller spinnerbaits.

- Anglers using a large number of crankbaits, plugs, and surface lures often opt for the storage capacity and sorting ability of multi-tray boxes.

- Stay with one lure per slot in each tray; trying to get away with several lures in each slot results in tangled hooks and dropped lures.

- Designate each tray, or tray section, for specific kinds of lures.

lures can readily be found.

How you figure this out, of course, hinges entirely on how you operate as an angler. Some people set up their tackle boxes and bags based upon where they fish, while others organize their tackle by lure type and then by size. Some also create generalized tackle boxes that have a bit of everything, knowing that something in there will work when they fish a water they don't know well.

ZOOM

Many anglers refer to an artificial lure as a "bait," such as "swimbait" or "buzzbait," or use the term to differentiate "hard baits" (usually plastic-bodied lures) from "soft baits" (soft plastics like worms or salamanders). This might confuse some novice anglers, but is simply a more universal usage of the term "bait," indicating anything a fish might grab.

Tackle Chests

- Big, stacked tray systems are a necessity for the advanced angler who needs a lure selection for a variety of tactics.

- An angler covering a lot of ground or water, by truck or boat, will need a lure selection that can cover numerous situations.

- Large chests and tray systems are intended for stationary use—in the garage, truck, or boat.

- Some chests and bags utilize covered, removable trays that can be swapped out for different situations.

Hanging Lure Box System

- A hanging system works well for the angler with many versions of similar hard-body lures, such as medium-size plugs in a variety of colors.

- The advantages to a hanging system are efficient use of space and ease of organization.

- Many hanging systems are adjustable to accommodate varying sizes for a given lure type, such as medium to large freshwater spoons.

- Such a system wouldn't work well with long soft plastics, such as worms, or with spinnerbaits. that wouldn't fit the slots.

ASSEMBLING TACKLE

27

FEATHER BOXES: ARRANGING FLIES

Be sure you've got enough room for several flies of the same pattern

Organizing your flies hinges on the same criteria as organizing lures: What fish are you pursuing, and what do you think they might be eating? Often, however, the freshwater fly caster also has to consider insect activity, as thousands of fly "patterns" (the technical term for an individual design) are intended to mimic various insects that dwell in or alongside trout streams and become active at certain times of the year, and are thus the fish's food of choice.

For freshwater, these nearly weightless lures fall into these groups: dry flies ("drys"), nymphs and emergers, streamers, attractors, terrestrials, and poppers; on occasion, a single fly can be ascribed to two groups, such as a dry fly tied as an attrac-

Dry Fly Box

- Many dry fly boxes have clear windows that let you locate a fly before opening the box.

- In general, organize dry flies according to size, shape, and color, as that's often how the fish are assessing them.

- Don't overfill compartments; put in enough flies to let you pick one without spilling the others.

- With larger dry flies, be sure you can close the box top without mashing upright wings.

Day Box

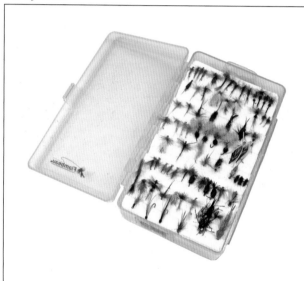

- On some occasions, you'll want to carry a variety of flies in one box.

- Such a "day box" lets you travel light and contains enough picks for a full day's fishing.

- Cull a number of possibly successful flies from your type-specific boxes to create a box that is destination or time-of-year specific.

- This is easiest to do with a foam-lined box so you can embed the hook points and observe entire rows of various flies at a glance.

tor pattern. Dry flies imitate both newly hatched and mature insects (mayflies and caddisflies, mostly) with full wings, and are fished on the surface. Nymphs and emergers are larvae-imitating patterns fished in the water column, nymphs at various depths and emergers just under the surface. Streamers are longer-bodied flies that imitate mostly baitfish or leeches.

Attractors are larger surface-riding flies that generally resemble big insects. Terrestrials imitate grasshoppers and other nonaquatic insects. Poppers—with their feather tails and cup face (which "pops" against the water)—imitate baitfish or insects on the surface. Most saltwater flies are designed to look like inshore baitfish, crustaceans, or various worms and are tied on much heavier-gauge wire hooks than freshwater flies. These require larger fly boxes.

One thing about flies is that you're going to lose a lot of them. You'll snap them off on tree limbs, submerged rocks, and, occasionally, the hard strike of a big fish. So having a half-dozen individual flies of the same color, size, and pattern is standard procedure. Freshwater flies aren't particularly expensive, depending on size. Saltwater flies are a bit pricier.

Large Fly Box

- The longer the fly, the bigger the box, and large streamers will fill a couple boxes quickly.

- With saltwater and big freshwater streamer flies, you might opt for boat boxes that have significant capacity.

- Cull a streamer selection from a larger selection to create a one- or two-box day's supply.

- You can also create species-specific streamer boxes, such as an all-bass or all-pike box (with some poppers for the bass).

Saltwater Fly Box

- Most anglers set up species-specific saltwater fly boxes.

- Use floating fly boxes if you're casting from a boat and taking flies from boxes stashed in a jacket or cargo pocket.

- Some boxes for big saltwater flies are similar to clear plastic trays for conventional lures, and are fitted to the same kinds of bags.

- Get boxes big enough to contain the entire fly, and that prevent the feather points of large flies from sticking out and getting bent or broken off.

ROD PROTECTION: RACKS & CASES

Broken rods can be mended, but keeping them safe in the first place is a lot easier

Most rods and reels worth buying these days are also very well made. Reels could outlast their owner, if properly maintained and occasionally overhauled. Rods can last a long time, but have a higher mortality rate than reels owing to performance stress and accidents. (Hint: Double-check vehicle doors and windows when loading rods.) You should, of course, protect these investments while not using them or when transporting them.

The first key to protection is storing rods and reels out of the way at home, and keeping them secure where you put them. Stacking them in the closet or in a corner of the garage is asking for trouble. Many rods come with rod cases, and when you're

Indoor Rod Rack

- Always remove hooks and lures from the line before storing a rod indoors.

- Various wall-mounted racks hold rods vertically or horizontally; your choice depends on the space with which you have to work.

- A proper rack should support the rod so that it does not flex, or should allow the rod to stand freely.

- Multisection rods over 7 feet long should be disassembled and stored section by section.

Car Rod Rack

- Car rides are hazardous to unsecured rods, so consider some kind of rack if not using rod cases.

- A number of vehicle rod racks mount on the ceiling of the interior, holding rods above the seats, or across the bed of a pickup truck.

- Some interior rod racks reduce passenger room, depending on how they're mounted, so consider where you fish and who you fish with.

- Exterior racks with uncovered rods work fine for short jaunts.

done fishing, the best idea is to clean the rod and return it to its case. Some anglers prefer to leave reels attached to rods, however, and numerous storage racks allow for that.

Outside the home, various rack systems for vehicles allow for easy transport and access to rods while moving from spot to spot. For extended travel, reels (and backup reels) should be stored in the case or pouch that came with them and then tucked in a gear bag, preferably one with a solid exterior. Hard-sided rod cases are a must for extended trips with fishing rods, especially for air travel.

YELLOW ● LIGHT

The angler who flies will rightly choose hard-bodied (very hard-bodied) rod and reel cases if checking that luggage. Rods that break down into multiple sections, however, should be taken as carry-on if the rod case is short enough. Most airlines allow this, even if you have your one carry-on bag. Why leave an expensive rod to chance?

Equipment Bag

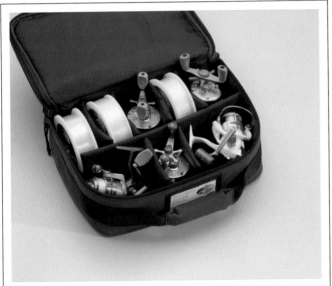

- On major trips, be sure to have at least two backup reels in an easy-access protective case.

- Don't overload a reel bag or you'll tend to drop it and damage reels.

- Nonadjustable storage compartments will be based on reel size, so don't try to jam larger reels into small- or medium-reel bags.

- Pick a case or bag that lets you see all its reels at a glance, rather than having to dig to find the one you want.

Rod Cases

- Numerous rod cases allow the reel to be left on the rod, but be sure the reel handle and body have sufficient protection.

- Soft cases, or rod bags, work fine for short car or boat trips and for carrying short distances.

- Multi-rod cases are an asset for the traveling angler headed out for multiple species.

- For extended travel, single-rod cases can be duct-taped together to form a single carrying unit.

ASSEMBLING TACKLE

CHOOSING EFFECTIVE KNIVES

Blade length, thickness, flexibility, and quality construction are key issues

While many anglers can and do manage with just one knife, having the right knife for a given task can make life a lot easier and safer. Given the variety of situations and cutting necessities you'll encounter while fishing, which can be anything from cutting cord or rope to cleaning and filleting fish, there are several different types of knives that you should possess.

You should first have a quality fixed-blade or single-blade folding knife with a strong 4-inch blade. This would be a general utility knife for jobs other than processing fish. After that, an old-style folding knife, often referred to as a "fishing knife," is a nice addition—it usually has a slender 4-inch blade that works well for cleaning fish (gutting, removing fins) and also

Utility Knife

- A utility knife need not have a blade much longer than 6 inches, and can have either a penknife- or drop-point-style blade.

- Be sure the handle fits your hand and provides an easy-gripping surface that doesn't slip when wet.

- A quality blade has a sufficient "tang" (the thickness of the top edge) and a cutting edge that holds its sharpness.

- When choosing a folding knife, select a model with a locking blade.

Fishing Knife

- Cleaning most freshwater fish does not call for a heavy knife, but one that can make fine, precise cuts.

- Choose a fishing knife that has a blade long enough to cut completely across or down a fish's body.

- With larger freshwater fish or saltwater species, a thicker, longer blade will be necessary.

- Keep fishing knives as sharp as possible, so that cutting is easy when you're trying to hold on to a wet or slimy fish.

a fish scaler that, if made properly, works well. Lastly, you will want a fillet knife, which has a blade of a very specific and flexible design that allows for the deft cutting necessary to make a perfect fillet.

Learn how to sharpen a knife and keep all your knives as sharp as you can get them. A sharp knife cuts easily and cleanly, and that allows you to make smooth strokes with a minimum of effort, without jerking or shoving the knife, which can tear fillets or steaks.

Fillet Knife

- A fillet knife's cutting edge should span from the bottom edge of the fish's body to its dorsal fin.

- The fillet blade also needs to be flexible, with an easy bend, so that the cutting angle can change as the stroke is made.

- About an inch of the blade tip should protrude from the fish's dorsal as you make a fillet cut.

- Don't cut through heavy bone or make steaks with a fillet knife—use a heavier fishing knife for that.

Sharpening Knives

- Numerous devices are available for sharpening knives, some very simple to use, but learning to use a sharpener is an essential field skill.

- Stroke the blade at a 20-degree slant on a sharpener, in a smooth, steady arc across its entire length.

- How hard the metal of a blade is and whether it's stainless steel or not will affect how easily it will sharpen.

- Never sharpen a knife blade on a motorized grindstone, because that can damage it permanently.

33

OUTFITTED: THE COMPLETE ANGLER

Follow these basic setups tailored to various waters to focus yourself and your tackle

After reading about all this gear, you might wonder how it all comes together when you want to go fishing. Clearly, what kind of fish you're after is your starting point, and that affects everything else: the type of rod and reel, the line, lure size, lure boxes, and tackle- and gear-organizing systems. But what kind of angler you want to be also influences how you

complete your outfit.

This spread is intended to give you a model of how to assemble your tackle and gear for some general situations: small and big freshwater, the surf, and angling from a boat. The three things you want to maximize in all situations are efficiency, safety, and success. The one item you must have

Small Freshwater

- Don't overstuff small tackle boxes; if you like to go basic but want to maximize capacity, combine a light vest with a carry box.

- Choose better footwear than you think you'll need, because you'll probably step in some very wet or muddy places.

- Wear long pants and take effective bug repellent and sunscreen.

- Put your tackle box in a secure, level place before you open it, and don't leave it open while you fish.

Big Freshwater

- Practice casting with your vest or pack on, and adjust it until you can cast comfortably, without interference.

- Some fishing shirts come with a Velcro-closure rod loop so you can secure your rod and change lures while wading.

- Cinch your chest waders' belt snugly—this will prevent a complete deluge of water if you fall.

- Put your line clippers on a lanyard attached to the front of your shirt or vest so you don't drop them.

with you in all circumstances is a good first-aid kit. There are numerous pre-made kits that you can buy, or you can assemble your own, based upon how large a kit you can carry.

While this book does not explore how to choose and operate a motorboat, your interest in fishing might arise from the fact that you already own a boat and have increasingly wanted to use it for fishing. See below for some basic guidelines for fishing from a boat.

ZOOM

If you fall in shallow water and your waders fill up, you'll waste energy trying to get out of them while in the water. Rather, walk out and take them off on the bank. However, if you fall in current, water-filled waders could pull you under into deep water where you have to swim. Drop your belt and suspenders and kick your waders off if they take you under.

The Surf Caster

- Wear a light waterproof jacket over your chest waders to prevent wave splash from dropping inside.

- Put your pliers in a sheath on your wader belt, and attach them securely with a lanyard.

- In the cold, wear latex surgical gloves under woolen gloves, or don a pair of waterproof gloves.

- Pick a rod with sufficient length and backbone to cast lures out far enough, but not one so stout that your shoulder wears out after fifty casts.

Fishing from a Boat

- In any boat, always use a personal flotation device (PFD); many are slim and stay out of the way of casting.

- Given how much water you can cover, maximize your lure selection with well-organized, tray-fitted tackle bags that are easy to use on board.

- Keep seats, decks, and angling surfaces clear of tackle, gear, and line, as any small snag or trip could get you wet.

- Always pack rain gear and a good windproof shell on larger lakes and river systems.

ASSEMBLING TACKLE

EASY CASTS: FIXED SPOOLS

A lot of fishing can be accomplished with spinning and spincasting reels

Spincasting and spinning reels are highly popular and widely available, due mainly to their ease of use and great applicability. You can use either one for just about any species of freshwater and small inshore fish, and for nearly every kind of freshwater lure and fishing-catching tactic. Both are fixed-spool reels: The axis of the nonrotating spool is parallel to the rod, and the line slips over the spool edge when cast. Rods must be matched to either type of reel, as spincast reels sit atop the rod and require smaller line guides, while spinning reels hang below the rod handle and call for much wider guides.

Spincast reels are usually the best starter reels for kids, as

Standard Spinning Reel

- A turning bail and line roller wraps line around a central spool; the spool moves in and out on a shaft as the bail turns so line is wound uniformly.

- To cast, flip the bail open and catch the line with a finger, holding it taut; then release it at the end of the cast.

- The drag-adjustment knob is usually atop the spool, or at the back of the reel.

- Many models allow for the hand crank to connect to either side, for left- or right-handed cranking.

Spincast Reels

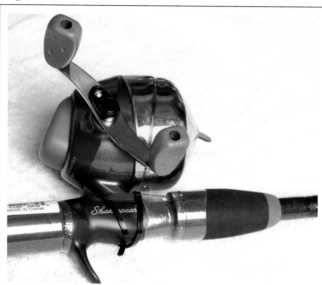

- Most spincast reels are intended for freshwater fishing, and thus don't have excessively strong drags or high line capacity.

- Set the drag using a star-shaped dial on the hand-crank mount, or a circular dial embedded in the reel body.

- Nearly all come with an anti-reverse mechanism, which keeps the spool from turning backwards during casting.

- With the first turn of the crank after a cast, the spool-release button snaps back into place, ready for the next cast.

they are easily understood and operated—just push the line-release button and cast. Such reels are most often paired with line from 4-pound test up to 12-pound test and work best when matched to a lure or sinker that weighs from ⅛ to ¼ ounce.

The best light and ultralight reels are often spinning reels, designed for very light rods, lines, and lures. Larger freshwater spinning reels can be easily matched to 15- or 20-pound-test and can cast lures or sinkers weighing up to 1½ ounces.

Choosing a Rod

- A pistol-grip rod works for one-handed casting; a longer handle allows for more leverage with a two-handed grip.

- Rods often come with information about what size lures they can handle, and that in turn will tell you what size reel and line to select.

- For most spincasting, you won't need a rod that is much over 6 feet long; for kids, a 5- to 5½-foot rod is plenty.

- Rods will range in retail price from relatively inexpensive to moderately expensive.

Freshwater Spinning Rods

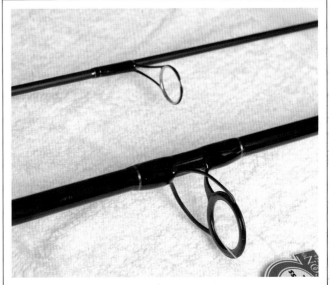

- Most spinning rods have a fixed reel seat, where the reel mounts to a specific point and is locked in place with a single adjustable ring.

- The line guides extend to align with the reel, reducing "line slap" (the rebounding of line against the rod at the end of a cast).

- Many spinning rods are tailored to casting certain kinds of line to certain species of fish.

- Most spinning rods range from 5½ to 7 feet long, depending on application.

SPINNING & SPINCASTING

HARDWARE: REELS TO RODS

The right reel and rod will make a single, natural unit that's easy to use

In the last twenty years, leaps in angling technology have led to a rapid multiplication of types of fishing lines and the design and availability of scores of reels and rods. You could easily have three or four different outfits—a matched rod and reel, with proper line—intended for just one species of fish, such as crappie or steelhead.

As you start out, you'll most likely depend upon one outfit to do a lot of fishing, or possibly two if you pursue very different species. What you want is a quality reel matched to the right rod, making for a balanced, easy-to-handle outfit. You don't have to spend piles of money to do this, but you do have to spend some time doing a bit of research, look-

Loading the Reel

- Spinning reels will handle a variety of line types— monofilament, fluorocarbon, firelines, and certain braided lines.

- Choose the line that gives you the best casting performance, but which can also optimize spool capacity and strength.

- Load the spool with enough line so that it comes off the spool smoothly during a cast, but don't overload it.

- Load the line under tension so that it wraps snugly and evenly.

Attaching Line to the Spool

- Spincast reels operate best with monofilament line, but also work with fluorocarbon lines and superlines.

- Braided line can work on spincast reels but isn't the best choice, as it sometimes wraps a bit too limp for the spool.

- Instructions that come with the reel will tell you how much line of a given test strength that you can load.

- Use a clinch knot to attach the line to the spool (see pages 214–15).

ing through tackle catalogs and asking questions at the retail shop.

Pick a reel that is right for the species of fish you're pursuing—i.e., it has the proper gearing and can cast lures of the necessary size—and load it with a type of line with which it will perform well; for most reels, regular monofilament works fine. Match this reel to a rod that balances well with the reel attached; neither the rod section nor the handle should prove to be significantly heavier than the other.

Line Guides

- The first line guide should be wide enough and hang low enough to let the line pass through with minimal tension.

- If the line forms an angle from the first guide to the reel, the reel is probably too large for the rod.

- If the rod handle seems to affect the movement of the rod, even when not casting, the reel might be too large or too heavy.

- In general, choose lighter rods and reels, and maximize line strength.

Handles

- For one-handed casting, be sure a short, pistol-grip handle gives you enough control of the rod but is also comfortable enough for push-button casting.

- A "blank-through-the-handle" design means that your index finger will contact a section of the rod body inside the handle so you can feel fish strikes easier.

- Choose handles of quality cork or durable foam that fill your hand sufficiently.

- Spincast reels can be mounted on rods with longer handles for two-handed casting.

ROD ACTION: MAKING CASTS

Putting a lure in the right spots calls for a bit of talent that you'll refine over time

Using both spinning and spincasting outfits is very easy, this being the main reason for their wide popularity. You need minimal ability to learn how to cast them, and the skills that you learn come quickly and can be rapidly improved upon. Of course, when you're propelling fish hooks through the air at 40 miles per hour, you do need to take a bit of care to do it right.

The main hazards of casting with a spinning reel are not flipping the bail completely open, or forgetting to do it, or having a damaged bail that flops back. When this happens, the line remains secured and you will most likely snap off your lure because the force of the cast has nowhere to go. The same will happen in spincasting if you fail to depress the

Gripping the Rod

- Fit the real stem between your finger in way that gives you a balanced grasp.

- Most spinning reels can be set up for either left- or right-hand casters.

- Use the index finger of your grip hand to secure the line for casting, and use your other hand to flip open the bail.

- Grab the line with your index finger before you flip the bail or the weight of the lure will pull out line.

Spinning

- Have roughly 4 or 5 inches of line hanging from the tip of the rod in preparation to cast.

- With most rods, casting is a quick hammering motion from about 9 to 11 o'clock high and back.

- Start the cast by looking at your target, and keep your eye on it as you complete the cast.

- Stop the forward motion when the rod tip points slightly higher than the target, and let the line slip off your finger.

line-release button completely and then try to cast.

With a spinning reel, you can keep your index finger extended to brush it against the spool and slow or stop a bad cast. With a spincaster, you can place your free hand alongside the reel as you cast and tender the line with your index finger.

Another main factor is, obviously, the rod you choose. A flexible rod requires a slightly slower casting action than a stiffer one, but you might be able to cast more accurately with a somewhat stiffer rod. Before actually purchasing a rod, test-cast a number of them (with the reel you intend to use on the rod) to see what kind of length and flex you prefer.

Spincasting

- The reel should sit low enough in its seat that your thumb presses directly into the center of the line-release button.

- Keep the line-release button depressed under your thumb through the entire cast.

- Start the cast with 4 or 5 inches of line hanging from the tip of the rod, not counting the lure's length.

- Keep your index finger secure in the trigger grip (on the underside of the rod) throughout the cast; this helps with controlling rod motion.

Spincasting, Continued

- The cast motion is a hammering-a-nail stroke, moving the rod from roughly 9 o'clock to 11 o'clock, and back.

- Release the push button just as you complete the cast and are aiming the rod tip slightly above the target.

- Most spincasters use their major hand to both cast and reel, switching the rod to their minor hand after the cast.

- Grip the rod handle with your minor hand whichever way gives you best control for reacting to fish strikes.

ON TARGET: MASTERING CASTS

Your favorite fishing spot might make some demands on your casting abilities

In the previous page, the "9 to 11 o'clock" casting arc—the direction the rod travels back and forth—is a basic format and assumes that you have enough open space around you to work the rod over the shoulder of your casting arm. Such optimal situations, however, are not always possible in various fishing locations.

Once you're on the water, you'll have to deal with tree limbs, brush, distance, and the need for accuracy. The sight of bobbers and spinners lodged in branches and logs clearly illustrates the difficulties you will often face getting bait or a lure into just the right spot. But as you get more comfortable with your various rods and reels, and start to hone your skills

Two-handed Spincasting

- Two-handed spincasting can give better control and imparts greater accuracy and power.

- Fit the palm of your minor hand (your least dominate hand) along the reel body or at the base of the handle—whichever gives you better control.

- Use your index finger to feather the line as necessary after your thumb lets up the line-release button.

- The motion for both arms is still basically the same: all wrist, forearm, and elbow action—no shoulder or raising the upper arms.

Sidearm Cast

- Use this cast to clear brush and limbs, or when the wind is strong enough to hinder an overhead cast.

- The arc of the sidearm is the same as the overhead, about 9 to 11 o'clock, but flat and out to the casting-arm side.

- Don't open up your arm from the elbow much—flex your wrist as you turn your hand outward to make the cast.

- The flat trajectory isn't in line with your eye, but you'll learn how to maintain accuracy.

as you make even more casts, you will be able to adapt your casting methods.

There are a number of approaches that can help you deal with obstacles, targeting, and distance with your spinning or spincasting outfit. The point isn't to get fancy or tricky, but rather to discover simple ways to apply the capabilities of your rod and reel outside of the most basic, direct forward cast. Greater rod skills means more photographs of you and fish.

Underhand Cast

- Use this cast when you have space below you, such as on a riverbank, but limited space above and to the side.

- Hold the rod in front of you, angled down, and then flex it upward with wrist action to about 10 o'clock.

- Keep the line-release button depressed, or the line around your index fingers, as you stroke the rod downward so the tip points at the water.

- Bring the rod upward briskly, and as the rod comes almost level, release the button or the line from your finger (with a spinning reel).

Flip Cast

- Use this approach in situations of very thick cover that allow for minimal rod movement.

- Start out as if making a brisk sidearm cast and quickly build up speed, but then stop halfway through.

- Rotate your wrist down and back around (forward) in a quick snap so the rod tip travels in a fast, tight semicircle.

- As your wrist comes back around, point the rod at the target and release the line.

TAKING FISH: ROD SELECTIONS

Different fish species call for differing techniques supported by a variety of rods

As you expand your spinning and spincasting endeavors and go after different kinds of fish, you're going to learn more and more about how rod and reel selection matter in terms of the strategies you have to employ to be successful. And the more you look through tackle catalogs, the more you will see a multitude of rods designed for specific species or approaches.

Can you succeed with a budget-limiting number of rods and reels? The answer is yes, if you match the tackle to the fish and are willing to use a variety of lines and rigs. Let's say you actively pursue farm-pond bass and big-river catfish, and sometimes trout in mountain creeks. That's calling for three different basic outfits: ultralight or very light (trout), medium-

Picking the Right Rod

- Rigs with sizable sinkers—up to 2 ounces or more—require casting strength mixed with a bit of finesse.

- Heavier spinning outfits rigged for catfish or other big species fished from boats shouldn't require long casts if you position the boat correctly.

- Stout rods might be a bit easier to control with a sidearm cast rather than the usual overhead cast.

- Big spinning or spincasting outfits still have to strike a balance between rod and reel.

Noodle Rods

- Long, super-flexing rods are designed to cover a lot of water when you can't get close.

- Big rivers with deep water or serious currents are the typical situations when such specialty rods are most useful.

- Spinning for steelhead and salmon on big western rivers is the main use for long "noodle" rods, as they're sometimes called.

- Such specialty rods work well for their given duty, but will not serve as all-around trolling reel.

light (bass), and medium to slightly heavy (catfish). If you load some stronger line on that bass rod, you can easily use it for the catfish, though it might not have as much backbone as you may want for casting heavier sinkers or beating big fish. And you could also get away with putting some heavier line on the trout rod and using it as your backup bass rod.

You can always push a rod's performance with the right line and rigs, but you'll never be able to swap extremes: That catfish rod is too much for the trout, and that lean, whippy trout rod will give out on big water with big fish. And notice that

expression, "backup rod." Your first-string rod is going to bear the brunt of the wear and tear. Quality tackle can handle that, but all things break, under the right circumstances. Ultimately, if you often fish a lot of hours for a certain quarry, you'll want to have an equivalent backup rod, probably two.

Spinning & Spincasting in Streams

- Learn to cast quickly and accurately with both overhand and sidearm casts with a light- to medium-action outfit.

- Select a target—a rock, an undercut bank, or a shady spot—where fish can conceal themselves and observe prey.

- Work the target with several casts, moving downstream, from 10 o'clock to 2 o'clock.

- If a fish strikes, or you see a fish move but it doesn't strike, "rest" the fish for a while and then try the same spot again.

Ultralight Rods

- Matching an ultralight rod and reel to a superthin "fireline" monofilament can create a very sensitive outfit with significant strength.

- Spinning and spincasting gear that won't overmuscle panfish and small trout maximize angling pleasure, especially for kids.

- Ultralight rods aren't much more than 5 feet long, but a good caster can send a lure a significant distance when necessary.

- Given the nationwide range of various panfish species and the fun they provide, a very light or ultralight outfit is a must-have.

CARE: STAYING OPERATIONAL

Just like your car, your fishing tackle needs some basic upkeep to stay fish-worthy

Barring accidents or abuse, the maintenance necessary to keep your spinning and spincasting reels and rods functional won't be costly over the short run. In the long term, however, major parts will have to be replaced on heavily used reels and rods.

With reels, you should lubricate with oil or grease those moving parts that take a lot of stress. Reels will probably come with an instruction manual indicating exactly where to put lubricants. Visually inspect the reel for marks or nicks, especially on the spool, and then test the reel by winding the handle and by pulling the line to test the drag. You shouldn't feel any rough spots or hear any scratches or grinding. If you

KNACK FISHING FOR EVERYONE

Oiling the Bail/Gears

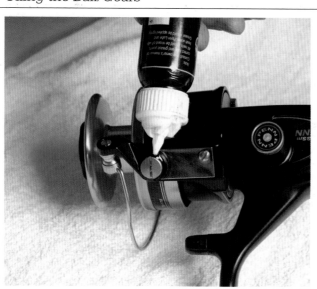

- Using the spinning reel's instruction manual, locate all the parts that need lubrication; don't get lubricant on parts or surfaces that don't need it.

- Lubricate the main shaft by removing the spool; lubricate the point where the bail hinges (the arm joint).

- Once or twice per season, remove the side plate to lightly grease each cog tooth of the gear system.

- Oil the moving surfaces of the handle, the spring inside the drag knob, and the anti-reverse switch.

Cleaning Spincasting Reels

- Remove the hood to be able to oil the main shaft, which is under the spool.

- Also oil the spool's spring and rotary pin (locate these using the instruction manual), and the inner mechanism of the push-button line release.

- Remove the side plate or hood to check and lightly grease the gear cog teeth.

- Check the line release—the spool top should press the line against the inside of the hood—and also the anti-reverse mechanism.

do, you'll need to open the reel to find and clean the problem.

Clean your rods with warm, soapy water and a soft cloth, being sure to run the cloth through the line guides and over the handle. The reel seat, locking rings, and threads should also be cleaned. Once this is done, inspect the rod under a bright light and look for cracks in its body or in the ceramic centers of the line guides. Check the coatings on the line-guide thread wraps to be sure they haven't cracked or partially broken away; bare thread will quickly indicate this.

Making Repairs

- You can remove a slightly bent bail arm and gently reshape it manually; carefully note its parts and how it came off the spool housing.

- Check/replace worn-out drag washers on the spool or in the gearbox of a spinning reel, and under the star-drag wheel in a spincaster.

- Damaged spools in both types of reels and damaged line-rollers on spinning reel bails should be replaced.

- Remove bent handles and wrench them gently back into shape, or replace them.

Reconstructing Rods

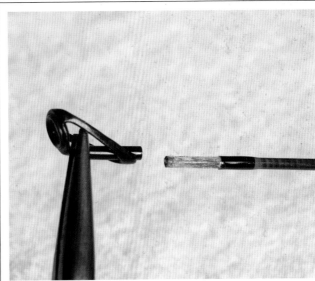

- The tip-top (the top line guide) can be removed and replaced if damaged, using epoxy glue and a replacement part.

- Holes in cork handles can be filled in with a mixture of cork dust (from a wine cork) and waterproof carpenter's glue.

- In the field, temporarily replace broken line guides with guides fashioned out of light, smooth steel wire, attaching them to the rod with duct tape.

- Cracked ferrules can be fixed temporarily with a binding of electrical tape.

SPINNING & SPINCASTING

47

OLD STYLE: HORIZONTAL SPOOLS

Lots of anglers still use the current form of a classic design

Reels with a horizontal, rotating spool that releases line at a right angle to itself predate spinning and spincasting reels by many years. Such reels and those used for fly casting were the two main types of reels in America for much of the late nineteenth century and first half of the twentieth century. The tricky casting of these old convention reels—which often suffered tangles of overrun, unspooled line, called "backlash"—led many anglers to take up spinning and spincasting gear.

But state-of-the-art baitcasting and conventional reels are now widely used in America, with baitcasting reels taking a lead role in professional bass fishing, and the larger, heavier conventional reels seeing continual use for big catfish, salmon, and saltwater species. The term "baitcasting" is a misno-

Baitcaster Features

- A defining feature of the baitcaster is the level-wind guide that travels along the spool to layer the line evenly.

- The line guide, is carried by a pawl that travels in a groove called the "worm gear" that turns as the spool turns.

- Gearing is housed in the reel sides, while drag washers are usually located under the star-drag knob at the base of the wind handle.

- Many baitcaster models have a spool-release clutch for casting, similar to the line-release button on spincasters.

Baitcaster Designs

- Baitcaster body designs vary from the low-profile, ovoid reels often used in bass fishing to reels with rounded sides, depending on the gearing configuration.

- Reel bodies are often aluminum, or sometimes or titanium-coated aluminum, with aluminum spools and

- Teflon-coated drag discs.

- While mostly associated with bass, baitcasting reels allow you to fish successfully for any species.

- Many baitcasters have adjustable spool-brake systems on their spools that reduce backlash.

mer, however—such reels are more often used with artificial lures than natural bait, but the name hung on from years ago (probably to differentiate these reels from fly-casting reels).

Baitcasting reels designed for freshwater use have better cranking power than spinning or spincasting gear and can thus handle some serious fish. They are also quite accurate for casting, and some models have adjustments for true precision casting. Conventional reels, especially when designed for saltwater, come with heavy-duty drag and gearing systems that are meant to smoothly handle very strong, fast fish.

ZOOM

If you're looking for precision casting control and strong cranking power in a small package, baitcasting might be the way to go. Learning thumb-and-spool control for casting isn't easy but can be mastered by most anglers, and the overall method of use might greatly appeal to some anglers.

Casting a Baitcaster

- To cast a baitcaster, depress the spool-release clutch with the thumb of your casting hand.

- As you depress the clutch, slide your thumb forward so it presses against the spool, securing the spool so it won't turn.

- Depressing the clutch creates "freespool"—the gears are disengaged and the spool can release line very easily.

- Use thumb pressure to control the spinning of the spool as you make your cast, this being the trickiest part of baitcasting.

Conventional Reels

- Conventional reels frequently lack the level-wind mechanism, and the angler must manually direct the line onto the spool.

- Conventional reels can pay out line to send lures or bait deep, or for trolling, and can be cast from shore by experienced hands.

- While often used for saltwater fishing, conventional reels are not true big-game reels, which are larger and have very powerful drag systems.

- Use a glove or wrap the thumb with tape when manually directing line on a conventional reel.

RIGHT STUFF: BAITCASTING OUTFITS

Anglers can create nice combinations of reel power and rod-casting accuracy

Just like in spinning and spincasting, baitcasting or conventional reels are matched to various rods to create a balanced outfit. Most baitcasting reels are roughly the same size, generally ranging from 6 to 9 ounces in weight, but can differ in their line capacity, gearing, and number of ball bearings. With many quality models, you can choose combinations of

weight, line capacity, gearing, and cranking power. The varying sizes of conventional reels also depend on their application and differ mainly in their line capacity and gearing.

A terrific advantage of baitcasting reels is the fact that just about any kind of line works with them—monofilament and superbraids or other superlines. This gives the angler a sig-

Types of Line

- Various baitcasters have quick-remove spools, in case you need to switch quickly from monofilament to more sensitive braided line.

- Most baitcasters release braided line easily, but can still be subject to some backlash due to angler error.

- Braided line is ideal for heavier-duty applications when fishing from boats and using bottom rigs for big fish.

- Monofilament works best with baitcasters when fishing soft plastics and also works very well with hard-bodied lures and spinnerbaits.

Loading (Spooling) a Baitcasting Reel

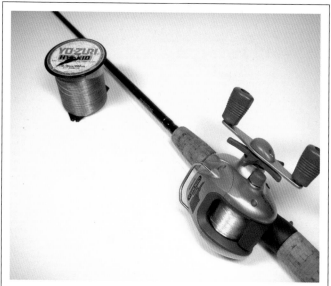

- Load a baitcasting reel with line under slight tension, with a steady, moderate reeling speed.

- Attach the line end to the spool with a short clinch or improved clinch knot (see pages 214–215).

- Be sure the line guide is loading the line evenly along the entire length of the spool.

- Check the reel's instruction booklet to find out how much line of a given test you can load onto the spool; don't overload the spool.

nificant range of performance, depending upon the kinds of lures or rigs being used. Most conventional reels are loaded with monofilament line, and some saltwater reels are loaded with wire line for tougher species.

There is a huge number of baitcasting and conventional rods from many different makers. Rods for baitcasters are designed for casting, while those meant for conventional reels are often referred to as "boat rods"—rods meant not so much for casting as for paying out line—surf rods, or trolling rods (see Zoom sidebar).

ZOOM

A variation on the conventional reel is the trolling reel, which often contains a beefed-up drag system and bearing, in addition to an analog or digital line counter mounted on the reel body so you can accurately reach your depth. Trolling rods range from 7 to 10 feet long.

Picking the Right Rod

- The target fish species and lure selection often dictate the length and action of a baitcasting rod.

- Rods with a trigger grip underneath the reel seat and short handle are designed specifically for one-handed casting.

- Baitcasting rods range from 5½ feet to 7½ feet, depending upon the casting distance and fish-fighting strength you need.

- Baitcasting rods incorporate small-diameter line guides on top of the rod.

Conventional Rods and Reels

- Conventional reels have a lever switch to put the reel into freespool, but press your cast-hand thumb onto the spool first.

- Given line capacity, you can sometimes replace just the first 100 yards of line using a line-to-line knot (see pages 230–31).

- You can pair conventional reels with both long surf rods and shorter, stouter boat rods.

- Casting a conventional reel with a surf rod calls for effective spool control using your thumb, something that takes time to master.

SPOOL CONTROL
Accuracy comes from the baitcasting angler's ability to manipulate the duration of the cast

Few people can pick up a baitcaster and make proficient casts right away. The touch, timing, and coordination of baitcasting give it a bit of a learning curve, but the accuracy that you can derive by using your thumb to regulate the spool and outflow of line is tough to match with other tackle.

Practice casting with the lures, reel, rod, and line that you

intend to fish with the most. Buy practice weights that approximate most of the lures that you'll use for baitcasting, anywhere from ¼ ounce to ½ ounce. Also, if you have a reel that comes with a built-in spool-braking system, which slows the spool's spinning right at the very end of the cast to prevent overruns ("backlash"), turn this system to its lowest set-

Working with the Spool

- Fill the spool with line to the correct full capacity so that you don't have to reach with your thumb to tender the spool.

- Place the index finger of your casting hand around the handle or trigger grip, and press your thumb to the spool.

- The spool-release clutch, if your reel has one, should be right under your thumb.

- If you wish, cast with two hands, gripping the rod handle behind the reel with your non-casting hand.

Baitcasting: Step 1

- Rotate the casting hand inward slightly so the knuckle of your index finger points upward.

- This slight turning of the casting hand allows the wrist to flex thoroughly and do the necessary work to cast.

- Using just wrist and forearm, take the rod tip from 9 to 11 o'clock, stopping the rod without going over your shoulder.

- Be sure the rod fully flexes, or "loads," putting a bend in it at the top of the cast.

ting or disengage it entirely so that you're learning from an unfettered spool.

If you use a baitcasting rod with a true "pistol grip"—a trigger grip coupled with a short, hand-filling handle—you're going to be making one-handed casts. However, many casting rods have trigger-grip handles that extend well beyond the reel seat and allow for a two-handed grip. Most professional bass anglers use these longer handles, as they aid in rod balance and control.

Baitcasting: Step 2

- Your thumb leaves the spool briefly as you finish the forward stroke and the lure takes flight.

- Once the rod unloads and the lure is moving, immediately put your thumb into contact with the spool to control the lure.

- As the lure arcs downward to the target, press your thumb back into the spinning spool to control the lure's drop.

- When the lure is just about to reach the target, press your thumb into the spool until it stops.

Baitcasting: Step 3

- Most anglers switch hands after the cast—the casting hand moves to the crank, and the other hand holds the rod.

- Hold the rod just behind the reel, your index finger in the trigger grip and your thumb atop the handle.

- Try palming the side of the reel with part of your hand, your fingers wrapping under the reel seat, as you reel with your casting hand.

- Hold the rod directly in front of you, elbows at your sides as you reel.

HORIZONTAL SPOOLS

DROP ZONE: PERFECT FLIPPING

When the bass are in thick cover, the baitcaster has a way of reaching them

The sidearm, underhand, and flip casts that work for spinning and spincasting outfits (described in Chapter 4) can also be readily accomplished by the baitcasting angler. In fact, along with mastering spool control, these approaches can produce highly accurate lure placement, despite the angler being crowded by brush or having to cast around tree limbs overhanging the water.

Baitcasting reels matched to the right rod also offer another excellent technique: "flipping" (sometimes referred to as "pitching," and not the same as a flip cast). This technique, which arose out of largemouth bass fishing, uses a short, pendulum-like cast to deliver a weighted soft-plastic lure or

Flipping: Step 1

- Flipping does not cover distance—it's an accuracy cast—so get close to the target.

- You must stand to make this cast because of how you use both arms and move the rod.

- Let out as much line as the rod is long, up to 8 feet, holding up the rod tip.

- Use your free hand to draw line off the reel, holding it between your thumb and index finger, stopping your hand just off your hip.

Flipping: Step 2

- Dip the rod tip as you pull back the outgoing line with your free hand, extending your arm.

- Raise the rod tip again, building up speed, and swing the lure (think of a wrecking ball) forward to the target.

- As the lure swings forward, move your free hand forward, letting the line shoot between your index finger and thumb.

- Finish the cast by pointing the rod at the target, extending it as necessary to reach the target.

jig to heavy cover, usually from a boat. With this method, an angler can tuck the lure right into a spot where he thinks a bass might be waiting.

Flipping requires two-handed coordination: the casting hand that works the rod and the other hand that handles the line. Flipping is a smooth, deft, easy cast that should quietly drop the lure. This is a technique that works only with a lure that has enough weight to carry the pendulum action of the cast—a jig or weighted worm, not a plug or popper.

Flipping: Step 3

- Release the line from your free hand, and move that hand to the lower section of the rod.

- Using your casting hand, work the jig or plastic worm vertically or dart it amid the cover (roots, branches, weeds).

- Strikes, usually from bass, can often come very quickly when flipping, and you'll have to muscle a big fish out of the cover.

- Fish the lure slowly, especially in heavy cover, but don't spend too long working one spot.

The Flippin' Switch

- To pitch the lure to another spot, point the rod at the lure and grab the line with your free hand.

- Pull the line with your hand as you raise the rod, turn to face the new target, and perform the wrecking-ball motion again.

- Some baitcasting reels have a "flippin' switch," which allows you to flip with just your casting hand.

- Engage the flippin' switch and depress the spool clutch; line pays out but the gears are still engaged.

OPERATIONAL MAINTENANCE

Look for serious wear and tear on gear that gets regular or heavy workouts

Most quality baitcasting or conventional reels and rods hold up very well these days, though they also cost a lot more than they did twenty years ago due to the quality of materials and level of technology that go into them now. If you really fish hard with your tackle, you're going to have to tend to it regularly. Hundreds of casts on the bass lake several week-ends in a row, or lots of hard work hauling in big bluefish in the bay, call for proper attention to maintenance.

Given the gearing necessary to generate the cranking power that these reels have, major fixes to the gear system are best left to professional tackle shops or to manufacturer maintenance programs. But basic upkeep of reels is within

Checking & Lubricating the Gear

- Check all moving parts of a reel to be sure they operate smoothly and are not worn.

- The pawl on the level-wind (the pin that moves in the level-wind worm gear as line is retrieved) endures a lot of wear, so check this often.

- Don't oil the level-wind worm gear, but if you replace this part, give it a touch of grease.

- To grease a baitcaster's gears, remove the side plate and put a bit of grease on the tooth of each gear.

Inspecting Worn Gear

- Inspect baitcasting and conventional rods for cracks or weak spots, especially after some heavy use.

- Cracked or splitting rod-guide wraps should be cut away, and the guide rewrapped.

- Carefully check reel seats for cracks or warped parts, especially on conventional rods that endure heavy fish-fighting stress.

- Duct tape is a temporary fix for weakened reel seats, but a broken seat will need a major fix or professional repair.

the ability of most anglers.

The items on baitcasting rods or rods for conventional reels (boat rods and surf rods) that require the most troubleshooting are the line guides, because these are focal points of great stress. If a rod were to lose one or two guides under the stress of fighting a big fish, that would greatly throw off the effectiveness of the rod and put more tension on the line, risking the loss of the fish.

Specific Reel Maintenance

- With baitcasting reels, oil the handle shaft, drag system, and the spool shaft bearings (on both sides).

- If your reel has a flippin' switch and anti-reverse switch, lightly oil these.

- With conventional reels, oil the drag lever or star drag, the spool shaft, the handle shaft, and the anti-reverse switch.

- Conventional reels sometimes have sophisticated gear systems, so follow exactly the manufacturer's instructions for greasing gears.

Cleaning the Rod

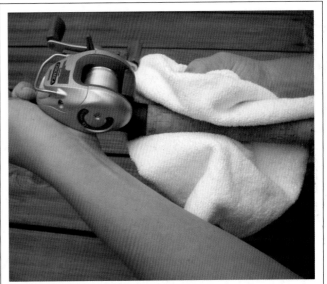

- Soiled rod handles have to be thoroughly cleaned, as embedded dirt will slowly cause breakdown of the handle material.

- Use a small scrubbing brush and warm, soapy water to remove dirt from rod handles.

- Seriously stained or soiled spots in cork or foam can be worked out with very fine sandpaper.

- The cap on the butt of the rod should be replaced if it becomes cracked or loose.

HORIZONTAL SPOOLS

SURF TACKLE: TOUGH STUFF
Casting over crashing waves is a bit of work, but the quarry are worth it

Surf casting originated on the East Coast, but anywhere there's breaking water on a beach or jetty, you'll find people casting lines. It is unlike anything else, as you must deal with waves, tides, and the trickiness of fighting and pulling a fish in from the breakers. It requires a bit of stamina and strength (and sometimes a beach-worthy vehicle so you can cover some ground), but when you're tied into a powerful striped bass or drum, you'll find that it's a real blast.

Surf casting calls for a good deal of serious tackle and gear. You can't really outfit yourself fully with just one medium-size tackle box, a workable rod, and some decent pliers. You could fish for a few hours that way, walking along the suds

Choosing the Right Rod

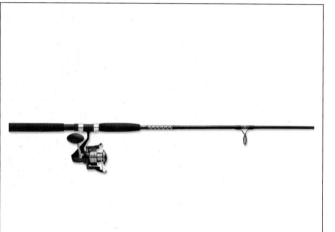

- For casting lures along the surf (i.e., "pluggin"), choose a spinning rod light enough to make numerous casts all day.

- Such a pluggin' rod will be roughly 7 feet long and have a bit stiff, and it might also double as a strong freshwater bass or pike rod.

- Heavier spinning rods can work for brief periods of casting lures, but are more suited for heaving weighted bait rigs.

- A dependable surf-casting spinning rod will vary from moderately to very expensive.

Surf-cast Spinning Reels

THUNN

- A surf-cast spinning reel should be loaded with a minimum of 12-pound-test line, up to 30- or 40-pound test at the max.

- A monofilament main line tied to a heavy mono-filament or wire leader can handle most surf-casting species.

- Look for reels with strong drag systems, with upwards of six disc washers, made of stainless steel or Teflon.

- Just as with spinning reels for freshwater, hand cranks can be switched for left- or right-handed retrieve on numerous surf-casting reels.

and casting plugs, but to cover the array of fish, necessary rigs and lures, and the demands of the sea itself, you'll need an assortment of rods, reels, tackle storage systems, and good tools.

Conservation plays a big part in surf casting, often because a number of the species pursued on the surf also comprise commercial fisheries. In recent years, various eastern states have officially declared striped bass a gamefish, thus giving it a beneficial legal status. Other places have considered calling for a saltwater fishing license to create conservation funding.

Various Types of Spinning Reels

- Some surf-cast spinning models forgo a bail, allowing the angler to pluck line from the roller to cast quickly.

- High-end models, made of tough, lightweight alloys, are meant to endure hard use in the salt.

- Numerous models are designed for "live-lining"— letting out line with the bail closed while fishing live, swimming bait (usually bunker).

- Various surf-cast spinning reels come with high-performance drag systems for superbraids or other small-diameter lines.

Conventional Reels

- Casting a conventional reel into the surf calls for thumb-on-spool control just like baitcasting.

- Look for a conventional reel with an anodized aluminum frame (often a one-piece frame) and spool, and instant or continuous anti-reverse ability.

- A number of manufacturers now make light-duty inshore reels very similar to freshwater baitcasting reels, with low profiles and spool-release clutches.

- A conventional surf-casting reel can vary from moderately to very expensive.

BAIT DELIVERY: THE RIGHT RIGS
Various hook, leader, and sinker configurations fit multiple situations and species

Experiencing a fish smash into your lure is quite exciting in the surf. However, using bait is usually much more productive than casting plugs and jigs, and is often necessary. Casting bait also calls for numerous considerations, including the species you're targeting, the bait selection and method of presentation, and choice of correct hook. Many tackle shops sell premade rigs intended for specific species, but a lot of surf casters prefer to make their own rigs to their specifications.

Leader sections for smaller inshore fish, such as croaker or small weakfish, can be from 10- to 12-pound test. For serious fighters of some size, like bass or drum, leaders can range from 30- or 40-pound monofilament up to 80-pound test for

Fish-Finder Rig

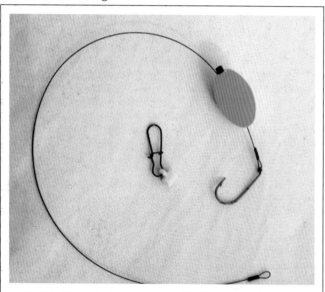

- The fish-finder rig allows a fish to grab the bait and move without feeling the weight of the sinker.

- The main line and leader slides through a sleeve connected to the stationary pyramid sinker.

- The float on the leader keeps the bait off the bottom, but a short line to the sinker puts the bait in numerous fishes' feeding zone.

- This works best with live (swimming) bait, or with circle hooks that don't require an immediate hook-set.

Surf Rig

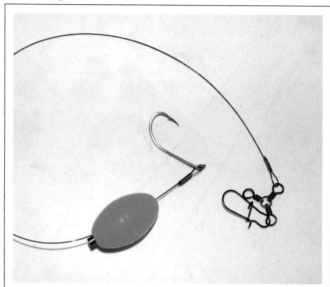

- This is the most basic rig for fish feeding along the bottom of the surf, and works well with clam as bait.

- The bank sinker lets you reel in the rig slowly, but a wire-pronged bank sinker can be used when you want something that will grab the sand.

- The leader from the three-way swivel to the hook should be at least 12 inches long, up to 36 inches.

- Use a duolock or crosslock snap to attach the sinker to the three-way swivel.

big fish. Nylon- or Teflon-coated leaders, or wire sections, can be used for toothy or sharp-edged species like bluefish.

Hook choice depends on fish size and their strike and mouth hardness. Larger-size claw and Kirby hooks work well with bait, and O'Shaughnessy hooks can also be used in surf rigs. Many anglers have switched to using circle hooks, which have a shorter shank and wider gap than regular hooks (which are often called "J-hooks" because of their shape), because circle hooks catch in the corner of a fish's mouth, allowing for easier release.

Top-Bottom Rig

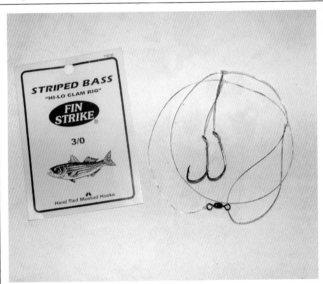

- Space the two hook leaders 6 to 15 inches apart, with the bottom leader about 6 inches above the sinker.

- The leaders should be 12 to 18 inches long and can be left bare or fitted with floats or bucktail jigs.

- Attach the leaders with dropper loops; these can be on the same or opposite side of the sinker.

- Fit this rig with different-size hooks to target smaller to medium-size inshore species, and bait it with squid or fish strips.

Spreader Rig

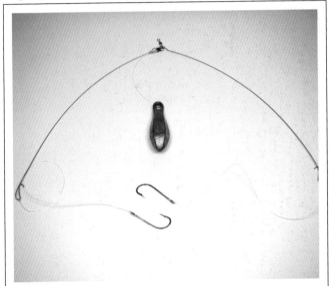

- Used most often for fluke or flounder, this wire-bodied rig is usually a store-bought item.

- The main line ties to the center of the wire, with leaders tied to the opposite ends of the wire.

- Cast this rig off jetties or into channels—places where gamefish corral schools of baitfish against the structure.

- Use a pyramid sinker with a spreader rig to anchor it, but not one that is too heavy so that you can't feel strikes.

SURF ESSENTIALS: GEAR & BAIT

Good choices minimize the usual hassles and hazards found in the sand

The beach is a pretty rugged place, actually. The wind, crashing waves, and shifting sand can tax a surf caster, so gear choices have to be durable, smart, and convenient—items that help save time and energy, and aid the angler in making the right moves to catch fish.

Dropping a reel in the sand can put it out of commission for the rest of the day, and a rod that gets dropped often half-disappears into the sand and can be stepped on. So various devices that secure your outfits and let you easily tie on lures or bait your rigs are must-haves.

How you clothe yourself is also of major importance. A lot of surf casting takes place in the fall and spring, when the

Sand Spikes

- Sand spikes are essential for setting up rods after casting out baited rigs.

- You can make them yourself by cutting 40-inch lengths of 3-inch PVC pipe, cutting one end at an angle to pierce the sand.

- Use a rubber mallet to pound the spikes into the sand at a 90-degree angle; don't angle them much toward the water.

- Set a spike next to your truck or chair so you can conveniently change bait or lures.

Using Four-Wheel-Drive Vehicles

- In many places during the fishing season, anglers can buy a pass to drive 4WD vehicles onto the beach.

- Rocket-launcher rod racks, attached to the front bumper or the top of the cab of a truck, are too useful not to have.

- Remove lures and rigs from your rods before transporting the rods in the rocket launcher.

- Bumper trays provide a highly useful place to stow a cooler, and can be easily removed after the season.

water can be cold and the shoreline wind nippy. You need layers under your waders, a wind-resistant outer shell, and the overall ability to keep your skin dry.

Your bait selections can also make or break your day. Fresh bait is best, and most often the tackle shop where you buy your bait will be a good source of intelligence on which gamefish species are moving around and what they're eating. Have several kinds of bait on hand to be able to target various species of fish.

The Surf Angler's Outfit

- In chilly weather or surf, opt for warmer neoprene waders instead of rubberized canvas.

- Wear a waterproof shell over your waders so splashing wave water won't go down your waders.

- Zip your shell all the way and be sure your neck is covered, so that wave splash doesn't drain down your neck and chest.

- On jetties or on shoreline boulders, wear metal-studded sandals called "corkers" that you can lace around your wader boots.

Surf Baits

- Create a place—a table or the tailgate of a truck—where you can easily sort and cut bait on a heavy-duty cutting board.

- Have two sharp knives, one for large cutting tasks and one for finer slicing.

- Keep bait packages sealed and out of the sun when not in use.

- Be sure the bait is legal where you're fishing; most store-bought baits are fine, but some baitfish species are protected—check your state's regulations, which are often online.

CLEAN UP: PRESERVING HARDWARE

The surf angler needs a bit of extra dedication to maintaining equipment

Maintenance habits are often overlooked by anglers, but given the amount of money you will put into decent equipment, you'll be helping yourself by tending to its mechanical health. Additionally, there is probably nothing else on earth short of battery acid that corrodes and destroys equipment faster than the saltwater environment, so the hardware you use in surf casting needs a lot of attention when you're done.

Saltwater tackle must be tended to after every use, and sometimes even while you're using it. Put together a cleaning kit of dry rags, toothbrushes, oil, grease, and a spray lubricant that you take with you to the beach as a kind of first-aid bag

Washing Reels and Rods

- As you change lures or rigs, occasionally give reels a dunking in the bucket of freshwater, then dry them.

- Turn the handle, listening and feeling for grit or sand that has lodged in the handle mounting or spool.

- A reel dropped in the sand needs immediate dunking and inspection; with some washing and lubrication, you can probably avoid trouble.

- When done fishing, wash rods with warm water and mild soap, rinse, dry, and inspect for cracks.

Driving on Sand

- Driving on the sand requires a drop in tire pressure to about 20 psi; you'll get stuck if you don't soften your tires.

- Have a small shovel in your vehicle to dig the vehicle out of ruts or holes if you get stuck.

- Once off the beach, hose off the tires, wheel wells, and undercarriage of the vehicle, or drive through a convenient rain puddle.

- Don't forget to reinflate your tires before driving home on the paved road.

for your hardware. Also set up a good-size bucket of fresh-water in the back of the vehicle (this chapter must assume you're driving a truck, Jeep, or SUV on the sand) for cleaning.

One thing that's going to happen to your beach vehicle is that you're going to get a lot of sand inside it. This is an un-avoidable factor of surf casting, so don't worry about it—you can vacuum it out later. You'll probably have to clean out fish slime, butt ends of submarine sandwiches, and spilled cof-fee, too.

ZOOM

For surfcasting information on the East Coast, try www.surfcaster.com, www.stripersonline.com, www.mssa.net, and www.stripersurfclub.com. On the West Coast, go to www.sport-fish-info.com, www.scsurffishing.com, and www.westcoastangler.com. Be sure to check out the links page on each of these Web sites—they can direct you to location-specific sites or conservation groups.

Basic Reel Maintenance

- Check the reel gears after any period of sustained use, especially if you were fight-ing fish.

- You might have to lightly re-grease reel gears halfway through a season of heavy use, first wiping away dirty or clumped grease.

- Replace the working section of line after every outing, or at least weekly if fishing just once or twice a week.

- At the end of the season, unspool all of the line on your reels and discard.

Preventing Corrosion

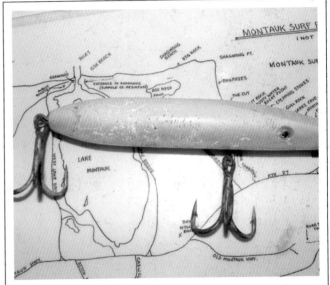

- When done with a lure, dunk it in the bucket of freshwater and blot it dry with a sponge (not a rag).

- Have an assortment of re-placement treble hooks and split rings, as these often corrode on lures no matter how much you wash them.

- Dunk bait rigs in the fresh-water bucket; lead sinkers don't easily corrode, but snap-swivels and hooks do.

- Wash, dry, and then oil and wipe dry pliers and knife handles, blade sides, and tangs after use.

SALTY TOSS: EFFECTIVE CASTING

Good casting form and enough rod will put your bait in the right place

Casting a surf rod is unlike any other casting you'll do, but it isn't difficult if you focus on technique without overemphasizing strength. Depending on the configuration of the sandbars in front of you, your cast will have to travel anywhere from 100 to 150 feet, maybe more. That might sound a bit far, but with the length and strength of most surf rods, and

the heavier weight of saltwater lures and rigs, you'll hit such distances. The main thing is to cast into the zone where most coastal gamefish cruise a sand beach.

This zone is called the "slough"—a channel between the outer sandbar and the breakers at the edge of the beach. If you look out at the water, you'll see waves crest perhaps 50 or

What to Do Before You Cast

- Before casting, take a quick look around you to be sure you've got room and won't hit anyone.

- You don't need to scamper over the sand to try to create casting momentum; just stand and cast.

- Make your cast from the wash of the waves on the sand, not by walking into or past the breakers.

- Be doubly sure with a spinning outfit that the bail is locked open and won't flip back as you cast.

Surf Casting with a Spinning Outfit

- Grip a spinning rod handle at the reel and butt, pointing the rod almost level back over your shoulder, facing your target.

- Feet apart, bring the rod over your shoulder, pulling down the butt, your reel hand pushing forward rapidly.

- Create power with your arms and shoulders to sweep the rod through the cast.

- As the rod comes past vertical, release the line from your finger, and stop the rod at about a 45-degree angle.

70 yards off the beach, almost breaking as they pass over the outer sandbar, and then flattening slightly and rolling toward the beach, where they break. Between the outer sandbar and the area of foamy white breakwater is where the gamefish will cruise. Of course, you have to consider the tide (high or low), the wind, and the shifting sand. Sometimes a "cut" will form in a sandbar, creating a channel from deeper water directly into the slough, which gamefish will readily travel.

YELLOW LIGHT

Casting in the surf is a bit hazardous. Time your casts with the waves so that you don't turn into a breaking wave. Beware of the force of undertow, which can quickly alter your footing. Breaking waves can quickly rise up to your knees, so take care to notwade out an unnecessary distance.

Surf Casting with a Conventional Outfit

- Open your hips and shoulders, extending the rod behind you almost level, thumb on the spool, the other hand on the rod butt, your weight on your back foot.

- Sweep the rod upward, pivoting your shoulders and hips to speed the cast, turning your body toward the water.

- Release the spool as the rod reaches 12 o'clock, and continue the forward cast.

- Extend your rod-hand arm completely, shifting your weight to your forward foot.

Finishing Your Cast

- You should be facing the water as you finish a cast with a conventional reel.

- If you finish off balance, you didn't open your hips and shoulders enough at the start of the cast.

- Keep the reel on freespool as you walk from the water's edge to the sand spike (with a spinning reel keep the bail open as you walk).

- Put the rod in the sand spike, engage the spool and drag, and tighten the line until you put a slight bend in the rod.

FINDING & HANDLING FISH

Keep an eye on the water surface and the birds, and beach fish with a little footwork

The first step in successfully landing a fish in the surf is to know your species. Are you casting to a fish that strikes hard, or picks up a bait and slowly moves off? Does the fish have a hard mouth or a softer mouth? Are you fishing circle hooks instead of J-hooks? And most importantly, how big and strong could your target species be?

The answers to these questions will tell you how heavy your line should be, how to strike the fish, and how to play it. When a good-size fish hits your lure or bait, it can turn for deeper water or go chugging down the beach, which can take your line directly into the lines of other anglers, a very tricky situation. So the main issue in fighting a fish in the surf is to get

Keep an Eye Out for a Blitz

- A "boil" is the splash of a single fish feeding on baitfish it chased to the surface.

- A "blitz" is a fast-moving school of gamefish, usually bluefish, chasing a school of baitfish along the beach.

- When a blitz comes down the beach, every angler will run for it, so pick your spot and be careful of your cast.

- You should always keep an eye on the seagulls and terns, as they follow the baitfish and gamefish.

Night Fishing

- Night fishing on the surf can be greatly productive for certain species like drum and striper.

- Fishing live-rigged eels and bunker chunks on a heavy outfit are tried-and-true approaches for big striped bass at night.

- Fish react negatively to bright lights shined on the water, so avoid this with headlamps and truck lights.

- Use headlamps that can be angled to shoot light on your hands, but choose dimmer settings, or green or blue light.

maximum pressure on the fish immediately and keep that pressure on through the entire fight.

With most bait rigs, a fish will hit hard enough to hook itself (or hook itself with circle hooks). But with a fish-finder rig, you'll have to take up some slack before you can set the hook. Most fish that strike a lure immediately hook themselves but your reaction to a hard strike also helps set the hook.

RED ● LIGHT

Unfortunately, many inshore gamefish have dangerous levels of PCBs (polychlorinated biphenyls) and mercury in their fatty tissues, where such industrial wastes tend to collect. Years of dumping waste at sea have led to this. Note the local warnings about fish consumption. Pregnant women should probably not eat any surf-caught fish.

Fighting in the Waves

- Wave action will make your rod nod and bend rhythmically, but when a fish hits, the thrashing is obvious.

- Pull the rod out of the sand spike, keeping it vertical as you quickly reel up any slack, and then sweep it back to set the hook.

- Keep the rod tip high and a strong bend in the rod as you fight the fish.

- Crank the fish in steadily, without stopping, keeping constant rod pressure.

Beaching a Fish

- Fight your fish to the point where the waves rise before breaking onto the beach.

- Pick an incoming wave, and as it raises your fish, reel in quickly and jog backward several steps, keeping the fish just on the back of the wave.

- Don't let the fish tumble into the curl of the breaking wave.

- After the wave breaks, bend the rod to hold the fish in place on the sand as the wave water rushes back.

DELIVERING FLIES: RODS & REELS

A weighted line flung by a flexing rod is the essential part of fly casting

Fly fishing, along with conventional bait fishing and ice fishing, is one of the oldest forms of angling in America, predating spinning and spincasting by roughly a century. Put simply, this form of angling is a way to deliver a virtually weightless lure, a fly, to a fish by using a weighted line and a rod that flings that line. Most people think immediately of trout when they think of fly fishing—and that's sensible, as the origins of fly fishing are found in the effort to cast imitations of various insects to feeding trout—but nowadays people fly fish for everything from smallmouth bass to sailfish.

Fly reels hold line and put drag on running fish, and don't do much else. They have pretty simple mechanical systems,

Line Weights

- The line-weight system, from 0 to 12, is the basis of the tackle and relates to the actual weight of the line in "grains."

- Lighter lines, and thus smaller reels, range from 0 to 4; medium lines range from 5 to 7, with reels slightly larger.

- The heaviest lines for the largest species range from 8 to 12.

- A fly reel is loaded mostly with "backing," a thin-diameter line that fills the reel and backs up the 60- to 80-foot fly line.

Spools and Reels

- Most fly reels are "single action"—one turn of the handle creates one revolution of the spool.

- The spools on most reels are easy to detach from the frame so you can switch lines quickly.

- The spool arbor—the central, horizontal post around which the line wraps—can have an increased circumference for greater line capacity.

- Large-arbor reels are often used for very fast-running, hard-fighting fish, such as tarpon and steelhead.

though some use very strong disc-drags. They're made of polycarbonate, lightweight alloys, and aluminum. The fly rod is the more crucial piece of tackle. Typically made of graphite, fly rods are rated at various levels of "action," or flexibility: slow, or full flex; medium, or mid-flex; and fast, or tip-flex (the stiffest). In general, the slower models are lighter rods used for smaller species, mid-flex rods are used for a variety of medium to large species, and tip-flex rods are used for long casts with heavier lines for larger fish.

ZOOM

Smaller to midsize fly reels have a "click-drag" system that functions via two pawls that engage a gear, which puts resistance on the spool. Heavier-duty reels have a disc-drag system, which employs a "friction washer" housed between the reel frame and the spool that, when adjusted, presses against the spool.

Fly Rods

- Most fly rods are a tube of graphite from 7 to 9 feet long, and come in two- to five-piece models.

- Casting with a fly rod is done with one hand in nearly all cases except for "Spey" rods, which are two-handed rods.

- The style of handle grip depends on angler preference, but the handle should fill your hand and be comfortable to cast.

- Nearly every fly rod has a cork handle, though some big-game rods have foam handles.

Fly Reels

- Fly reels always mount on the underside of the fly rod, usually with an uplocking ring.

- The drag switch on many smaller reels is a dial at the base of the spool, turned left or right to increase/decrease drag.

- The holes in the sides of the reel allow a wet line to drain water.

- On the larger reels used for big fish, a dial in the center of the side plate tightens or loosens the disc-drag system.

CHOOSING FLY LINES & RODS

The various qualities of different fly rods and lines handle many fishing situations

Figuring out what line to use with which reel and rod is where fly fishing befuddles a lot of anglers. The difficulty probably arises from the fact that there are so many different configurations of fly line, and the crucial properties of rods differ widely size by size and from maker to maker.

Most anglers start with a mid-weight fly rod, usually a 5 or 6 weight, with moderate flexibility (medium action). Fly casters usually use a "weight forward" (WF) line—a line that has a larger diameter at the forward end, which makes that end heavier than the rest of the line. This weight carries the line using the force the rod gives it during a cast. Depending upon application, a fly line floats or sinks, slowly or quickly. A

Fly Lines

- Level and double-taper lines work for very short casts and very small flies, but are not in widespread use.

- The weight-forward line is the most popular, as it casts well over many distances.

- A shooting head, with its shorter, lighter midsection, is designed for maximum distance casting and is often used with sinking lines.

- Special weight-forward lines, like bass-bug tapers and certain saltwater lines, can help increase casting accuracy and distance.

Backing

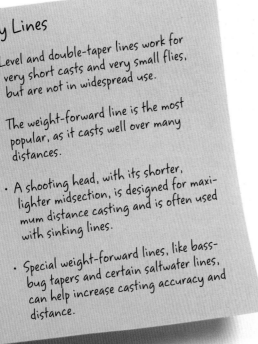

- A reel should come with specifications for the amount of backing it needs, depending on the fly line being used.

- Fill the reel with enough backing so that the fly line rises almost to the edge of the spool.

- Backing allows for retrieving and storing the fly line in large coils that play out easily, without being misshaped.

- Backing can be Dacron or a braided superline in sufficient strength for the fish sought; don't use standard monofilament.

weight-forward, floating line for a 6-weight outfit is abbreviated "WF6F," whereas a sinking line of the same size is "WF6S."

Rod choice connects to line performance. Casting a light, 3-weight floating line to small-stream trout calls for a quite flexible (slow-action) 3-weight rod. Casting a 9-weight sinking line on a big river requires some power, and for that you would select a 9- or 10-weight mid-flex or tip-flex (fast-action) rod, depending on your casting ability and style.

ZOOM

The term "taper" refers to the shape of the fly line as determined by its diameter across its length. But sometimes the term is used specifically in reference to the larger-diameter forward portion of a shooting head or weight-forward line. Bass-bug or striper-fly lines are often called "specialty tapers," referring to the modified weight-forward design.

Fly-Rod Action

- The thickness and diameter of the graphite tube determines how fast/stiff or slow/flexible a fly rod will be.

- A more flexible rod can require a somewhat longer casting duration.

- Fast-action rods work for big-water and saltwater conditions in which an angler needs to cast weighted lines or punch through wind.

- For short casts on small water, a 7-foot fly rod is all that's needed; longer casts on bigger water call for 9- or 10-foot rods.

Using the Equipment

- Generally speaking, line weight, reel, and rod all match by number.

- Most tackle can handle fly line one number higher: a 5-weight rod and reel can handle a 6-weight line, and so forth.

- A fly rod loads with the tension of the line as it comes off the water or travels through the air.

- When the rod flexes forward in casting, it unloads and imparts its energy to the line, propelling it to the target.

BUSINESS END: LEADERS & TIPPETS

The "presentation" of a fly hinges on the qualities of the final length of line

The leader in fly fishing is a bit specialized. A leader's length, strength, and diameter are very particular, given that you might be casting a small fly that must be tied to a very light "tippet"—the terminal section of the leader—but you might be fishing for big trout that can really fight, so you need a leader of some strength. Freshwater fly leaders are also quite a bit longer than usual, anywhere from 7 to 12 feet, while saltwater fly leaders are often constructed of different sections of different strength.

A fly leader is usually constructed of monofilament or fluorocarbon. You can make leaders by connecting lighter and lighter sections of monofilament with blood knots (see pages

Fly Leaders

- The butt end of the leader attaches to the end of the fly line with a knot or loop-to-loop connection.

- The short butt section ranges from 20- to 30-pound-test line that quickly tapers to a lighter section.

- A sectional leader can be constructed of five or six pieces of monofilament or fluorocarbon.

- A leader must taper evenly and thoroughly enough to complete the fly cast by turning the fly over and putting it on or into the water.

Choosing the Right Leader

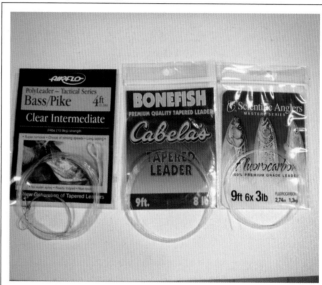

- For floating flies, especially for wary trout, a longer leader of about 9 or 10 feet is necessary, possibly longer.

- Shorter leaders, around 7 or 8 feet, work all right with subsurface flies, such as nymphs or streamers.

- In general, with small, floating flies, tippets need to be light—4X to 6X—and 24 to 36 inches long.

- When casting big flies to tough freshwater species, such as big largemouth bass, a short, strong tippet works best.

228–29), or you can buy premade tapered one-piece leaders that get thinner and thinner down to the last 30 inches or so, which is the tippet section.

Freshwater fly leaders are classified by their tippet size, usually from 0 to 6; the higher the number the thinner the diameter. Tippets also have an "X" suffix: 1X, 2X, 3X, etc. The X is a holdover from the days when leaders were passed through a razor-sharp tool to make the tippet thinner and thinner; for example, a 4X leader passed through the tool four times. Tapered monofilament leaders are now created chemically.

Leader Types

- Monofilament leaders are just slightly denser than water and will sink slowly.

- Newer fluorocarbon leaders are significantly denser than water and sink steadily, and they work well with quick-sinking fly lines.

- A "level leader," a single 7- or

8-foot section of monofilament or fluorocarbon, works for aggressive species that aren't wary about the leader.

- You can sink a subsurface fly using just a monofilament leader with a floating fly line, as the fly's weight will take it down.

Shock Tippet & Saltwater Leaders

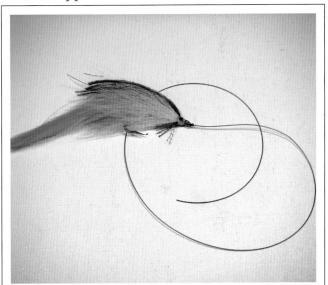

- Numerous manufacturers offer species-specific saltwater leaders with a tippet of correct strength.

- Handmade saltwater leaders must taper effectively like freshwater leaders, but are much heavier and stronger.

- A "shock tippet" is often tied

to the end of a saltwater leader to handle the fast, hard strikes of certain big species.

- The shock tippet combines a heavy monofilament tippet, shock-absorbing knots, and a section of hay wire or very heavy monofilament connecting the fly.

FLY ESSENTIALS

Casting a fly is often as good as, and occasionally more effective than, standard lures

Just like any other fishing, fly fishing is about the right presentation of the correct lure. While there are applications, such as casting poppers to largemouth bass or streamer flies to trout, that can be easily matched with conventional lures cast from spinning or baitcasting outfits, there are some things that only a fly caster can do, such as hook trout that are entirely focused on mayflies, or cast an imitation shrimp to a very particular, very wary saltwater species, such as bonefish.

A big part of the value of fly fishing is in the methodology. The demands, limitations, and advantages of casting these kinds of lures this way makes you think about fish and fishing in wholly new ways. Your casting ability will also change

History of Fly Fishing

- Fly fishing evolved in England in the nineteenth century, with braided horse-hair and silk lines, and greenheart-wood rods.

- The earliest lures of fur, feather, and hook were intended to imitate various insects, hence the name "fly" fishing.

- Other early British patterns imitated baitfish to catch salmon and pike.

- Several thousand insect patterns now exist, imitating all stages (nymph, emerger, hatching adult, and grown adult) of mayflies, caddis flies, stoneflies, and other species.

Streamer Flies

- Streamer flies, similar to original salmon-fly patterns, imitate various baitfish and also big nymphs, leeches, and crustaceans.

- Streamers are comparable to plugs, spoons, spinners, and jigs but are sunk by the fly line and their own weight.

- The body materials of a streamer—various kinds of feathers, fur, and synthetics—impart a swimming action or profile that attracts fish.

- Streamers can be cast and stripped in by hand, drifted over the bottom, or trolled from a boat.

greatly, and will most likely improve, when you learn how to quickly put a fly on a specific spot—a task that has specific challenges in every size of fly, line, and rod.

Catching a particular kind of fish on a fly under particular conditions can be quite an achievement. At the same time, smart anglers take along all the effective tackle they know they might need, and many switch between fly rods and spinning or baitcasting rods as conditions change, fish move, and different challenges arise.

For many years, flies were made from the feathers of various wild and domestic fowl and the fur of different wild mammals. A number of those materials are no longer in use due to conservation of the species from which they derive. In the past twenty years, however, numerous synthetic materials such as Mylar, plastic foam, and epoxy have taken fly tying and fly performance to new levels.

The Fly Rod

- A basic fly cast requires more room than making a cast with a spinning, spincasting, or baitcasting outfit.

- Fly rods are much longer than regular tackle, as the fly rod needs more leverage to power the line.

- Fly rod line guides, called "snake guides," are S-shaped curves of wire that create little line friction.

- The larger, bottom guide is called the "stripping guide," as the angler pulls line by hand from below that guide.

Floating Flies

- Anglers must consider currents and slack water when casting floating flies and lines.

- Fly lines can be manipulated in the air, with rod action or pauses, to throw slack in the line to deal with varying currents.

- Both upstream and downstream casts call for slack to get the floating fly to drift naturally.

- When a floating fly is pulled against the current by the moving line, this is called "drag" and it scares fish away.

ROD WORK: MAKING CASTS

With fly lines and rods of any size, the basic casting motion and shape are the same

The first few times you try fly casting, you'll probably have line lashed everywhere, but the basic motion will start coming to you sooner than you think. Imagine a wooden dowel with a long piece of very light string attached to the end; flick that dowel back and forth, between 10 and 1 o'clock, using just your arm and elbow, and watch how the string forms the

same shape—a flat line with a tight loop at the end—going backward and then forward. That's the basis of every cast, and it starts with the backcast.

To learn the motion, extend about 20 feet of line from the end of the rod, take up the proper grip and stance (as described below), and simply work the rod back and forth,

Proper Rod Grip

- Hold the rod handle with your thumb on top; keep your wrist in line with your forearm.

- The tip-top of the rod should be at eye level, with line out in front of you, as you make the backcast.

- Keep your elbow slightly away from your body, about 2 or 3 inches, and your biceps almost touching.

- Raise the rod swiftly and smoothly, your thumb knuckle coming up almost in line with your ear and your wrist straight (as if hammering).

The Backcast

- The elbow is the pivot point of making the backcast and forward cast.

- Don't tilt your wrist backward at the end of the backcast; keep it in line with your forearm as you stop the rod at 12 o'clock.

- You must wait for the backcast to unroll behind you before you come forward; this pause gets longer with more line.

- When you feel the line load the rod with a slight tug, that's when your arm should come forward.

keeping the line in the air. Don't try to force it or go quickly, and be sure to stop the rod at a near-vertical position. The more line you have in the air, the more time you must give to the backcast—the backward motion of the rod that pulls all the line from in front of you and transfers it behind you, and thus loads the rod for the forward cast.

The Forward Cast

- The "hammer and nail" motion will be most clear on the forward cast; keep your wrist and forearm straight.

- Speed up the rod as you come from 12 o'clock down to eye level again, using your forearm and shoulder to power the stroke.

- If your elbow comes away from your body a little bit, that's all right.

- Finish the cast crisply with a bit of hand strength, but keep your wrist locked—don't cock it downward.

Completing the Cast

- As you finish the cast, use your hand to aim the tip-top just slightly above the target.

- Cast the line out over the water, not into the water, so that it falls evenly as the loop of leader unrolls.

- If your forward cast comes forward sloppily, the line probably touched the ground behind you because you opened your wrist on the backcast.

- If the cast collapses completely, you didn't pause long enough for the backcast.

ADVANCED CASTING: LINE CONTROL

You can manipulate a fly line with rod and hand to increase accuracy or distance

Manipulating a fly line as you make a cast and while it's on the water are often necessities, frequently having to do with the varying speeds and directions of current, and streamside cover. Other times, you'll manipulate the fly line to increase line speed and thus improve your distance.

Discussed here are four major line-control techniques for freshwater: the roll cast, for when there's too much cover behind you for a normal backcast; line mending, to reduce current drag on the leader and fly; the slack cast, to throw slack into the line before it lands on moving water; and the double haul, a way to impart more speed to a floating or shooting-head line. Each method has its nuances, but the

The Roll Cast

- Put the rod tip as far behind you as you can, lower than normal, with the line on the water alongside you and extending outward.

- Your rod hand should be a bit below your shoulder as you stop the rod behind you.

- Stop the rod behind you so the line stops on the water, as you need the surface tension to load the road.

- Make a normal forward cast, which will unroll the line off the water.

Mending Line on a Stream

- Before mending, throw some slack into the main line by wiggling the tip-top, which will pay out some line.

- Don't pull too much slack from your leader, something you're already trying to prevent.

- Make the upstream mend with a quick, smooth roll of the rod (like a slow jump rope) that picks up the bowed section of line and drops it up-current.

- There should still be slack in the leader, and a drag-free fly.

fundamentals are easy to comprehend. The double haul will seem tricky, but basically you shorten the line with your line hand on the backcast by "hauling," or pulling on it; you then put line into the backcast and then haul the line (shortening it) again on the forward cast.

Saltwater fly-casting techniques are much more demanding in two aspects: dealing with accuracy over distances and dealing with wind. This is the realm of the truly advanced caster, and is detailed in a number of the books mentioned in the resource section.

Throwing a Slack Cast

- Strip a length of slack line off the reel, pinch the line with your index finger against the rod handle, and make a cast.

- As the line flows forward, release the slack line and wiggle the tip of rod sideways before you finish the forward cast.

- Complete the cast by bringing the rod tip down parallel to the water, as this will maintain the slack in the line.

- The line should fall evenly on the water in a slack-filled squiggle shape.

The Double Haul

- Start a backcast, with no slack in the line and holding the line with your line hand.

- As you raise the rod, haul the line down past your waist with your line hand (shortening the entire line).

- As the rod reaches vertical, with the line flowing behind you, bring your line hand up almost level to your rod hand.

- On the forward stroke, haul the line down past your waist again, and then release it as you finish the forward stroke.

HARD-BODY LURES

Crankbaits, poppers, and plugs take multiple fish species in all kinds of waters

There are probably more makes and models of artificial lures than there are brands of beer. Their development in America really took off in the late nineteenth century. The creation of various plastics through the mid-twentieth century, and the computerized designs and high-tech materials of the late twentieth century, brought about light-bodied, high-performance

lures that look and act a lot like those things they're intended to imitate: mainly baitfish, but also worms, amphibians, and crustaceans.

You can cast artificial lures with any kind of outfit—even a fly rod can launch very light soft-plastic lures. As mentioned in earlier chapters, most any rod will come with instructions

Crankbaits

- Used to target bass found at specific depths, crankbaits are intended to imitate a fleeing baitfish, like a small shad or perch.

- Such lures are made of plastic or balsa wood and can incorporate internal noisemakers that rattle.

- The size of the lip of the crankbait determines its diving depth: the larger the lip, the deeper the dive.

- Most crankbaits are designed to wobble to varying degrees while "cranked" through the bass's strike zone.

Lipless Crankbaits

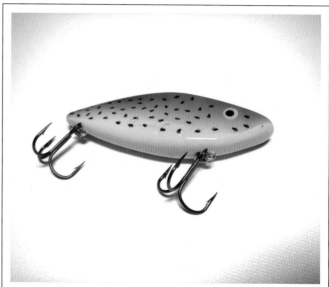

- Lipless crankbaits are shaped similarly to regular crankbaits, but have a lipless, pointed nose and flat, slimmed flanks.

- Often used to search for feeding fish, such lures can be fished with varying speeds and retrieves.

- These lures are usually fitted with very loud internal rattles to send out vibrations similar to those of moving baitfish.

- The body design of lipless crankbaits gives them a fast wobble that maximizes bright, glinting body colors when retrieved quickly.

printed on the lower section indicating how heavy a lure it can cast properly. Trying to launch a 4-ounce pike lure with a spinning rod designed for lures not heavier than 1¼ ounces will make for a difficult day.

Numerous lures are species-specific, while others attract strikes from any kind of fish. Spinnerbaits are mostly intended for various bass species, and secondarily for pickerel and pike. You won't see many catfish caught on a spinnerbait (though don't rule it out), but a single spoon in the right color can nab trout, bass, pike, and salmon.

ZOOM

Various crankbaits and plugs allow for what is called "tuning"—adjustments to the diving lip or the angle at which the line attaches to the split ring—to alter the action of the lure during the retrieve, thus creating more or less wobble depending upon the situation.

ARTIFICIAL LURES

Poppers

- The concave face of a popper throws up a small splash of water and makes a distinctive popping sound.

- A popper's action is meant to imitate a wounded baitfish on the surface, or a baitfish attempting to escape a predator below.

- Some cigar-shaped surface lures are designed to waggle their tails while spitting a bit of water from a slightly concave face.

- Surface lures are highly effective for largemouth bass after sundown.

Plugs

- Longer hard-bodied lures that float or sink slowly and are reeled in with a steady retrieve are often referred to generically as "plugs" or "minnow-style" baits.

- Floating models dive and dip off the surface, while sinking models drop to a desired depth and are then cranked through the strike zone.

- Plugs can have jointed bodies, or even articulated flexible bodies that waggle attractively during a retrieve.

- Floating plugs can also be twitched or jerked across the surface.

SPINNERS, SPOONS, & JIGS
Combinations of flashiness and swimming action of metallic lures make fish notice

Spinners, spoons, and jigs are some of the oldest lure designs in America, but there is now an incredible variety of these elemental lures. Spoons are probably the most simple of all—just an oblong, rounded piece of light, thin metal, painted or unpainted, sometimes dimpled or curved. They have a lively wobble when fished, and mostly imitate a fleeing baitfish.

Spinners also imitate fleeing or wounded baitfish, with a metallic or plastic blade that spins rapidly around the wire shaft of the lure. But fish might also mistake small, dark spinners for aquatic insects. Jigs come in a tremendous variety but have a basic configuration: a metal head (usually lead) fused to a hook, with an attached body of bucktail, feather, or soft plastic.

Spinners

- Quality spinners incorporate brass parts that are silver-, copper-, or chrome-plated, and stainless steel main shafts.

- Blade shape varies from oval to oblong, depending upon performance and overall spinner size.

- Most spinners have a single treble hook and can be dressed with feathers or fur to create a flowing skirt around the hooks.

- Spinners have to be retrieved fast enough to get the blade spinning, as this sets the swimming action and path.

Spoons

- Spoons made for regular casting and retrieving can also often be trolled, and some spoons are meant to be "jigged" (retrieved vertically).

- Spoons can have a finish as simple as stamped, silver-plated brass or have inlaid holographic reflectors.

- Most spoons are fitted with a single treble hook, but some spoons come with a single hook with a weed guard.

- Many spoon patterns have one, two, or three imitation eyes either painted on them, or bead eyes.

These three kinds of lures in various sizes can be fished for just about all North American gamefish when casting to midlevel depths or going to the bottom. Spinners catch a ton of trout and salmon, and larger bucktailed versions catch muskie. Spoons take bass, pickerel, and pike, and jigs are a traditional lure for smallmouth bass and crappie. It's all a question of what you think the fish are eating at what depth, and if you have a lure that will imitate that food in appearance and movement.

ZOOM

Jigs and spoons play a major role in ice fishing, in which they are fished vertically and jigged by raising and dropping the rod tip, with minimal use of the reel. Ice-fishing-specific spoons and jigs are often Day-Glo colored with highly iridescent finishes as visual attractors.

Jigs

- Small jigs—from $1/32$ ounce to $1/16$ ounce—in all kinds of colors, and sometimes fit with spinning blades, effectively target panfish, perch, and trout.

- Bucktail jigs from $1/4$ ounce to $3/8$ ounce work well for larger perch, smallmouth bass, and walleye.

- Jig heads vary greatly in shape, from round to football- or bullet-shaped, depending on the desired depth and swimming action.

- Jigs are very effective when slow, probing fishing is necessary—something that quick-swimming lures can't handle.

Largemouth Bass–Specific Jigs

- Largemouth bass–specific jigs feature big, blossoming latex skirts and heavy weed guards.

- These jigs are intended for casts to thick cover, such as weeds and lily pads, and swim toward the bottom with a lot of motion.

- The swirling, pulsating skirt on such a jig is what entices strikes from largemouth bass.

- Fish such a jig in a yo-yo fashion, getting it to rise and then drop to maximize the action of the skirt.

SPINNERS, BUZZBAITS, & PLASTICS
Some lures look like art projects, while others are meant to be near-perfect copies or strange creatures

Anyone who watches professional bass fishing, live or on television, knows how big a role spinnerbaits, buzzbaits, and soft-plastic baits play in that endeavor. Just about every serious bass angler has a wide assortment of these highly versatile lures.

Spinnerbaits and buzzbaits don't look like any kind of natural bait. Their flash, motion, and sound are what induce strikes. Spinnerbaits can be fished shallow or deep, fished to the bottom and jigged up, or fished in a stop-and-go fashion, and can nab smallmouth bass, crappie, pickerel, and pike, as well as largemouth bass. Buzzbaits ride in the surface tension and their propellers spin, making noise and commotion.

Spinnerbaits

- Color choice is a major consideration, but finding the right depth to fish a spinnerbait is just as important.

- Most spinnerbaits use willow leaf or Colorado blades, singly or in combinations, and blade size and color have a significant impact on fish attraction.

- Anglers often affix a soft-plastic grub or worm section to a spinnerbait hook, in the center of the skirt.

- Spinnerbaits should swim without wobble, and can be "tuned" by bending the body wire to achieve this.

Buzzbaits

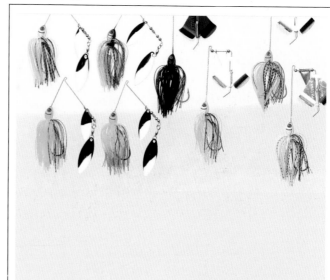

- Use buzzbaits to search out bass in muddy waters or when other lures don't produce.

- Pick a buzzbait that can be fished as slow as possible but with the blades still turning and spitting water.

- Buzzbaits are productive in calm, warm water, and in hot conditions under cloudy skies; use darker colors for murky water and light colors in sun.

- Bass that short-strike a buzzbait can be nabbed by adding a single trailer hook to the main hook.

These lures are mainly for targeting largemouths. Originally buzzbaits were "in-line" lures, much like big spinners, but changes in design brought about the mobile-like configuration of one or two wire arms that hold up the prop blades over the skirted main body.

Soft-plastic lures can be either near-replicas of various natural foods—worms, frogs, and fish—or alien-like things with tentacles that swirl and squiggle in the water. There's a soft-plastic lure for every situation and most major gamefish, including numerous variations for salt water. Such lures work very well in heavy cover, but you can also jig them, crawl or bounce them along the bottom, or do a yo-yo retrieve (up and down). Two important soft plastics are the worm and the lizard (that imitate a salamander or mud puppy), which have been around for a long time. These can be fished weighted or unweighted, deep or shallow. Plastic frogs, in a variety of forms, can be retrieved across weeds and lily pads. "Tube baits" are a form of hollow soft plastics, and you can fish these in much the same way. Some larger tube baits have become serious big-bass producers.

Plastic Worms

- Bass are caught on plastic worms of various sizes, but in general the longest worm fished correctly takes the bigger fish.

- Suppleness and softness are the most important qualities in a soft plastic.

- Plastic worms come in a huge variety of colors—picking the right color requires a little research and trial and error.

- A worm's body shape, tail configuration (curly tail, paddle tail, etc.), and thickness often determine the way to fish it.

Various Soft Plastics

- Flipping a big, ugly soft plastic into heavy cover has become a major tactic of largemouth bass fishing.

- Dragging a tube bait over the bottom or over rocks and structure is a highly effective approach for smallmouth bass.

- Soft-plastic "jerkbaits" look like worms with a fattened belly, but are designed to dart and drop, imitating a wounded baitfish.

- Many soft plastics are scent-impregnated with natural ingredients so they really stink.

PLASTIC WORM RIGS

Emphasizing the tempting swimming action of artificial worms and a slower retrieve are key

The plastic worm has long been a mainstay of bass fishing. Few other fish are caught on such lures. The main point of rigging these worms in various ways is to capitalize on their suppleness and swimming characteristics, and move them through a bass's strike zone in a highly enticing way. They work best in warm water and warm weather, and for casting

to specific bass lairs or to fish at a particular depth. Unlike a buzzbait or lipless crankbait, plastic worms are not lures with which you can cover a lot of water or attract bass with sound.

When fishing these rigs, work them slowly to give the worm a chance to slither and dance. Use the rod tip to raise

Carolina Rig

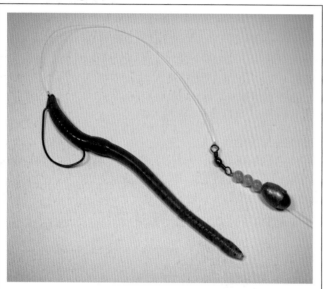

- Hook a worm through its head with a worm hook and embed the point.

- Tie 20 inches of leader from the hook eye to a barrel swivel; this can be shorter if fishing in thick cover.

- Push the main line through a cone-head or barrel sinker, then through a bead or two, and then tie the end of the main line to the top eye of the swivel.

- Slowly retrieve the weight along the bottom, as the worm suspends above the bottom.

Texas Rig

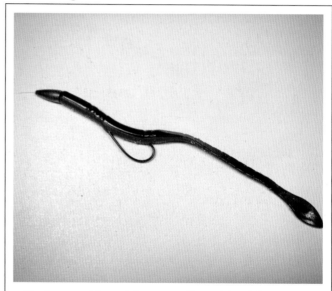

- Hook a worm through its head with a worm hook, embedding the point.

- Tie a leader to the hook eye; the worm can simply be fished this way weightless, if desired.

- For weight, slide a cone-head sinker down the leader to the hook eye; you can leave it sliding, stopping it with a bead, or secure it to the worm head.

- Work this rig through shallow cover.

then softly drop the worm, moving the tip from flat in front of you (9 o'clock) to 11 o'clock, then back down, reeling up the slackened line as you go. When bass take a plastic worm, the sensation is more like a quick thud or rap on your line because the fish inhale the slow-moving worm, as opposed to striking hard a fast-moving plug. Learning to sense a bass's strike on a worm, and the difference between that and the worm or sinker bumping a submerged tree limb, comes with experience and patience.

ZOOM

Numerous brand-name hooks are designed specifically for use with worms. These hooks have kinked shanks or elongated bends to allow you to rig worms in a variety of ways, with or without the point embedded. "Worm hook" is a generic reference to a kink-shank hook used with Texas or Carolina rigs.

Wacky-Worm Rig

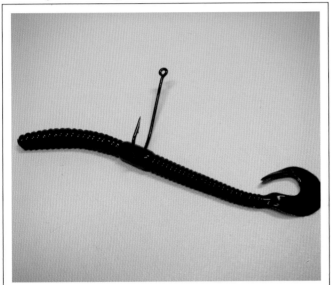

- The wacky-worm rig often involves a thick, shorter worm with evenly tapered ends.

- Hook the worm through the center of its body, or cinch a small rubber O-ring around the worm and slip the hook through that.

- Use a light, 20-inch leader tied to a small barrel swivel, and as light a main line as possible or a superline.

- Let the wacky worm slowly descend without any rod motion, then give it very light twitches with a very slow retrieve.

Drop-Shot Worm

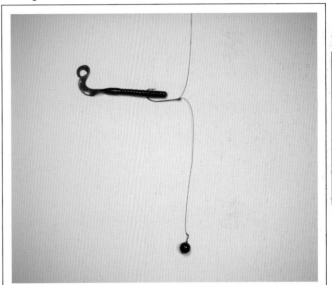

- At the intended depth, tie on one or two hooks with dropper or Palomar knots (see pages 216–17) directly to the main line.

- Tie the end of the main line directly to a casting or bell sinker heavy enough to hold bottom.

- Pick a worm that flutters in the water, and hook it through the nose.

- Drop the sinker to the bottom, keeping an almost vertical connection while lightly vibrating the line with the rod tip (don't lift the sinker).

BIG BITE: SALTWATER LURES

The key to selecting saltwater lures is to match the size, color, and profile of the bait

Most saltwater lures imitate saltwater baitfish: shad, bunker, sardines, silversides, or eels. Other saltwater baits—clams, crabs, squid, sandworms, and shrimp—are not often imitated (though some soft plastics imitate crabs, squid, and shrimp); these things are simply fished in their natural state. The fast, steady retrieval of a plug, swimbait, or top-water lure easily

imitates the flight of a baitfish running from a predator, and some saltwater jigs might pass for squid or shrimp.

Except for rigs and lures for various big-game species, saltwater lures mostly resemble freshwater lures but tend to be a bit bigger or heavier, as saltwater baitfish are a good deal larger than their freshwater cousins. A spoon that works in a

Saltwater Plugs

- Saltwater plugs come in as many color schemes as any freshwater model, and can be solid bodied, jointed, or have articulated, flexible bodies.

- An all-black diving plug works well at night and in the hours before dawn, in the surf and inshore.

- A switch to a bright orange or orange-yellow diving plug just after sunrise can sometimes prove effective.

- Just as with freshwater lures, the larger the diving lip, the deeper the plug will dive.

Surface Lures

- Surface lures that spit a lot of water make a popping sound that attracts various gamefish.

- These lures are sometimes bottle-shaped or pencil-shaped, or have a wide, cupped face, and contain rattles to accentuate their fish-calling ability.

- Fish surface poppers with a stop-and-go action, using the rod tip to yank the lure with enough force to make the lure throw water.

- Saltwater top-water baits, or stickbaits, are worked just like in freshwater, with a retrieve that emphasizes their herky-jerky action.

freshwater lake, however, could just as easily catch inshore saltwater species. And a big saltwater soft-plastic lure—one of those fitted to a lead-cast fish head—could work for striped bass in a large freshwater reservoir.

Hooks on saltwater lures, however, need to be tough, sharp, and of heavy-gauge wire. You will find that having an assortment of extra treble hooks, split rings, and a ring-eye tool on hand when you fish in salt water will be a big help, as various fish will blunt and bend lure hooks in all kinds of ways.

Saltwater Jigs

- Saltwater jigs from 1 to 3¾ ounces can be tipped with a large, dark soft-plastic worm to attract larger gamefish.

- Drop a jig down to the bottom, especially along the edge of a drop-off, raise it up with the rod, and then drop it again.

- Tip a jig with strips of squid or fish fillet, or a shrimp tail.

- Heavier jigs (2 to 4 ounces) are best cast from a boat so they can be worked vertically over bottom structure.

Skirted Teaser Rigs

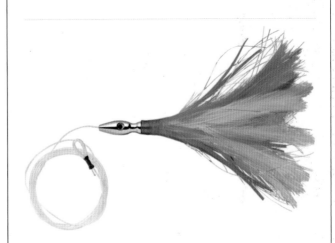

- Skirted teaser rigs of different sizes can be trolled to varying depths, giving them a dancing-swimming action.

- Most often, teasers are rigged with a hook baited with a natural (dead) or soft-plastic baitfish, and trolled in spreads of six or eight.

- Multiple hookless teasers can be trolled as attractors to bring gamefish into specific rigged teasers or lures.

- Teasers work on a multitude of species, from king salmon to dolphin to billfish.

ARTIFICIAL LURES

WEIGHTLESS LURES: PICKING FLIES

The variety of flies now available to the angler are thousands more than those in use not long ago

Although the lure on the end of a fly line can range from a tiny puff of feather to a length of surgical tubing shaped into a baitfish, both of these lures and everything between these limits of design can be called a "fly." Flies are measured on a scale that matches standard, even-numbered hook sizes, from 2 (big) to 28 (very small) for freshwater flies, and 0 (pretty big) to 4/0 (bigger) for saltwater flies.

The great advantage to flies is that if an angler also knows how to tie a fly (an art all its own), he or she can perfectly match the lure to the actual natural creature. And unlike buying lures in a store, if you can tie flies, you can make the thing exactly as you think it should be made.

Dry Flies

- Dry flies imitate various winged aquatic insects (newly hatched or adults) sitting on the water's surface.

- Most dry flies range from a size 12 to a size 22, but can get even smaller to imitate the tiniest aquatic insects.

- Dry flies must be fished "drag free," requiring careful slack management and line mending.

- "Matching the hatch"—a popular catchphrase— involves comparing a dry fly to a natural to see if it is a close imitation.

Nymph Patterns

- Nymph patterns imitate the larval, or nymphal, stage of aquatic insects and are fished in the water column or along the bottom.

- Nymphs are sometimes tied with a metal bead head (which possibly resembles an air bubble) that can help sink the fly in current.

- Because actual nymphs swim actively in the water, nymph patterns can be retrieved with short strips of line.

- When there's no insect hatch occurring, nymph patterns can be used to locate trout.

Discussions of flies tied to imitate various insects often refer to "artificials" (the lure) and "naturals" (the actual, real bug). A "recipe" is a formal set of ingredients for tying a particular fly, resulting in a "pattern" of definitive color and configuration usually identified by a proper name; for example, Black Ghost streamer, Griffith's Black Gnat, or Olive Woolly Bugger. Materials used to tie flies range from feathers of special chicken breeds to squirrel fur to Styrofoam. Saltwater fly patterns often incorporate small metal heads (like jigs) to sink the fly faster and farther.

ARTIFICIAL LURES

Bass Bugs

- Bass bugs can mimic a baitfish fleeing on the surface or a swimming frog when retrieved with a stop-and-go action.

- Some bass bugs have cupped faces to make a popping sound, while others have bullet-shaped bodies for subtler noisemaking.

- Being heavier than most flies, some bass bugs benefit from fly lines designed specifically for them.

- Smaller bass-bug-style patterns in black, white, and bumblebee colors work very well for big sunfish.

Streamers

- Streamers can be tied with a variety of materials and are mainly intended to imitate various baitfish species.

- The word "streamer" refers to a freshwater fly, but many saltwater patterns are simply beefed-up, streamer-like flies.

- Most streamers are fished from mid-depths to the bottom and retrieved with quick strips of the line.

- Just about any streamer can be weighted so it sinks faster, especially in fast currents, and rides just over the bottom.

MAIN BAIT: RIGGING WORMS
When in need of a fail-safe bait, look no further than worms

The worm on a hook is an icon of fishing. Just about anyone who has ever fished has opted for this simple and highly successful tactic, surely as a child and perhaps often as an adult. Earthworms of various kinds are very good natural baits, as many gamefish species readily take them.

The two most popular kinds of worms for fishing are night crawlers and red worms. Night crawlers are preferred for their size—anywhere from 6 to 9 inches—and 3- to 4-inch red worms are often easily found at bait shops (supplied by worm breeders). Anglers also use garden worms, a 5- to 6-inch earthworm species found in damp soils, and 3- to 4-inch manure worms, a species found in farmland soils.

Rigging a Worm

- A worm should be as natural-looking and lively as possible on the hook.

- Don't thread a worm onto a hook so far that its body bends with the shank or is otherwise kinked.

- With smaller fish, you can sometimes use just half a worm by breaking off the tail section and rigging that.

- Hook a whole worm through the collar (the light-colored band behind its head) using a hook with a long shank.

Rigging Nightcrawlers

- A whole night crawler can be rigged Texas style, with a Z-bend worm hook through the nose, with or without weight.

- The hook point can be embedded or rigged slightly exposed, depending upon how thick the vegetation is.

- Whole night crawlers work well for big bass when fished slowly through cover or along the bottom.

- In some places, worms fished deep for trout are so effective that they're considered to be unfair or unsporting.

Worms are usually easy to find in moist, rich soil, not far under the surface. They can also be found in layers of decaying leaves along the edges of woods. Night crawlers can be caught at night, especially after a light spring rain. Use a flashlight with a red-colored beam, or a flashlight covered with red cellophane, as worms are highly sensitive to white light and will retreat from it. When you spot a night crawler, grab its front end and slowly pull it free from the soil.

Rigging Two Worms

- Two red worms or smaller garden worms can work on one hook, but rigging multiple worms is a waste.

- Fish will tear into multiple worms, eating much of your bait before they get to the hook point.

- Multi-hook dropper rigs can be used to fish more than one live worm close to the bottom or in the water column.

- The smaller the worm, the smaller the hook; but still use a hook with a shank long enough for hook-setting.

Carolina-Rigged Worm

- A Carolina rig is much like a "worm harness," two leader-rigged hooks that secure a live worm but let it act lively.

- A night crawler can be Carolina rigged with or without weight; beads and a spinner blade can be added above the top hook knot.

- Shorter earthworms—from 3 to 5 inches—can easily be Carolina rigged with smaller hooks.

- Don't hook a night crawler in its tail—let that be free to swim and curl, enticing fish.

NATURAL BAITS

HARD SHELLS: CRAYFISH & SHRIMP

Wherever they are found, crayfish and shrimp are high on the fish menu

North America is home to dozens of different species of crayfish—which are also called crawfish, crawdads, and mudbugs—ranging from 2 to 6 inches in length. Largemouth and smallmouth bass readily devour these lobster-like crustaceans, as bass find them in a variety of environments and can capture them easily. But fishing small live crayfish can

also work well for panfish and, in some situations, trout.

Most anglers buy their crayfish at bait shops, as collecting a large number of them can take some time. But a small, half-day supply can be collected by hand in streams and lakes where crayfish are abundant (and capture is legal). Keep captured crayfish in a water-filled bait bucket with a short layer

Crayfish

- Crayfish in their soft-shell (molting) phase are even more enticing to fish, so use these if you can find them.

- A crayfish might be small, but its pincers can still give a nasty pinch, so be careful of this crustacean's aggressiveness when caught.

- Fish a crayfish with minimal weight on the line—maybe just one or two very small split shot about 25 inches above the hook.

- A crayfish bait must be on the bottom to be effective, but a float that allows the bait to reach bottom can be used.

Hooking Crayfish

- Use a long-shank hook with enough gap for sufficient hook-sets, depending on crayfish size.

- Don't hook a crayfish through its main body, as this will injure it and prevent it from staying lively.

- If casting a crayfish from a boat, affix the hook straight up and down to the tail.

- If casting from shore, hook the crayfish in the tail lengthwise.

of ice on the bottom and some moss or a layer of weeds on top. Replenish the water hourly to keep the crayfish oxygenated.

Ghost shrimp, or sand shrimp, are often used in coastal rivers in the West to catch incoming steelhead and salmon. Freshwater grass shrimp are also used effectively to catch perch, crappie, sunfish, and bass. Like crayfish, most shrimp are store-bought, but you can catch them in some places using nets. Keep them in the water in which you caught them, not tap water, and change it a few times as you fish.

RED ● LIGHT

While crayfish and shrimp often appear on the dinner plate, don't eat bait-shop crayfish and shrimp. This might sound obvious, but in the name of economy and hunger, some people might consider a bait-shop crawdad as good as a fish-market crawdad. They're not the same, however. Leave them to the fish.

Shrimp

- Cast shrimp along the edges of weed beds or sight-cast them directly to schools of panfish.

- Use a few small split shot for better casting distance and to get light-bodied shrimp down in the water column.

- Use a light-wire, long-shank bait hook in a size that matches the shrimp, anywhere from size 6 to 12.

- Don't rig a shrimp through the middle of its body, but through the very front of the head.

Hooking Shrimp

- A shrimp can also be rigged through the tail with the barb up, or with the barb down (weedless) if cover is thick.

- An unshelled tail section secured with a bait loop can be fished deep effectively for many gamefish.

- Make a bait loop by tying the leader to a hook using the uni-snell knot (see pages 222–23).

- Before finishing the knot, insert the shrimp tail in the knot loop, close the loop, and put the barb in the tail end.

NATURAL BAITS

SERIOUS PROTEIN: USING BAITFISH

Effectively targeting big fish often calls for a bait worth the effort to eat it

Often, the largest local gamefish primarily eat baitfish or other, smaller gamefish. While a largemouth bass might love big worms and crayfish, many of them most readily devour shiners, sunfish, and shad. Smallmouth bass and big trout inhale sculpins and dace, and crappie and walleye attack minnows. Channel catfish and flathead catfish eat any fish they can get in their mouths. Pike and muskie are much the same, and also eat their own kind; many a juvenile pike or muskie turn up in the digestive system of an adult.

The terms "baitfish" and "forage fish" indicate a species that isn't very high on the food chain and is a regular meal for dominant fish species. The word "minnow" has become a

Rigging Minnows

- In general, minnows from 3 to 4 inches work as bait for most larger gamefish, such as trout and bass.

- Small minnows, from 1 to 2 inches, fished on size 8 or perhaps size 10 hooks, work for sunfish, perch, and crappie.

- Hook a live minnow in a way that won't interfere with its ability to swim and breathe underwater.

- Affix a hook just deeply enough in a minnow's tail, dorsal fin, or back to hold it.

Fishing with Rigged Minnows

- In shallow waters, fish a live minnow on enough line to let it a move naturally along the bottom.

- When gamefish are suspended at a certain depth in deeper water, use a light float to set the minnow to that depth.

- To search for fish, use a light float and pay out line as the minnow swims along.

- In deep water, a small bank sinker on a sliding cuff (with a bead stop) will let a minnow swim along the bottom.

generic term for any small (1- to 4-inch) freshwater baitfish, but this includes chubs, dace, true minnows, shiners, and sculpins—fish of a wide variety of colors and shapes.

Crappie, walleye, and smallmouth bass anglers probably make the most active and frequent use of minnows as bait, and often carry aerated live-wells on their boats to keep minnows fresh and active. A small, covered bucket will work for brief periods for the angler on foot. Tackle-shop baitfish are often shiners, fathead minnows, suckers, and other forage fish legal for use, and you can review their condition at the time of purchase.

Rigging Dead Minnows

- Dead minnows can be rigged for cast-and-retrieve or trolling by using the leader to secure them.

- The leader can be passed through the gill and down the body, or through the gill and wrapped once around the body.

- The leader can also be pushed through the minnow's mouth and out its vent, and tied to a single or double hook.

- A dead minnow still-fished on the bottom is very effective for catfish and trout.

How Gamefish Strike Minnows

- Most gamefish will strike a small live minnow aggressively and the hook-set will be quick.

- Larger live baitfish, such as a shiners or shad, will swim away from pursuing gamefish, so wait for the strike.

- Sometimes gamefish don't get an entire large baitfish in their mouth on the strike, and a quick hook-set fails.

- Wait for the fish to move with the big bait, pause to eat it, and move again, then set the hook.

NATURAL BAITS

CRUNCHY SNACKS: INSECT BAITS
Few gamefish will pass up a tasty bug if it's easy to get

Being terrifically opportunistic feeders, fish won't turn down most insects, which are rich in protein. Given the incredible variety of insects that flourish in or around streams and lakes, there are many different kinds of insect baits the angler can use. While some of these baits can be store-bought, often you can collect insects readily, in good numbers, in natural settings. The key is to collect those bugs that fish can't pass up or those that the fish are actively eating.

Insects must be rigged as unobtrusively and fished as naturally as possible, with hooks that aren't too large (given the size of the insect) and that allow the bug to be lively. Insects that land on the surface, such as beetles and grasshoppers, should be fished on the surface, and aquatic insect baits, mainly large nymphs, should be fished along the bottom.

Grasshoppers & Crickets

- Grasshoppers attract panfish, trout, and bass when hooked through the collar and fished on the surface, using a very light leader.

- Quietly and softly cast, or just lower, a hopper along the edge of a grassy bank; a small bobber can give weight for a cast.

- Crickets, hooked shallow behind the head, point up, can be drifted subsurface with a small split shot to trout and bass.

- A light or ultralight spinning or spincasting outfit works best for casting most insect baits.

Hellgrammites

- Hellgrammites, the nymphs (larvae) of the dobsonfly, are found under stream rocks and are a primo smallmouth bait.

- Like a hopper, hook a hellgrammite shallowly through its collar, but beware its pincer jaws.

- Affix enough split shot to the line to get the nymph near the bottom, but use a float to keep it off the bottom.

- Cast hellgrammites over rocky bottoms or around larger rocks, and in riffles and along seams of currents.

Some insects that fish eat readily can't be fished naturally and must be imitated, usually with flies. Winged mayflies and caddis flies are simply too delicate and light to be hooked—trout will ignore such a strange thing. Bass eat dragonflies and damselflies, but these fast-flying, strong insects are tough to catch and get rigged on a hook. But those bugs that can be readily hooked are beetles, wax worms and grubs, grasshoppers, crickets, and hellgrammites, among others.

Beetles & Cicadas

- Fish focus on the water under tree limbs or near reeds, where wind blows beetles and bugs onto the water surface.

- Larger beetles can be rigged just like hoppers and fished on the surface, using a small bobber.

- Cicada hatches attract a number of gamefish, including big trout, but these insects are tough to catch and rig.

- Don't hook beetles and insects so low that the hook becomes a part of the bug's silhouette when fish look up.

Wax Worms and Grubs

- Grubs, wax worms, and mealworms are all larvae of winged insects, and are excellent baits.

- Grubs are abundant in rotting logs, and can be hooked crossways or threaded onto a hook.

- Wax worms (maggots) and mealworms are readily available in bait shops and pet stores, and can be rigged two or three at a time.

- These larvae can be fished deep or shallow, or used to tip jigs, for panfish, bass, trout, walleye, and perch.

NATURAL BAITS

CANNED FOOD: MAN-MADE BAITS

Temptations from the kitchen and laboratory take their share of fish

For years, both pre-made artificial and homemade baits have been used in lieu of natural ones, although these baits have mostly been targeted at catfish, carp, panfish, and trout. Many of these baits arise out the use of old recipes involving dough and cheese for catfish, and dough, cheese, and corn-kernel baits for trout. Contemporary processed baits are fished in

their own way, often with bottom rigs, but the approach is the same as it is for not real baits: Get the baited hook into the fish's strike zone.

Are these processed and homemade baits as effective as or more effective than natural baits? Under certain circumstances, they can bring about as much success as natural baits, or even

Synthetic Trout Baits

- Most synthetic trout baits are buoyant and meant for still-fishing in lakes or very slow streams.

- Bait the hook with a salmon-egg-size amount, which should float just enough off the bottom to be visible.

- Some synthetic trout baits tend to fly off the hook with hard, fast casts, so lob the rig to the target.

- If a trout bait doesn't work after a short time, try selecting a bait of a different color.

Dough Balls

- Heat cornmeal, flour, and water to make a consistent paste for dough balls for carp fishing.

- Add corn syrup or maple syrup, vanilla extract, and spices/sweeteners to the paste for flavor, scent.

- Mold the dough balls into a size no bigger than a gum ball and let them harden in the refrigerator.

- Dough balls should be rigged on a single hook small enough to be buried in the ball with a little of the point exposed.

greater success with some species. Their advantage is in their widespread availability and the fact that any leftovers go into the refrigerator, where they can stay fresh for some time. Many new artificial baits, in dozens of colors, also give off a potent scent that is much stronger than that of most natural baits.

Technically speaking, salmon eggs are a naturally occurring bait, but the salmon eggs you buy in the bait shop have been culled, cured, and are often colored and sometimes flavored, so they are quite a bit removed from their natural state. These processed eggs are used mainly for trout and salmon fishing.

Salmon Eggs

- Salmon eggs can be fished singly or in pairs just above the bottom while still-fishing, or drifted in current.

- Short-shank, rounded hooks called "egg hooks" are specially made for use with salmon eggs.

- Multi-egg setups can be made using dropper rigs and small sinkers, and colored beads can work as attractors.

- Fishing eggs in current calls for a float, but use enough weight to make the cast and to get the hook down in the water column.

Egg Sacks

- Egg sacks come in fishnet bags; both the eggs and the bags are colored to look like fresh roe.

- For salmon fishing from a boat, use a rig with a float fixed near the hook to keep the sack off the bottom while fishing in current.

- Use a float and a hook snelled with a bait loop to secure the sack when casting egg sacks from shore.

- Egg sacks are great for king salmon throughout the Great Lakes region and on the Pacific coast.

NATURAL BAITS

SEA FOOD: SALTWATER BAITS

Fish in the surf and offshore will take a variety of naturally occurring foods

Whether fishing off the beach or from a boat inshore or far offshore, natural baits play a major role in saltwater fishing. Sometimes catching fish hinges on using natural bait and nothing else, especially at certain times of the year when bait species are more plentiful due to breeding cycles or migrations. Various small fish species, worms, mollusks, and crustaceans can all be rigged in a number of ways and fished at varying depths, although putting a highly effective bait on the bottom at night, such as clams, can guarantee a strike.

A key element in using saltwater baits is selecting the correct hook for the kind of bait that you use and the species of fish you seek. Circle hooks work well with several baits and species, but

Eel Rig

- Targeting large striped bass along coastlines and in river deltas often calls for a live-rigged eel.

- Make a fish-finder rig (see page 60) without the float, and connect to it 28 inches of 40- or 50-pound monofilament leader.

- Tie a 6/0 or 4/0 bait-holder hook or octopus hook to the leader, and hook an 18- to 24-inch live eel through the bottom and then top lip.

- Fish this rig along drop-offs to deep water, in holes, and around structure.

Bloodworms, Clam Worms, and Sandworms

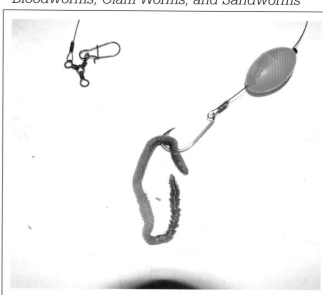

- Bloodworms, clam worms, and sandworms are abundant coastal worms that can be store-bought or collected.

- You can rig these whole just like a plastic worm (see pages 88–89) on surf rigs, using worm hooks or octopus circle hooks, or rig parts of them.

- Spinner blades and colored beads can be added to the leader above whole-rigged worms as attractors.

- A big sandworm (18 inches) can be rigged just like an eel and fished from a drifting boat.

long-shank or wide-gap J-hooks are necessary for larger baits or for gamefish that need to be struck hard and quick. "Octopus" hooks have a bent-back eye, which is optimal for snelling because this gives a good in-line direction of pull for hook-sets.

Bait rigging for saltwater big-game—marlin, sailfish, and tuna—is a specialty in itself. Whole dead mackerel, mullet, bonito, and ballyhoo are rigged in numerous ways, sometimes weighted orrigged with teasers, or sewn up with big-game hooks inside them. Saltwater big-game fishing also makes use of circle hooks for effective catch-and-release.

Crabs

- Use blue crabs, fiddler crabs, calico crabs, green crabs, and sand fleas (not true crabs) with various saltwater rigs.

- Crab baits work for croaker, drum, perch, permit, tarpon, tautog, snapper, and grouper.

- Hook whole or half crabs on bait hooks through the side-point of the shell or behind a back leg; hook a sand flea through the back end of its shell.

- Fish crab baits close to the bottom; fish half crabs and small crabs under a float.

Rigged Baitfish

- Live-rigged baitfish can be highly effective for striped bass (bunker or mullet) and fluke (killifish).

- Hook a live baitfish through the dorsal fin, nose, or back with a bait hook or octopus hook.

- Strips of baitfish fillet can be fished with bottom rigs or fish-finder rigs, drifted from a boat.

- Small strips of fish fillet can be fished under a float along jetties, from piers, and in flat surf.

NATURAL BAITS

105

LARGEMOUTH & SMALLMOUTH

The major bass species are two big reasons why anglers get up in the morning

More people pursue, catch, and celebrate largemouth bass in America than any other fish, and the smallmouth bass has long been heralded as one of the most terrific fighters in freshwater. In years past, these species were referred to collectively as "black bass," an all-encompassing term for a variety of freshwater bass, which belong to the sunfish family.

The green-colored largemouth bass, also referred to as "bigmouth" bass, "bucketmouth," or Florida bass, is found across a large swath of the United States, from New England to California. The species does not thrive above the 42nd parallel and prefers warmer, still waters—lakes, ponds, and reservoirs—but does inhabit the slowest waters of warm riv-

Largemouth Bass Body Markings

- Body markings vary, but most largemouths have a lateral stripe of black splotches down their lateral line and black patches on their cheeks.

- The corner of a largemouth's jaw extends past the back of its eye socket, a key identifying feature.

- Largemouths tend to have bulkier heads and shoulders and a more rotund gut than smallmouth bass.

- Largemouth bass have a visibly more shallow separation between their first and second dorsal fins than do smallmouths.

Largemouth Bass Habitat

- Largemouths prefer thick cover in lakes or ponds, an essential part of their ambush method of predation.

- Forage fish and smaller gamefish comprise most of the largemouth's diet, but bass eat a wide variety of live prey.

- Largemouths can tolerate temperatures from about 35 degrees Fahrenheit up to 90 degrees, but prefer 65 to 85 degrees.

- Spawning can begin in late winter in places where the water warms to 60 degrees, but usually occurs in mid- to late-spring.

ers. The Florida subspecies is the heaviest. Most anglers catch largemouths from 4 pounds up to 10 pounds.

The smallmouth bass, nicknamed "bronzeback" for its bright, olive-gold coloration, thrives in cool, even cold, rivers and streams and big northern lakes. It is often found near trout water, but not in many places in the South or Southwest. Smallmouths that inhabit larger, nutrient-filled waters can reach some size—a 6-pound smallmouth is a big one. Largemouths sometimes leap when fighting, whereas smallmouths often go airborne within seconds of being hooked.

George Perry and the World-Record Bass

- The largest bass on record is George Perry's 22-pound, 4-ounce giant caught in 1932 in Georgia's Montgomery Lake.

- Perry caught the fish on a Fintail Shiner plug and weighed it on a certified postal scale.

- Only one known photograph of what experts believe to be the Perry fish exists; Perry and his family ate the fish.

- Perry's bass won its category in the 1932 *Field & Stream* big-fish contest; he won again in 1934 with another, smaller bass.

Largemouth Bass Characteristics

- Largemouth bass size and growth rates are influenced by many factors, but southern fish tend to be larger.

- In optimal conditions, with a significant amount of forage fish, largemouths can grow rapidly.

- Largemouths can tolerate a lot of turbidity in the water in which they live, and in some places even inhabit brackish waters.

- As table fare, largemouth fillets are very good, flaky white meat when taken from fish that lived in clear waters.

FRESHWATER BASS

CATCHING LARGEMOUTHS

Anglers love the bigmouth bass for all its toughness and trickiness

The widespread range of largemouth bass makes them a very popular and accessible fish, but what wins over most anglers is the fish's great predatory aggressiveness that leads it to strike many different kinds of lures and baits. An added bonus is the largemouth's determined, bull-dogging fight—the fish tend to run quickly for cover, and pull fiercely once there.

Baitcasting, spinning, and spincasting outfits all work very well for largemouth bass. Largemouth lures run from ¼ ounce to 1¾ ounces, and light- to medium-action rods can handle most any lure or bait necessary. Aside from the "flippin' switch" that some baitcaster reels have, any quality reel designed for medium-weight freshwater fishing should be

Soft Plastics

Crankbaits & Spinnerbaits

- Soft plastics can be as good a fish-searching lure as spinnerbaits around piers, docks, and other man-made structures.

- If bass are striking at but missing surface plugs, cast a weightless tube bait instead, with a slow, jerky retrieve.

- In colder water or with pressured fish, fish a straight-tailed, lightly weighted medium or short worm, twitching it on a slow retrieve.

- For murky conditions, use black, purple, or blue soft plastics with curly tails, split tails, or other appendages.

- You can fish a crankbait in brush or timber, but slow down your retrieve and stop when the lure bumps a snag, and let it float up.

- Prospect with spinnerbaits and crankbaits around brush and flooded timber first before casting into the cover.

- After prospecting around brush and timber without success, flip or pitch soft plastics or jigs into the cover.

- Fish the outer root branches of a big stump first, and then work your way in.

enough to match a largemouth's fighting, though a smooth, finely adjustable drag system is a good idea.

Bass are not terribly line shy, but in clear water they can be wary of a heavier line. A 4- to 8-pound monofilament or braided main line will be fine in farm-pond situations (although farm ponds regularly turn up big bass). Waters known for larger bass call for an 8- to 12-pound-test line. A fluorocarbon leader in a strength a step up from the main line works well.

Swimbaits

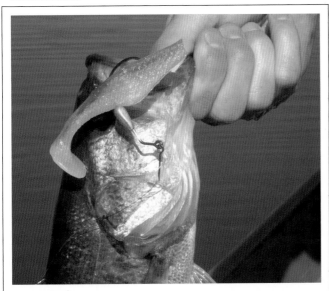

- Using big "swimbaits" for largemouth originates from the use of saltwater lures for big bass in southern California.

- Resembling forage fish and other gamefish, solid-bodied and soft-plastic swimbaits are fished mainly in lakes at various depths.

- Larger swimbaits, up to 10 or 12 inches long, call for stouter rods and braided lines.

- Soft-plastic swimbaits can be rigged in multiple ways: weightless, Carolina style, or with a jig head, to name a few.

Bass: Under Varying Conditions

- Generally speaking, a rise in barometric pressure will send bass deeper, while during a falling barometer, they will become active.

- When a cold-weather front comes in, or bass have been pressured, try switching to smaller, ¼- or ⅛-ounce crankbaits.

- In big, open water, search for bass at various depths with crankbaits, swimbaits, and plugs.

- On days of high barometric pressure, try "finessing": small worms (4 or 5 inches, max) fished very slowly in cover or along the bottom.

SMALLMOUTH BASS
The "bronzeback" takes the prize for high-energy angling

There was a time when northeastern trout fishermen considered smallmouth bass to be a "trash" fish and would have happily eradicated them. Fortunately, such erroneous thinking never caught on completely, and the smallmouth is now a highly valued gamefish across its current range, from Maine to the West Coast and some southwestern states. The smallmouth does not appear in many waters in the deep South.

The smallmouth clearly differs from the largemouth, with its more gold-bronze coloration and vertical olive or brown bars mottling the sides of its body. Some lake-dwelling smallmouths can become quite dark, with a rich, brown tiger-striping. The corner of a smallmouth's jaw does not extend past the back edge of its eye socket, and its dorsal fins are connected in a slightly shallow dip, unlike the deeper cleft

Smallmouth Bass Food

- Few anglers keep small-mouths for the table, and the species is pursued almost entirely for sport.

- Smallmouth bass, however, are edible, and when taken from clear waters are as tasty as largemouths from clear water.

- The smallmouth's main diet consists of baitfish—minnows, small perch and sunfish, and juvenile bass.

- Smallmouths also readily eat crayfish and a variety of nymphs, leeches and worms, and various insects.

Smallmouth Bass Habitat

- Smallmouth and large-mouth bass do occur in the same lake in some places, but will seek different habitat.

- In deep lakes, smallmouths stay in cooler depths, whereas largemouths will be found in warmer, shallower water.

- Smallmouths spawn later than largemouths, usually in late spring or in the early summer.

- A smallmouth spawning bed will be made over gravel or rock bottom, and can be as deep as 10 or 12 feet.

between a largemouth's dorsal fins.

Smallmouths live in both small and large streams and in deep lakes. They prefer a rocky or gravel bottom, and in rivers tend to seek slower sections of water along main current seams. In lakes, smallmouths seek the cooler levels and won't be found in warmer surface layers in summer. They might live close to trout in small streams, but in rivers avoid the colder, faster trout waters.

ZOOM

"Black bass" is an outdated expression that was once used to describe any freshwater bass, which are fish that belong to the sunfish family, *Centrarchidae*. In addition to largemouth and smallmouth bass, this family includes spotted bass, Suwanne bass, redeye bass, and Guadalupe bass—all similar in body shape and fin configuration.

Smallmouth Feeding Tactics

- The ideal water temperature for the smallmouth is from 60 to 70 degrees Fahrenheit, but it will tolerate lower temperatures.

- Smallmouths feed through the entire water column, taking insects off the surface, and picking crayfish and nymphs off the bottom.

- Smallmouths will sometimes trail behind rooting suckers or turtles, grabbing insects and crayfish that escape the lead animal.

- Reservoir- and lake-dwelling smallmouths usually grow faster and get bigger than smallmouths in streams.

Size of Smallmouth Bass

- Most smallmouths in streams and rivers reach 1 or 2 pounds and don't get over 15 inches long.

- The biggest smallmouths come from larger rivers and deep lakes where forage fish levels are good.

- A whopper smallmouth reaches 4 to 6 pounds; smallmouth in the 8- or 9-pound range are rare catch.

- The American record smallmouth bass is an 11-pound, 15-ounce fish caught in 1955 in Dale Hollow Reservoir, Tennessee (above).

FRESHWATER BASS

SMALLMOUTH FISHING
Smallmouths can be picky, but when they hit, you know it

Fishing for smallmouth bass calls upon an arsenal of lures that is something of a crossover of largemouth bass and trout lures. Jigs, crankbaits, spinnerbaits, and soft plastics can be highly successful, and so can diving plugs, spoons, and spinners. Natural baits include minnows, crayfish, hellgrammites, and worms, and should be fished live, if possible. Crayfish are a main bait in waters where the crustacean is plentiful.

Jigs and crankbaits are the most widely used lure for locating smallmouth bass in lakes. Successful searches along rocky edges or drop-offs and vertical presentations to deep points often make use of bucktail or plastic-skirted jigs and jig heads fixed with curly-tailed soft plastics. Crankbaits matched to local forage-fish colors or crayfish crank patterns can work well; crayfish-imitating crankbaits need to reach the bottom and

Crankbaits

Jigs

- Crayfish-pattern crankbaits come in such a variety that making a match to the local crayfish population can be close.

- A crayfish crank is usually a mid-depth lure, diving to bottom from 4 to 6 feet, as crayfish don't live much deeper.

- In clear waters, bright, rattling crankbaits fished stop-and-go at lower depths are a good searching lure.

- Crankbait patterns that produce well for smallmouth also imitate local forage fish, usually shad and perch, in silver, white, and yellow.

- Work bucktail or feather jigs with an up-and-down action, using the rod tip to raise and drop the jig.

- A nearly vertical presentation for jigs is best, but they can be cast from shore on creeks and rivers.

- Bounce a skirted jig fitted with a soft-plastic crayfish along a rocky bottom with a slow, up-and-down action.

- Weedless football-style jig heads (3/8 ounce) fitted with brown latex skirts or a V-shape of brown rabbit fur also imitate crayfish on the bottom.

flutter along the rocks.

Light spinning and baitcasting outfits work fine for small-mouth, with monofilament or braided line on a lightweight reel. A braided line allows a better touch with jigs fished deep or crankbaits close to the bottom, and a low-visibility fluo-rocarbon leader in very clear water is a smart move. Small-stream fishing for smallmouth bass is entirely an ultralight endeavor, done well with a spinning outfit.

ZOOM

Trolling for smallmouths works well on larger lakes when you need to search out fish. Mid-depth or deep-running plugs, spoons, and bait rigs can all be trolled; setting the depth, however, is crucial. Target rocky points, drop-offs, sandy places, and deep structure. Troll just fast enough to create proper lure action.

Surface Lures

- A soft-plastic jerkbait retrieved on the surface with quick twitches of the rod can induce very hard smallmouth strikes.

- Try top-water lures on a very calm lake surface early in the morning and at sun-down, varying the speed of the retrieve.

- Small buzzbaits can also bring strikes early and late in the day.

- A "walk-the-dog" retrieve for certain surface lures calls for a downward twitch of a lowered rod tip, a quick reel-up of slack, and an-other downward twitch.

Lure Alternatives

- When lures aren't producing strikes, switch to a whole night crawler rigged with a few split shot above the leader.

- Hook a live minnow through the dorsal fin, and cast this below a float to small-mouth structure (rocks, sand patches, drop-offs).

- A creek chub or redtail chub from 5 to 8 inches long rigged live can take trophy-size smallmouths.

- Target smallmouths holding in deep water—20 or 30 feet down—with a drop-shot rig baited with small plastic worms.

FAT FEATHERS: BASS FLY FISHING

Bass on a fly rod are great fun when the fish are eager about the offering

Anglers have used flies specific to largemouth and smallmouth bass for as long as there has been fly fishing in America. Many of the earliest patterns, from as far back as the 1800s, are long forgotten and current flies do not resemble them at all. But long before there were baitcasting outfits and bass boats, people cast flies to these popular fish.

Current bass fly patterns are fished on the surface, subsurface, and along the bottom. Bass flies most often mimic the fish's favorite food—baitfish—but also imitate frogs, leeches, crayfish, and nymphs. Such flies are tied with a wide variety of materials, including fur, bucktail, synthetics, and feathers. A 6- to 8-inch length of brown or red chenille can flutter in the

Big Poppers

- Largemouths readily take frog-patterned and baitfish-patterned poppers cast to lily pads and weed patches.

- At twilight on some rivers, white poppers cast to eddies and slow riffles nab smallmouths looking for moths.

- Let a popper sit for a short time after it lands on the surface, and then give it a few light pops before slowly stripping it in.

- Strip a popper in a stop-and-go fashion, pulling the line crisply enough to get the "pop" sound and splash.

Woolly Buggers and Clouser Minnows

- Woolly Buggers in olive, brown, and black most likely mimic a leech or big nymph in the smallmouth's eye.

- A big (size 8) black or brown Woolly Bugger ticked along the bottom will also nab largemouth bass.

- The Clouser Minnow, developed specifically for smallmouth, sinks quickly and swims along the bottom.

- Color combinations of white, yellow, green, and red in streamers tend to get a smallmouth's attention, but an all-black leech pattern also induces strikes.

water as nicely as a soft-plastic worm. Poppers, as mentioned here and on page 83, are a highly popular fly for both largemouth and smallmouth bass.

Most fly-fishing tackle for largemouth and smallmouth bass is either slow or medium action, with rods and lines from 4 to 8 weight. A number of fly lines are weight-forward lines designed specifically for use with poppers, while sink-tip lines are often used with streamers to take them deep in the water column. Fly reels for freshwater bass fishing rarely need much backing, as these fish are brawlers, not long runners, and don't cover too much ground in battle, although big smallmouths can make short, streaking runs. An 8-weight rod is called for only with the biggest bass—fish that might break 6 or 8 pounds.

While some anglers might not seriously consider this, a fly rod can cast lighter soft plastics like smaller worms and grubs. A number of fly patterns are making use of soft-plastic tails, such as the Woolly Grub, as more and more materials are adapted to fly tying.

Catching Largemouth Bass

- Heavier tippets are necessary for big largemouths that lurk in cover, and tapered fluorocarbon leaders work well.

- On smaller bass waters, an 8-foot fly rod is a little easier to handle than the usual 9-foot length of many rods.

- A variety of flies called "divers" work well on big bass; they float on the surface, then dive under when retrieved.

- Nighttime fly fishing with size 6 or 8 dark poppers and divers can be very successful for largemouth bass.

Catching Smallmouth Bass

- Smallmouth streams are usually shallow enough to wade with hip waders.

- Medium-size lakes and rivers are the right places for fly casting from an inflatable or kayak.

- Nymph patterns that would otherwise be cast for trout can work well for smallmouth bass, if matched to the local insects.

- Smallmouths can be finicky about tippets and leaders in clear water, so go as light as you can with low-visibility fluorocarbon leader and tippet material.

BEST BASS: TOP WATERS

Major waters with optimum conditions for bass growth are rarely a secret

Largemouth and smallmouth bass are so widespread across America that anglers will encounter many good, medium-size fish, and then a few big ones here and there—largemouths that reach or break 8 pounds and smallmouths that surpass 3 pounds. Those waters, however, that can offer up big fish after big fish become national hot spots.

Two main components for such quality bass waters are the level of forage and the cleanliness of the water. Lunker largemouths and smallmouths get big by eating good meals all the time, and this usually means that baitfish populations are very healthy. Pollutants must be nonexistent or in very low levels for either species to thrive, as pollution will cut into the

The Everglades

- With thousands of channels and backcountry lakes and grass flats, the waters of Florida's Everglades hold a great number of quality largemouth bass.

- Fast-moving crankbaits, top-water plugs, plastic frogs, snakes, big worms, spoons, and buzzbaits all produce in the Everglades.

- During spring and summer, twenty- to thirty-fish days are possible, in the right location, but fishing early and at dusk is a good approach.

- Largemouths reaching 20 inches are frequent, and 5-pound fish are common.

Southern California

- Lake Casitas produced two of the ten biggest largemouth bass in the world, one in 1980 and one in 2002.

- Located in the Ojai Valley, Lake Casitas is easily accessed from Malibu; the lake is surrounded by a large recreation area.

- Fishing tactics often involve big trout-imitating swimbaits fished deep in the late winter and early spring.

- Two other major largemouth destinations, Castaic Lake and Lake Dixon, are within easy driving distance.

food chain, affecting the bass diet.

Conservation also plays a major role in creating quality bass waters, and not just conservation of fish but also conservation of watersheds—the soils, trees, and tributary waters surrounding main rivers or lakes. Many potentially good largemouth waters in Florida are threatened by changes in drainage due to land development and agriculture, a particular setback given that Florida-strain largemouths are the biggest (they were the fish stocked in southern California to create a series of trophy-bass lakes in the 1990s).

ZOOM

A number of lakes across northern and central Mexico hold some seriously big largemouth bass, with Lake Huites and Lake Bacurato often at the top of the list. But Cuba has long had a premier largemouth bass fishery, and in the post-Castro years, as travel restrictions ease, some serious lunkers could be caught on this large island.

Dale Hollow Reservoir

- Dale Hollow Reservoir in Tennessee produced the current world-record smallmouth and still consistently produces big smallmouths.

- Targeting trophy smallmouths in the spring with spinnerbaits, jerkbaits, and crankbaits has been highly successful.

- When smallmouths go deep in the reservoir, get down to them by drop-shotting soft plastics or with jigs and deep-running spoons.

- Smallmouths from 15 to 18 inches are caught with some frequency, and state-mandated slot limits have helped increase trophy potential.

Penobscot River

- Maine's Penobscot is an old logging river, full of sunken logs and deep holes that contain numerous smallmouths.

- Soft plastics and tube baits, while not traditional New England smallmouth lures, are highly effective here, especially in high water.

- Curly-tailed grubs on jig heads heavy enough to beat the current and get down along the gravel are go-to lures.

- For fly-fishing approaches, try white-and-green Clouser Minnows, black leech patterns, and olive-gold Woolly Buggers.

FIRST FISH: BLUEGILL

Highly populous and widespread, a variety of sunfish provides tons of opportunities for the angler

A sunfish is usually every angler's first fish, especially for those who start young. Various sunfish species, such as bluegill and pumpkinseed, are found nationwide and generally have strong local populations. The fact that they inhabit the shorelines and shallows of ponds, creeks, lakes, and slower rivers puts them in easy reach of the shortest cast. Sunfish can be a little skittish

close to shore—they'll move away if you approach with heavy footfalls—but offered the right bait, they can be terrifically aggressive fish and make a very willing quarry.

Given sunfish's preference for shallows, anglers can often sight-cast to them and watch the strike, an added plus for young anglers, who get a good lesson in fish behavior and

Bluegill

- The bluegill is called a variety of names across its wide range—bream, brim, blue sunfish, and sun perch.

- Bluegills usually have greenish bodies with dark vertical bars, an orange breast, and a black-tipped gill cover.

- Some bluegills can become a dark blue-purple, or even black along their backs, depending upon their habitat.

- A good-size bluegill reaches 10 or 12 inches in length and will have a full, oval shape, but won't have a fat gut like bass.

Pumpkinseed

- Turquoise-blue streaks cover a pumpkinseed's head from its nose across its gill plate, and many amber and blue spots cover its sides.

- Two key identifiers are the pointed pectoral fin that extends above the eye, and the red-orange mark on the point of the gill cover.

- The pumpkinseed's range covers most of the Northeast, South, and Northwest, but it doesn't appear much in the Southwest.

- Most pumpkinseeds range from 4 to 8 inches, with a big specimen reaching 10 inches.

reaction time. Most species exhibit a diving, corkscrewing fight and continue an angry thrashing once in hand or net. The lightest possible tackle—ultralight spinning or spincasting outfits, or 0– or 2–weight fly-casting outfits, with short rods—is all that an angler needs to pursue sunfish. Monofilament line of no more than 2 or 4 pounds is necessary.

A wide variety of baits and lures work for sunfish, just as long as they're small enough for the fish to get in their mouths. Hooks much larger than size 6 don't work, with sizes 8 and 10 usually the right choice.

Redbreast Sunfish

- Also called "redbelly" and "robin" in some parts of its range, the redbreast sunfish's brightest markings occur during the spawning season.

- The redbreast's gill point (or "lobe") is solidly black or blue-black, differing from other species with a similarly long lobe.

- Generally found in the East, southward to Florida, and in parts of the Midwest, the redbreast prefers rocky sections of small rivers.

- More tapered in shape toward the tail than most sunfish, redbreasts can reach 7 or 8 inches.

Redear Sunfish

- Also known as "shellcrackers," redear sunfish possess small teeth that allow them to break the shells of freshwater mollusks.

- The redear is a bit more tapered and pointed at the snout than other sunfish, and has an olive-green body with numerous darker spots.

- Redears are found all across the South, and into the Midwest and southwest to Texas.

- Matching the size of bluegills, redear sunfish can reach 9 inches or larger in optimal habitat.

LIGHT TOUCH: CATCHING SUNFISH

Given the chance, bluegills, pumpkinseeds, and other sunfish fight as gamely as bigger fish

The kind of tackle necessary for sunfish is the lightest around—short, whippy rods and small spinning or spincasting reels being the most ready and easy to use. There's no point using tackle that not only overpowers the fish but also muffles the sensation of the fight, so that all the angler is doing is striking and lifting fish out of the water. Sunfish put on

a show, but only the lightest tackle allows them full exercise. Long casts won't be necessary, usually, given that many sunfish prefer nearshore habitat. Bluegill and other species favor weeds, sunken logs, stumps, rock piles, and lily pads.

Just like largemouth bass, sunfish build nests in shallow waters and protect them, in the spring or when water tempera-

Ultralight Spinning & Spincasting Outfits

- A shorter rod works best for sunfish; anything from 5 to 6 feet long is all you need.

- Push-button spincast reels were made for sunfish, but small spinning reels work fine, too.

- If you have a very light baitcasting outfit, that can also work, but the reel need not be sophisticated or powerful.

- Store-bought or hand-fashioned cane poles work in a pinch for sunfish, but are a bit clumsy when it comes to landing fish.

Fishing for Sunfish

- A universal sunfish bait rig consists of a small float about 20 inches above a size 8 hook, with two small split shot just below the float.

- Hooks much smaller than size 10 might be too small and could be swallowed by sunfish.

- Sunfish will sometimes peck at a bait before biting it entirely, making the float twitch.

- Wait until the float or bobber moves off steadily or goes under, then set the hook with an easy turn of the wrist.

tures get into the mid-60s. And just like bass, sunfish can be easily targeted while on their nests, but again, the individual angler must determine how sporting this is, and whether pressuring adult fish guarding nests is reasonable.

In clean waters, bluegill, pumpkinseed, redbreast, and redear sunfish are usually quite palatable when cooked properly, with white, flaky meat. Bag limits on sunfish are usually pretty liberal in many places, given the various species' ability to reproduce in high numbers.

ZOOM

There is a saltwater sunfish, but it's nothing like freshwater sunfish. Oval-shaped, including the tail, and with one long dorsal fin and one long anal fin, the ocean sunfish ranges from 8 to 10 feet long and 10 feet high, fin tip to fin tip. Weighing up to 4,000 pounds, the ocean sunfish is the heaviest bony fish.

Sunfish Jigs

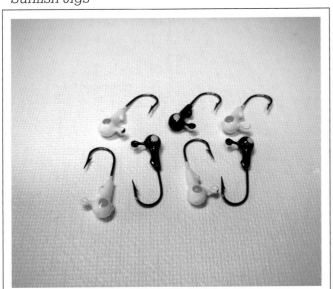

- Standard sunfish jigs have small, lead heads and slim nylon or feather skirts; fish these with a medium-fast up-and-down retrieve.

- Good-size bluegills and redears will chase small grub-tailed jigs and small spinners.

- Baiting hooks with worms for sunfish calls for just a section of a night crawler, as sunfish will pick apart a whole worm before getting to the hook.

- Whole grubs, mealworms, and whole small crickets also attract sunfish when rigged below a float.

Unhooking the Fish

- Sunfish can be difficult to unhook, given their small size (which makes them hard to grab) and small mouths.

- Use a wet rag or bandanna to cradle a sunfish, cupping your hand to hold the fish upright.

- Beware of a sunfish's dorsal-fin spines when unhooking it—the spines are quite sharp, so make sure the dorsal fin is lying flat.

- Removing a swallowed hook calls for needle-nose forceps to get down into a sunfish's narrow gullet.

PANFISH DUOS: CRAPPIE & PERCH

As popular as any gamefish, these species are pursued often for their food value

Four major panfish species that are always paired in anglers' minds are black and white crappie, and white and yellow perch. All four are premier light-tackle gamefish. The crappie looks a lot like a speckled hybrid of a bass and sunfish. Those markings, in fact, have led to the alternate names "calico bass," "speckled bass," and "speckled perch." The white perch is not a true perch, and is actually related to the white bass and striped bass. Yellow perch may have some bass-like attributes, but it is a true perch, in the same family as walleye and sauger.

Like their sunfish cousins, crappies have long played a major part in the angling and dietary history of America. Crap-

Black Crappie

- Black crappies appear to have a gold or olive body covered with irregular bluish or black specks, and can sometimes have solid-black backs.

- The spotted dorsal and anal fins are very similar in size and configuration, with seven to eight dorsal spines.

- A black crappie's tail fin is marked with irregular bands, and it has a slight indentation in its head just above its eyes.

- Black crappies range from 8 to 14 inches and grow up to 2 pounds.

White Crappie

- White crappies are lighter colored on their sides than black crappies, and have vertical bands of spots covering their silvery-green flanks.

- The dorsal fin of a white crappie usually has no more than six spines, and is also comparable in size and shape to the anal fin.

- The white crappie's tail fin has evenly marked bands across its rays.

- With a more tapered and slimmer body than the black crappie, the white crappie can reach 13 or 15 inches.

pie fillets have been considered so delectable that they were termed sac-a-lait, or "milk sack," by the Creoles. In some parts of the country, these fish are still referred to with the proper pronunciation—"croppie".

White and yellow perch are also frequently pursued in regions where they are abundant. White perch don't mind brackish water and are often found in estuaries and costal rivers, but also inhabit inland lakes. Yellow perch are found in a variety of waters but prefer large, clear lakes, which often makes them a major quarry of ice fishermen.

ZOOM

The word "crappie" comes from the French-Canadian word *crapet*, used to refer generically to a number of species in the sunfish family, *Centrarchidae*, which includes the black bass. The French crapet became "crappe" in early American usage, but its French-Canadian origins are unclear.

Yellow Perch

- Yellow perch have an unmistakable yellow-gold body and, during the spawn, bright yellow-orange pelvic and anal fins.

- Seven or eight vertical brown-black bars extend along the perch's body, from its back almost to its belly.

- A noticeable bump rises up in front of the first dorsal fin, but the snout tapers to a round point and the body slims through the tail fin.

- Most yellow perch run 8 to 10 inches, and sometimes reach almost 1 pound.

White Perch

- White perch have two dorsal fins, the first one comb-like with a number of spines, the second having a squared-off rear edge.

- The body of a white perch can be silver-olive or brownish gray across the back, with silvery sides and a white belly.

- White perch lack the speckles and stripes found on their closest relatives, the striped bass and white bass.

- Most white perch don't get much larger than 8 or 9 inches and a half pound in weight.

SCHOOLED FISH: MULTIPLE CATCHES

Some searching and thinking is necessary to locate these species

White and black crappies and white and yellow perch tend to form sizable schools, so the angler who catches a few is probably on to something. The hard part is locating the fish, but there are some essential approaches. As with sunfish, very light spinning or spincasting tackle is all you need.

For black crappie, look for deep weeds and brush piles,

flooded timber, and drop-offs to deeper water. Search out large schools in the pre-spawning stage in the spring. In hotter weather, black crappies will go deep to find cool water. White crappies seek the same kinds of structures as black crappies, but not as deep, and don't mind warmer water.

White perch in brackish waters are often found near the

Natural Baits

- The go-to natural bait for crappies is a live minnow hooked through the lips or dorsal fin, fished under a float.

- Crickets, wax worms, and grubs are also successful natural baits, fished on dropper rigs or below a float.

- Both black and white crappies have tender mouths and don't strike hard; smooth hook-sets are a must.

- Sometimes very slowly trolled rigged minnows (live or dead) can cover ground to locate a crappie school.

Crappie Jigs

- Small jigs with curly-tailed soft-plastic grubs are a go-to lure for crappie anglers, often in white or yellow.

- In-line spinners in size 6 or 8 tipped with a soft-plastic minnow is a workable, if larger, lure for crappies.

- Drop-nose jigs, with an Indiana spinner blade attached to the jig head and a feather or nylon skirt, also work.

- Work jigs, spinners, and spinnerbaits as slowly as possible to get proper swimming action with the lure, but no faster.

bottom and become active around structures (holes, river mouths) at tide changes. In freshwater lakes, the angler must target creek mouths, shelves, or channels between points of land. Sometimes white perch will chase baitfish to the surface, and such a feeding school will have to be approached carefully. Yellow perch roam open lake water in schools during the day, over a variety of bottoms—rocky, muddy, sand— and need to be prospected for. In the evening or at night, they sometimes venture up to more shallow water.

GREEN ● LIGHT

In many places, crappie and perch limits are very liberal, sometimes allowing upwards of a dozen keepable fish. In some places, in fact, so many fish are present that fishery managers want fish kept. But in those places where you're taking numerous full-size adult fish, avoid repeatedly maxing out your limit over several days.

Yellow Perch Tactics

- Fish lures for yellow perch slowly, getting them near the bottom and keeping them there through the retrieve.

- Small spinners, small jigs with nylon or hair skirts or tipped with curly-tailed grubs, and very small plugs work well.

- Cast whole small worms, whole grubs, or live minnows under floats but with enough split shot to get the bait down.

- Yellow perch holding in very deep water are best approached with a boat so that jigs can be worked vertically.

Catching White Perch

- Searching for white perch schools often requires a boat in order to cover enough water to prospect for fish.

- In freshwater lakes, try small diving plugs that match the local forage fish, small spinners, and jigs.

- Get lures near the bottom and work them slowly, and keep working areas where you find fish.

- For natural baits, drift live minnows and whole small worms under a float with enough line below to reach near bottom.

SMALL POPPERS: PANFISH ON FLY

Sunfish, crappies, and perch will inhale flies as quickly as any trout or bass

Fly fishing for panfish can be terrifically fun, especially for kids and new fly casters, because the casts need not be long and sunfish and other panfish are not too particular about the look of the fly. Sunfish are often close enough to shore that you need not wade, while crappies might be holding in deep water and thus call for a boat, kayak, or inflatable.

The lightest, shortest fly rods and lines used for stream fishing for small trout are all that's necessary for panfish; 2- and 4-weight rods and lines will do it. If you're casting from a boat on open water in the wind, however, go with at least an 8-foot rod to get some power against the wind, but in optimal conditions, a 7-foot fly rod works well. Very often, a

Rods and Terminal Tackle

- Given panfish size, a slow-action rod that's very flexible can heighten the action.

- For casting accuracy, find a rod with which you can accurately place small flies and poppers.

- The body of a popper creates more wind resistance than a feather fly, and will need a bit more force on the cast.

- Leaders for panfish should be 6 or 7 feet long with as light a tippet as possible, usually a 4X or 5X (see page 75 for tippet discussion).

Panfish Poppers

- Poppers for panfish range from size 10 to size 16, with top colors being black, white, red, and yellow.

- If sunfish hit a popper but you can't hook them, go down at least one size, from a size 12 to 14, for example.

- Crappies that are feeding on surface insects will take poppers and dry flies that are a close imitation in size and color.

- Larger bluegills will readily go after a rubber-legged popper that looks big enough for bass.

floating line will be fine for fly casting to panfish, but if fish are holding at depth, use a bead-head fly (weighted) or put a few split shot on the leader to get the fly down. A short sinking tip might also be necessary.

Keep in mind that as you cast for panfish, a largemouth bass might grab a popper that you meant for bluegill, or a rock bass or smallmouth bass might grab a small streamer meant for crappie.

Poppers & Attractor Patterns

- Poppers cast to panfish don't need to be retrieved—just twitch and pop them in place.

- Be careful of spooking sunfish when you pick the popper off the water for another cast—keep line splash minimal.

- Small gnat patterns, nymphs, and small Woolly Buggers fished in the surface film or subsurface can quickly attract sunfish and crappies.

- Smaller attractor patterns, such as a size-14 Stimulator, and hopper and cricket patterns can be deadly on calm summer ponds.

Crappie Flies

- Minnow-imitating streamers in sizes 10 and 12 fished along the bottom nab crappies and yellow perch.

- "Mini-jigs" are small, light lead-headed jigs that work well for crappie and can be cast with a fly rod.

- Tie a single square knot in the upper leader section, or secure a bead there, and then slide the tippet and leader through a slip float.

- Tie on the mini-jig; it'll sink when cast, and the float will stop at the knot or bead for correct depth.

127

COAST TO COAST: PANFISH WATERS
The real question might be, is there anywhere that panfish aren't?

Quality panfish waters can be found all over the country, and might very easily be in your own backyard—the classic neighborhood farm pond can produce big fish and offer lots of action. There are, of course, numerous renowned panfish waters worth investigating, but any given water that supports sunfish, crappie, and perch with enough food and a quality environment can hold significant fish, either in size or number.

Anglers in the Northeast can find sunnies, as they're known, in ponds, streams, and both deep and shallow lakes. Quiet eddies along riverbanks will also often hold sunfish. Southern impoundments and bayous are major hot spots for redear sunfish. Countless midwestern lakes from Arkansas to Missouri to Minnesota contain millions of big bluegills, and impoundments across Texas are also major sunfish destinations.

Santee Cooper

- The Santee Cooper impoundment system in eastern South Carolina could be a life's work for the panfish angler.

- Redear, or shellcracker, sunfish grow to significant size here, including the world-record 5-pound, 7.5-ounce shellcracker.

- Excellent numbers of crappies that often approach 2 pounds inhabit the brush piles throughout the creeks in the springtime.

- Pursuing the sizable bluegills and other quality panfish here calls for a motorboat, though angling from shore can be successful.

John Kerr Reservoir

- On the Virginia–North Carolina border, the John Kerr Reservoir continues to hold many big black and white crappies.

- Bordered by two Virginia state parks, this massive reservoir has many creek arms and coves where crappies hide and spawn.

- Pre-spawn fishing with small spinnerbaits over the numerous brush piles is a highly successful tactic.

- Given the reservoir's size and multiple hot spots, a boat is the only way to fish for crappie here.

In the West, California, Oregon, and Idaho have many very good sunfish waters.

Black and white crappies exist in every state. Excellent waters extend across the South and northward into Virginia, Maryland, and southern Pennsylvania. Lakes and oxbows across Louisiana and Mississippi are crappie powerhouses. Numerous waters in Oregon, Washington, and California also hold good crappies, as well as yellow perch.

Big lakes in New England and the Midwest are famous for their yellow perch, but this species also occurs in small, even shallow, lakes or ponds (sometimes the result of freelance stocking). Anglers searching for white perch should check out coastal waterways and lakes from Maine through southern Pennsylvania into the eastern Carolinas. Midwestern impoundment waters and Great Lakes watersheds also offer significant white perch fisheries. On the West Coast, white perch inhabit numerous California estuaries and inshore waters. In some places in the Midwest, however, the white perch is considered a nuisance species and is banned from import, and local-caught fish are quickly used as bait for bigger fish.

Top Perch Fisheries

- In the Northeast, Lake Erie, Lake Winnepesauke, Lake Champlain, and Lake St. Clair are top yellow perch waters.

- In the Midwest, Iowa's Mississippi River Pools 10 and 11, Minnesota's Plantagenette Lake, and Wisconsin's Lake Winnebago hold good yellow perch.

- Major white perch fisheries can be found all around Chesapeake Bay, especially in river estuaries.

- North Carolina's Lake Waccamaw and Albemarle and Pamlico Sounds and tributaries are good white perch spots.

Top Redear Fisheries

- Redears (aka shellcrackers) and bluegills in terrific numbers swim in the waters of the Lake Mitchell, Yates Lake, and Lake Jordan in Alabama.

- Anglers take redears of significant size from the waters of Tippah County in Mississippi and Caney Lake in Louisiana.

- In Florida, Lake Tarpon and Lake Guntersville have had very good shellcracker populations.

- Georgia's Lake Seminole has been the go-to place for shellcracker anglers on the Georgia-Florida border.

LIGHT-TACKLE CATFISH

Ponds, streams, and small lakes often contain fun, easily caught, smaller catfish species

Freshwater catfish occur all around the world. In the southern and midwestern United States, larger catfish species are about as popular as bass. Bullheads are the most widespread catfish, occurring in sluggish streams, ponds, and lakes across the country. The three main members of this family are black, brown, and yellow bullheads.

Bullheads do not take on much size, with a typical maximum length of 12 to 15 inches. They don't mind muddy waters and can stand very warm water with low oxygen. Like other catfish, bullheads can use their air bladders to breathe gaseous air in poor water conditions (they'll gulp air at the surface) and survive for a brief time when taken from the water. A high, lobe-

Black Bullhead

- The black bullhead prefers warm waters with muddy bottoms, and tends to occupy shallows.

- Coloration on the dorsal surfaces can be black or a dark green, with yellow or whitish flanks.

- Black bullheads have chubby bodies that are stubbier and stouter than brown or yellow bullheads, and tend to be bottom feeders.

- Maximum length for black bullhead is usually around 12 inches, with the weight 1 pound or less.

Brown Bullhead

- The brown bullhead has a more tapered body than the black bullhead, with less stoutness, but is also a bottom feeder.

- The dorsal surfaces are brown or yellow-brown, and the sides are a mottled yellow-brown or olive-brown.

- Brown bullheads will take to somewhat deeper water in lakes and streams than black bullheads, preferring weedy sections with gravel or mud bottoms.

- Most brown bullheads don't exceed 2 pounds and reach 12 to 14 inches.

shaped dorsal fin and eight chin barbels are key identifying features, but depending upon their range, the three major bullhead species can very closely resemble one another.

The white catfish occurs mostly in coastal rivers from the Chesapeake Bay to Florida and Texas. It doesn't mind somewhat brackish waters and seeks slower currents in streams and rivers, but the species also occurs in ponds or lakes. White catfish have been introduced to similar habitats on the West Coast. White catfish are a bit larger than bullheads, averaging 16 inches.

YELLOW ● LIGHT

Be wary of the dorsal and pectoral spines found on bullheads, white catfish, and other catfish species. The first spine of these fins can deliver a nasty poke to the hands. A species of small catfish called madtom, which are often used as bait, have actual venom sacs at the base of these spines and can deliver a painful sting.

Yellow Bullhead

- The largest of the three main bullhead species, the yellow bullhead can reach 2 or 3 pounds and 18 inches in length.

- Colored yellow-brown and mottled, the yellow bullhead has a rounded tail, unlike the inward-curved tail of the brown bullhead.

- The yellow bullhead also has white or yellow-white chin barbels, while black and brown bullhead chin barbells are all dark.

- Yellow bullheads prefer slow streams and lakes or ponds with soft bottoms, and scavenge for food at lower depths.

White Catfish

- The white catfish is easily identified by its bluish-gray dorsal surfaces, the distinct edge between its grayish flanks and white underside, and its lack of spots.

- A white catfish's body is more torpedo-shaped than the bullhead's, and its tail has a shallow fork.

- White catfish are not as elongated as channel catfish, and don't have as deeply a forked tail.

- Matching the biggest yellow bullhead in size, white catfish can reach 18 inches and upwards of 3 pounds.

CATCHING SMALLER WHISKERS

Young anglers who've had enough of sunfish easily move on to bull-heads and white catfish

The great thing about bullheads is that they are present in the same waters where young anglers are casting for sun-nies. White catfish are also often found in the same ponds and small lakes (there are numerous pay-to-fish operations that stock white catfish). Moving from sunfish, crappie, or perch usually takes a change in the terminal tackle, but the

rod and reel size and line weight will be enough.

Bullheads will bite during the day, but frequently tend to be more active at night and will reward the angler who stays on the water from dusk to midnight. These fish hardly ever strike any sort of lure, so still-fishing with bait—natural or prepared—is pretty much the standard for bullheads. The

Tackle for Bullhead

- An ultralight to light spinning or spincasting outfit loaded with 4- to 6-pound-test monofilament is perfect for bullheads.

- Use as little weight as possible with a bullhead rig—just enough to get on the bottom.

- Set up a drop-shot rig with 12-inch hook leaders, or a rig with a sliding sinker pegged with a bead or split shot.

- Use long-shank size-4 to size-2 hooks, and have pliers handy since bullheads tend to swallow baits, or use circle hooks.

Bullhead Bait

- Big bullheads take whole worms fished on the bottom, while a piece of night crawler hooked on a light jig head works for smaller fish.

- In early summer, small whole crayfish or crayfish tails also take bullheads.

- Leeches, strips of liver, and dough balls have proven effective for bullheads, but the worms are the main natural bait.

- Be sure not to get artificial odors on bullhead bait, such as grease or sun-screen—these unnatural scents turn bullheads away.

best fishing occurs in the spring and into the summer, when the water temperature is rising from the 60s (Fahrenheit) into the 70s. In the early spring, daytime fishing brings some success, but as water temperatures hit their peak, bullheads become more nocturnal.

White catfish are considered good eating (better than bullheads, certainly), and are frequently pursued for the table. White catfish become active as water temperatures get into the 70s. Daytime fishing can be successful, but pursuing white catfish at dusk and at night can have bigger payoffs.

Bullhead Fishing Techniques

- Often bullheads will just hold the bait in their mouths as they move off, without clamping down on the hook.

- If fishing on the bottom with a relatively tight line, let the bullhead move off a distance before a quick hook-set.

- When fishing a bait below a float, let the float completely disappear before setting the hook.

- If keeping bullheads for eating, pursue those in relatively clear waters and put the fish or meat on ice immediately.

White Catfish Bait

- White catfish feed mostly on baitfish, small crustaceans, and aquatic insects, and sometimes aquatic vegetation, depending on their environment.

- Targeting white catfish with a live minnow fished on the bottom with a dropper rig is the first thing to try.

- If minnows don't work, try a whole worm on the bottom, rigged with a sliding sinker.

- White catfish will take a host of catfish baits— dough balls, stinkbaits, chicken liver—which might be the local bait of choice.

BIG, BIGGER, BIGGEST CATS

The channel, blue, and flathead catfish deserve and get a lot of attention

Big catfish have a special place in American fishing history. Many a midwesterner has tangled with a monster blue catfish, and across many states, channel catfish are a species of angling and eating delight. And the bruising flathead catfish has become what you might even call its own "big-game" fishery.

Anglers find channel catfish in rivers, creeks, and lakes across the entire country, and even into northern Mexico and southern Canada. They have been introduced in many places and are a large part of fish-farming operations, and even comprise a major commercial fishery in some parts of the country. Channel cats prefer very clear waters and don't mind a little current.

Channel Catfish

- Often called the "spotted catfish," a very quick identifier of the channel cat is its deeply forked, V-shaped tail with pointed lobes.

- Along with its spotted sides, the channel cat's elongated, tapered body and less bulky head differentiate it from the bullhead.

- Body color varies, depending upon habitat; channel cats might be dark olive, or dark blue, or almost black on the dorsal sides.

- Most channel catfish range from 2 to 8 pounds; the 1964 all-tackle record was 58 pounds.

Blue Catfish

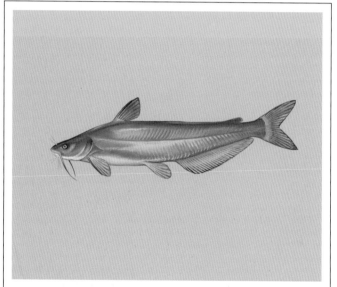

- Sometimes called the "Mississippi cat" or "silver cat," the blue catfish has a deeply forked tail with rounded lobes.

- The blue cat's body has no spots, and it has a longer anal fin and more rounded dorsal fin.

- Larger-size blue catfish develop a bulky head and a distinct humped back at the base of the dorsal fin.

- A blue cat's flanks can sometimes be a pale silvery-blue, and their underside is usually a clear white, or sometimes gray.

Blue catfish—so called for their coloration—are found in rivers and impoundments mostly across the South, from South Carolina to Texas, but still inhabit their original range in the Mississippi, Missouri, and Ohio Rivers. Like the channel catfish, they seek clear water, but with significant current.

Big waters are the home of flathead catfish, where the fish like to go deep in tailraces below dams on big rivers, or in reservoirs and large tributaries. Also called "shovelheads," these big cats can be found from western Pennsylvania across the Great Lakes drainages to the Dakotas and Idaho.

Of the 2,200 species of catfish worldwide, the longest is the European wels catfish, and the heaviest is the Mekong giant catfish. A wels caught in Romania reached 9.9 feet and 220 pounds. The Mekong cat record was a 9-foot, 646-pound fish caught in 1981 in Thailand.

Blue Catfish Records

- Most blue catfish weight from 5 to 15 pounds, with 50-pounders not uncommon in some places.

- The current world record, set in 2005, is a 124-pound fish from the Mississippi River in Illinois.

- The previous two world records were a 121.5-pound blue cat from Lake Texoma, Texas, and a 119-pound fish from South Carolina's Santee Cooper River in 1991.

- The biggest blue cat on record was a 150-pound fish taken from the Mississippi River (probably by a commercial operation) in 1879.

Flathead Catfish

- The flathead catfish, also called the "yellow cat" and "mud cat," has a squared-off, slightly rounded tail and square-shaped dorsal fin.

- The coloration of a flathead catfish varies, but in general has a brown dorsal surface, with yellow-brown mottling.

- As the name suggests, a flathead has a wide, spade-shaped flat head and a large, wide mouth.

- Flathead catfish regularly reach 20 pounds, with 80-pounders not uncommon in some places; the world record is 121 pounds, caught in Kansas in 1998.

135

BIG FISH IN THE HOLE

Look for deep river- and lake-bottom structure for major cats

Still-fishing from shore or at anchor and drift-fishing from a boat are the main ways to pursue big catfish, given their preferred station on the river or lake bottom, in holes and sometimes in heavy cover. Set lines (a heavy line, with a single baited hook, tied to a tree) and trot lines (a length of line tied to a float, with several dropper hooks) are still used in some places to catch big cats.

In rivers, focus on tributary mouths, deep drop-offs, deeply undercut banks, and deep pools, especially pools with stumps, sunken logs, or boulders at the head, as big fish like to position themselves behind these. Channel catfish are a bit more mobile than their larger brethren, and will move into shallows over gravel or rocky bottoms and can be targeted in current seams and at creek mouths. Reservoir catfish take to deep

Tackle and Baits

- Channel cats call for medium-action rods and reels—spincasting, spinning, or baitcasting—loaded with 10-pound-test line.

- Baits for channel cats range from fish strips to crayfish to chicken liver, on size 2 to size 1/0 hooks.

- For blue and flathead catfish, use heavy baitcasting rods and reels or conventional reels, loaded with 30- to 50-pound-test line.

- Live or dead shiners or shad, strips of fish, and chicken livers work for big blues and flatheads, on size-3/0 to size-5/0 hooks.

Rigs and Sinkers

- A slip-float rig using ¼-ounces of large split shot, or a ¼-ounce slip sinker (egg sinker) baited with a big minnow is very effective for locating channel cats in shallow water.

- A larger version of the slip-float rig with a heavier sinker and longer leader can go

deep for bigger catfish.

- Use flat-sided sinkers with river rigs, as current will roll a round-sided sinker.

- Offset, long-shank hooks are most often used for bigger cats, but size-3/0 to size-5/0 circle hooks aid catch-and-release.

flooded timber and to holes below inflowing tributaries.

Waters immediately below dams can be major catfish hideouts. Outflow from the dam creates an immediate, deep area of churning water, called a "scour hole," and below this will be mounds of gravel and debris, pushed there by the outflow. Big blues and flatheads will station themselves in the hole, depending upon where churned-up baitfish spill out, and also seek the slower water behind debris mounds, while channel catfish will cover the sides and up-current edge of the mounds. Wing dams also attract catfish; the cats will patrol the downriver edge of the dam, depending on how deep the water is, and sometimes chase baitfish around to the upriver side. Make use of topographic charts, depth gauges, and sonar to locate holes and hiding spots and determine their size.

Soft-Bottom Rig

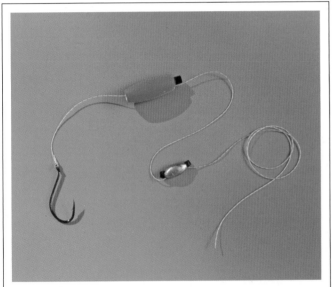

- With heavier rigs, use the lightest sinker possible that still keeps the bait stationary on the bottom.

- Over sandy or mucky bottoms, in water without strong current, use a pyramid sinker to punch into the bottom to hold the rig in place.

- Use a small float on the leader to keep the bait just off turbid, debris-strewn soft bottoms.

- In such a rig, the main line can be heavy-test braided line, while the leader can be a lighter-test monofilament.

River Rig

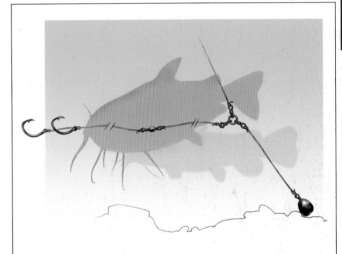

- For a river rig, pull a 50-pound-test superbraid through a three-way swivel.

- Tie a 24-inch 30-pound "big game" monofilament to the other barrel swivel eye, and snell this to a 6/0 octopus circle hook, possibly adding a swivel halfway down the leader.

- Tie a 5-ounce flat-sided or Bell sinker to the third swivel eye using 20-pound monofilament.

- If the sinker or hook snag, the lighter monofilament will break before the main line does.

CATFISH BAITS

Make and rig stinkbaits, dough balls, and fish strips for big cats

Catfishers can get into some serious dockside debates about two key things: 1) what kinds of odors attract catfish the best when using stinkbaits and dough balls, and 2) how big a live or cut bait should be. As with all things fishing, experimentation is inevitably necessary.

Across the country, many locally made catfish baits are available at tackle shops, concoctions that resulted from mad scientist work in garages and sheds, where catfish enthusiasts experimented with ground-up shad, pulverized shrimp, soap, lunchmeats, cheeses, and natural flavorings like vanilla extract. This has been going on for many years, owing largely to the willingness of big catfish to eat just about anything smelly or flavorful, and the willingness of anglers to use whatever they had on hand—like hot dogs, Vienna sausage,

Chicken Liver, Beef Lungs, and Hot Dogs

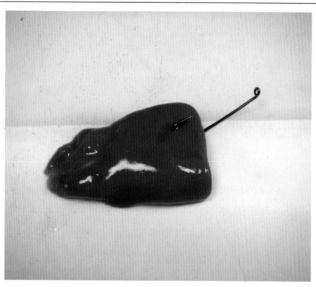

- Use slightly frozen raw chicken liver hunks; they hold the hook a bit better before getting soft when warmed.

- Coat hunks of chicken liver with garlic salt, let dry, and then mix with more garlic salt.

- Fill beef lungs (windpipe intact) with beef blood and hang in a cooler; when the tissue is fully saturated, cut the lung into bait cubes.

- Cut hot dogs into ¾-inch sections and soak in crushed garlic and garlic salt, or tuna oil.

Baitfish

- Baitfish for big catfish include suckers, sunfish, small bullheads, herring, gizzard shad, creek chub, and shiners.

- Rig smaller baitfish in front of the dorsal fin with a 3/0 Aberdeen hook, a finer-wire hook better matched to small baitfish.

- Rig bullheads through the tail with a 6/0 or 8/0 octopus hook or circle hook.

- To make shad strips, cut off the head and tail, and cut cross-sections (steaking) or fillet the shad and cut the fillets in half.

or hunks of fried chicken—to satisfy catfish hunger.

As for using rigged baitfish, some anglers swear by the rule "big bait, big fish," while others, including some who specialize in big cats on major rivers like the Missouri, stick with short strips of baitfish meat, nothing over 4 inches. Flathead chasers often rig an entire live gizzard shad, as flatheads prefer live bait and are not as partial to smelly prepared baits as blues and channel catfish.

ZOOM

"Noodling" is a way of catching big catfish, usually flatheads, without bait—by grabbing them by hand. Noodlers wade, swim, and even dive underwater to force their hand into a flathead's mouth and yank the fish from its hiding hole. Noodling is not an officially recognized method of fishing, although there are numerous noodling competitions.

Dough Balls

- To make dough balls, put 1½ cups of cornmeal, 1 cup of flour, and 4 ounces of anise oil into a pot.

- Add 16 ounces of a sweet, fruit-flavored soft drink (non-diet) to the pot.

- Stir the mixture continuously over medium heat until all the fluid is absorbed and the dough is sticky and stiff.

- Put the mixture on a floured board and knead, adding more flour until the mix isn't sticky; make grape-size balls and cool them before using.

Premade Catfish Baits

- Premade catfish baits are usually pasty substances that range in odor from sweet to horribly stinky.

- Mixtures of crushed fish and livestock liver, brains, and coagulated blood are blended with cheeses, garlic, barbeque sauce, and anise.

- Specially prepared "soap baits" are still found in some regions, as soap cakes were used to bait trot lines years ago.

- Channel catfish and flathead catfish have been known to strike deep crankbaits, jigs, and plugs, but rarely.

AMERICA'S TOP CATFISH WATERS

The South and the Southwest rule, but western and Canadian fisheries are worth the trip

All three bullhead species are so widespread that quality bullhead fishing can be found in just about any decent environment. The black and brown bullhead records come from New York, and the record yellow bullhead was caught in Arizona. A Missouri farm pond or an oxbow in Arkansas or a lake in Pennsylvania could easily turn up a new bullhead record.

As for the bigger species, the South, Southwest, and Midwest are the quality fish zones in terms of consistency and record-breaking size. The locations below are notable for producing abundant big fish (they also tend to be very large bodies of water), but there are other locations worth mentioning: The Susquehanna River in Pennsylvania is probably the best

Santee Cooper

- The Santee Cooper system, composed of Lake Marion and Lake Moultrie, is located in southeastern South Carolina.

- Target areas of flooded brush or timber and bottom structure like channel bottoms and ledges, humps, and sloughs.

- Try drift-fishing from a boat using whole, live threadfin shad or gizzard shad.

- The state record for channel catfish (58 pounds, 1964), flathead catfish (79 pounds, 2001), and blue catfish (109 pounds, 1991) all come from the Santee Cooper system.

Mississippi River

- Hot spots for big cats abound on the "Big River," including the waters near Rosedale and Yellow Bend, Mississippi, and Memphis, Tennessee.

- Favored baits are skipjack herring and shad for blue cats, live sunfish for flatheads, and shad innards for

channel cats.

- Jug fishing for catfish is popular on the Mississippi— anglers float rigged, empty plastic bottles like bobbers.

- Tennessee's Cumberland River and Tennessee River also rank as major big-cat hot spots.

northeastern destination for flatheads, and the James River in eastern Virginia is good for channel catfish. Arkansas's Lake Ouachita is a great channel cat spot, while Texas's Choke Canyon Reservoir holds good blue catfish. The Red River from North Dakota into Manitoba is known for abundant, sizable channel catfish (rules call for all channel cats over 30 inches to be released, if that gives you an idea). Brownlee Reservoir in Idaho has produced some massive flatheads, including the current record fish., In 2000 a 101-pound blue catfish came out of the San Vincente Reservoir in California. Take a look at the state fisheries Web sites for Oklahoma, Missouri, Kansas, and Kentucky for other catfish waters.

Flatheads, however, are not welcome everywhere. Their introduction into non-native waters disposed them to devour a great number of indigenous fish. In the Oconee River in Georgia, flatheads are causing declines of native bullheads and sunfishes. Flatheads introduced in South Carolina are eating up the Edisto River fish populations. Errant introductions of these catfish into waters in New Mexico and Pennsylvania have also done damage to resident fish populations.

Missouri Hot Spots

- Missouri River waters near Glasgow are full of catfish, and numerous guide services operate out of cities along the river.

- Float fishing on the Grand River from Brunswick to the Missouri River is a good bet for major catfish.

- Look for big blues in the Osage River from the Bagnell Dam to the Missouri River at Jefferson City.

- Drift-fishing with cut fish can work well for big channel and blue cats on Truman Lake, southeast of Kansas City.

Texas Hot Spots

- With a 98-pound flathead catch in 1998, Lake Palestine offers good chances at trophy fish on live bait, and abundant channel catfish.

- Easily accessed from Dallas/Forth Worth, Lake Lewisville has an excellent wintertime blue cat fishery in the old Lake Dallas section.

- Lake Texoma, on the Oklahoma-Texas border, holds trophy blue catfish that go after live shad, cut bait, and blood baits.

- Oklahoma's Grand Lake o' the Cherokee is also worth the trip for major blue catfish.

141

AMERICA'S OTHER MARQUEE FISH

Numerous species of trout are a mainstay in many anglers' sport

Trout are a highly contrasted counterpart to bass, in the ranks of freshwater gamefish. Both species have played central roles in the development of American fishing and have been pursued with equal gusto as esteemed, tricky, hard-fighting fish. Trout, however, are physically much different fish that don't readily inhabit waters that rise above 65 degrees Fahrenheit, and often prefer rivers and streams with steady current.

The term "trout" encompasses a varied group of fish that belong to the true trout genus, *Salmo;* the char genus, *Salvelinus;* and the Pacific salmon genus, *Oncorhynchus.* Brown trout are "true" trout, while brook trout, lake trout, and bull trout belong to the char genus. Western American species—the rainbow, cutthroat, and golden trout—are grouped in the salmon genus. But all of these fish share very similar traits:

Rainbow Trout

- Rainbow trouin catchable size from 14 inches to 12 pounds, with some regional populations even larger.

- Sometimes referred to as redband trout, the "rainbow" name was attached by northeastern fisheries managers stocking the fish in the late 1800s.

- Distinguishing marks are the lengthwise pink or red stripe, which can be pale or bright, and many small black spots on the fish's back and sides.

- Rainbow trout are found across the country, except for portions of the South.

Brown Trout

- American brown trout arose out of introductions of the indigenous European strain, with the first ones arriving from Germany in 1883.

- Brown trout have amber or silvery bodies with "coffee bean" black spots across their backs and red spots on their sides.

- Most brown trout range from 15 to 20 inches, but can reach 8 or 12 pounds in some locations.

- Brown trout are found across much of the East, Midwest, and West, but not the farthest South or Alaska.

lack of spines in their fins, an adipose fin (the small, thumb-like fin in front of the tail), and often very bright, highly detailed bodily markings at various times.

Rainbow trout and brown trout are probably the two most well-known species, given their extensive range brought about by stocking programs and their hardiness in varying environments. A number of trout, including cutthroat, rainbow, and brown, have a seagoing form that dwells in coastal rivers and lives in the ocean for periods of time.

ZOOM

Three of America's most rare trout are the Apache and Gila trout of the Southwest, found mainly in Arizona, and the Sunapee trout of Maine. Loss of range and competition with introduced trout species have put the Apache and Gila trout in severely threatened status. The Sunapee is hanging on in Maine through various reintroductions, but its New Hampshire populations are extinct.

Brook Trout

- Once called the "speckled char," the identifying marks of brook trout are their lower fins edged in white and the irregular yellow blotches on their backs.

- Its range covers the Northeast, into Canada, and down through the Appalachians into the mid-South;

it has been introduced in the West.

- Most brook trout don't get much larger than 15 inches, but bigger specimens can reach 3 or 4 pounds.

- When spawning in the fall, brook trout take on their most intense coloration.

Cutthroat Trout

- The term "cutthroat" is slightly generic, as there are fourteen different, identifiable variations within the cutthroat species.

- All of these fourteen subspecies range across western states, from Montana to New Mexico and over to California.

- In general, most cutthroat species range from 14 to 20 inches, with some fish breaking 4 pounds; coastal and lake-dwelling cutthroats get bigger.

- Cutthroats share their range with brown and rainbow trout, and hybridize with rainbows to make a "cutbow."

OTHER MAJOR TROUT SPECIES

When anglers need a variation on the browns and rainbows, these species provide the chase

The great variety of trout species in North America is an angler's boon. The extent of the environments where the fish occur—small streams, big streams, lakes, coastal river mouths—and these species' huge range provide all kinds of opportunities, some highly unique.

If you want to mix a little backpacking with your angling,

seek the golden trout. This smaller but very pretty member of the salmonid family lives in lakes and headwaters at elevations of 6,900 feet and higher, mostly in the Sierras of California and a few other western states. Another western species, the bull trout, is one of the bigger, more aggressive char. It is still endangered across much of its range in the Lower 48,

Lake Trout

- Called "mackinaw" in some places, the lake trout's dark to light green body, white spots, and forked tail are main identifiers.

- This highly edible cousin of the brook trout ranges from the Great Lakes and upper West across Canada to Alaska.

- Most lakers are under 10 pounds; the all-tackle record is 66 pounds, 8 ounces, and a 102-pounder was netted in Canada in 1961.

- Lake trout seek the coolest waters, ranging from 20 feet to 100 feet deep.

Steelhead

- Steelhead go to sea as juveniles born in freshwater, and five or six years later return to their home river as adults to spawn.

- Unlike Pacific salmon, the steelhead doesn't always die after its spawning run, but can return to the sea.

- In the sea, steelhead are bright chrome but take on rainbow trout coloration in freshwater.

- Most steelhead range from 4 to 12 pounds, but they can reach 20 pounds; the all-tackle record is a 42-pound, 2-ounce fish.

but appears to be mounting a comeback in some waters.

The steelhead is a larger, oceangoing version of the rainbow trout, found in many western coastal rivers. This fish has also been established in the Great Lakes. Terrific and aggressive fighters, steelhead call anglers to the river in droves when they arrive to spawn. The lake trout is a deep-dwelling char that can also take on some serious size and, in northern cold-water lakes of Canada, becomes a vigorous fighter. In the Lower 48, the "laker" is well worth pursuing for fillets for the smokehouse.

ZOOM

The Dolly Varden trout is a coastal Pacific char closely related to the bull trout and arctic char. Years ago the Dolly and the bull trout were confused as the same species. Usually a sea-run fish of 2 or 3 pounds, this trout supposedly got its name from a Charles Dickens character known for wearing colorful dresses.

Bull Trout

- Because of their endangered status, bull trout are the subject of major conservation and catch-and-release efforts where they occur in northwestern states.

- Bull trout often grab a smaller trout already on an angler's line, and then a serious battle begins.

- Most bull trout aren't more than 5 pounds, but 30-inch fish appear occasionally; the record is a 32-pound, 40½ -inch fish.

- Bull trout have big heads and long jaws, and elongated, tapered, green-colored bodies with whitish and pink spots.

Golden Trout

- A brilliant green-gold-red body coloration, a lengthwise row of lavender blotches, white-tipped dorsal fin, and a heavily spotted tail identify the golden trout.

- This smaller trout, rarely exceeding 1 pound, was originally found only in California's Kern River basin.

- The golden trout is part of the rainbow and redband trout group, and does have a slight lateral red marking down its sides.

- The species has been introduced successfully to Idaho, Washington, and Wyoming.

GETTING TROUT TO BITE
Trout can be notoriously fussy, but a wide variety of lures give the angler an edge

Trout have led to as much human thinking about designing tackle and fooling fish as any other species, sometimes even more, given the great variety of trout, their general trickiness, and waxing and waning moods. The angler can still fish, cast and retrieve, fly cast, troll, and go deep for trout, all depending upon the species and situation.

Trout will readily take bait. In fact, one of the biggest innovations in trout fishing of the past twenty years has been the introduction of clay-like, malleable artificial bait in numerous wild colors. In "put-and-take" fisheries, i.e., stocked trout that anglers usually keep, this is a go-to method. Wild fish might also grab such offerings, but are usually more attuned to nat-

Spin-Fishing and Spincasting Outfits

- For small-stream trout, an ultralight outfit that doubles as a sunfish outfit will work fine for trout under 1 pound.

- Casting on rivers will take a medium-action spinning rod with some length, upwards of 7 feet.

- Spincasting and spinning

reels loaded with up to 10-pount-test monofilament work well in most trout-fishing situations.

- Going deep for big trout calls for medium to heavy rods; steelhead require a long casting rod and spinning or conventional reel with strong drag.

Plugs

- Trout feed on baitfish found frequently in streams—shiners, sculpins, and dace—and fall for plugs that correctly imitate bait size and color.

- Plug fishing can be especially fruitful on bigger creeks and rivers and in lakes, where there are more large-size trout.

- Most trout are ambush predators that strike quickly, so keep a plug moving and fish it through the entire strike zone.

- In wintertime conditions, small diving plugs and crankbaits, called "peanuts," can take big rainbow trout.

ural baits, such as aquatic insects, worms, and leeches.

Among artificial lures, trout anglers have been using in-line spinners and spoons since the late 1800s. Most lures are designed to be retrieved in the water column or close to the bottom. When trout feed on the surface, they are almost 100 percent of the time feeding on insects, which must be accurately imitated by hand-tied flies. Poppers, floating stick baits, and plastic frog imitations are rarely elements of the trout tackle box (but that's not to say that a big brown trout patrolling at night wouldn't eat a frog or mouse—they do).

Other Baits

- Spinners need not be much bigger than size 3 to take trout of all sizes.

- Small spoons are also fine, and need not get much bigger than 3 inches long.

- For live bait, rig a small minnow forward of the dorsal fin on a size 6 hook, and use a small casting sinker to get it on the bottom.

- A salmon egg on an egg hook, or corn kernels or small worms on a size 8 hook, fished on the bottom are highly effective.

········· • GREEN ● LIGHT • ·········

Often, trout anglers will crush the barbs on lures and flies if practicing catch-and-release fishing. This allows for easier hook removal and less stress on the fish. Trout have bony, rough mouths, and barbed hooks can be very difficult to remove.

TROUT

Trolling

- To cover lots of water, anglers can troll spoons, small plugs, and streamers around big lakes.

- As the ice thaws, trout can be found in all levels of a lake while the water is still uniformly cold.

- When weather warms, lake-bound trout often seek deeper cool water, from the high 50s to low 60s Fahrenheit.

- Trout in lakes feed on baitfish and crayfish, so choose lures or baits that match the local forage.

TECHNIQUES FOR TAKING TROUT

A wide range of approaches is necessary for success with trout in their various habitats

In the classic rock-strewn river, trout seek places where they can take up a station without having to exert a lot of energy swimming against current. Trout lurk behind or along rocks and boulders, along ledges and undercut banks, behind fallen trees, at the back of an eddy, on the current seam between slow and fast water, and in pools below waterfalls. Rainbow,

brown, brook, cutthroat, and bull trout all follow this basic pattern, with local variations. Brown trout sometimes hunt in slower water than where you might find rainbows. The angler's goal is to present lures or baits in moving water in a way that uses the current to move the offering past these likely ambush locations. Often a cast is made upstream of the tar-

Fishing Lake Trout

- Most fishing for lake trout in Great Lakes waters and northwestern lakes requires deep jigging or slow-trolling with spoons and plugs.

- Lakers will sometimes come up to shallower waters to hunt forage fish around rocky ledges and points.

- Regularly changing the pattern of lure movement—slowing down, speeding back up, turning or bobbing—often induces lakers to strike.

- Juvenile lakers will come up to lake shallows in northern waters and can be taken with small jigs or spoons.

Fishing Steelhead

- In western rivers, spawning steelhead move through deep, fast-current sections, or stay behind boulders and in holes.

- Steelhead anglers often "back-troll" on rivers, moving with the current to slowly drift lures into the fish from a boat.

- Anglers target spawning Great Lakes steelhead in tributaries by wading, drifting in float tubes, or casting from the bank.

- Most steelhead spawn runs are from late winter into spring, but on the Great Lakes, trolling takes non-spawning fish in big water.

get, such as a rock or the front of an eddy, and then the bait is allowed to drift past, or a lure is retrieved through the trout's perspective. Imagine you're a trout, in the current's seam, and ask yourself, "Where would I look for food?"

On many western lakes, rainbow, brown, and sometimes cutthroat trout will patrol the bulrushes and weedy or marshy areas that ring the lake's margin. The water at this level must be cold enough for the fish (and often it is into early summer), and when it is, they will readily come close to shore. And unlike trout in streams that maintain a station, lake-

dwelling trout go roving and will cover a lot of ground in a day. There's no current to bring food to them, so they go find baitfish that live in shallows and can be corralled against the banks, or insects and invertebrates that inhabit the weeds. Often, lake water is clear enough for anglers on shore to see patrolling trout, or target them from an inflatable, casting toward shore.

High Mountain Lakes

- On high mountain lakes, look for gathered trout at stream inlets or outlets, or rocky drop-offs.

- Cliff faces or steep rocky banks are places where trout might circulate, looking for prey.

- On larger lakes at lower elevations, trout and even smaller, stocked steelhead will seek deep troughs were there is cold, flowing water from a feeder stream.

- Packing in a small inflatable and waders is probably the best way to approach mountain lakes.

Stocked Trout/Private Water

- Stocked trout provide many opportunities for anglers, although wild fish, where found, are prized.

- Access is a major issue on crowded waters, where pay-to-fish, privately owned sections often offer the best chance at good fish.

- Some stocked trout survive through summer, if they can find cold water, and become "holdover" fish that start to take on wild traits.

- Limestone streams, mainly in the East, stay cold through spring and summer to provide continued trout action.

149

TROUT ON THE FLY

Sometimes the original approach for *Salmo trutta* and its brethren is the only way to go

The original English feather-and-hook combinations were made largely for the salmon and brown trout (*Salmo trutta*) of the British Isles. That occurred out of necessity, as there were no industrial lure-making abilities in the 1600s. But the other necessity—a lure that floats just like a winged insect—remains to this day. When trout are keyed in on a mayfly, cad-

dis fly, or stonefly hatch, other baits or lures will interest them little.

The key to using insect-imitating flies is to identify the actual bugs that the trout are eating (Atlantic salmon will occasionally take insects; mature Pacific salmon don't). The phrase "match the hatch" refers to matching flies to hatching,

Dry Flies

- Trout will occasionally focus on a hatching insect so sharply that they will pass up other bugs on the surface.

- Other times, as a hatch fades, casting a dry fly of a different species will trigger a trout strike.

- When there is no visible hatch of insects, cast nymph patterns that mimic the local species, or try small (size 18) gnat-pattern dry flies.

- Have a couple damselfly patterns (dry flies) in your box, in case you see trout feed on these.

Streamers

- Drift streamers across the current so that trout see the full profile of the fly, suggesting a struggling baitfish.

- On a "dead drift" with a streamer, trout often hit it on the "swing" at the end of the drift as the streamer turns a tight arc.

- When stripping a streamer, pull it in with short, darting strips of the line, pausing between each strip.

- One of the best streamer patterns, the Muddler Minnow, comes in many versions and colors.

winged insects. But trout readily eat larvae, or nymphs, that live along the stream bottom or drift or swim in the water column, and these, too, must be matched to what is in the angler's fly box. This is the reason why you'll see fly fishers carrying several boxes bursting with flies—getting color and size correct is crucial.

Trout will eat, or "take," surface insects in a number of ways: a sipping take, a splashy take, and a rolling take. This all has to do with the size of the fly, the aggressiveness of the trout, and the water surface (calm or riffled).

Casting streamers for trout is also highly effective, given how much trout feed on forage fish. Streamers can be cast and left to "dead drift," letting the fly's feathers and other materials flutter in the current and do the work of attraction; or a streamer can be stripped in, making it dart like a fleeing baitfish. Certain trout streamers, such as the Woolly Bugger, imitate no specific species except for maybe a leech, a big nymph, or a small crayfish.

Picking the Right Dry Fly

- If your dry fly is the right color but trout pass it by, try going down a size smaller.

- Cast dry flies about 10 to 15 feet upstream of a trout's feeding station, being sure not to put the line over the fish.

- Trout will grab attractor patterns that don't mimic a specific species but can look like stoneflies floating on the surface.

- Foam-body flies that float, like the Chernobyl Ant, can also mimic big stoneflies and attract trout.

Nymph Patterns

- Cast nymphs upstream or downstream or cross-current and strip them like a streamer, as nymphs actively swim in the water column.

- The nymph pattern that a trout takes tells you what species of flies might be soon hatching.

- In the winter and early spring, midge (gnat) nymph patterns fished down in the water column can be highly successful.

- A "dropper" rig—a dry fly with a nymph pattern tied to the dry-fly hook—covers your bets.

TOP TROUT WATERS

Fishing for trout can take anglers to some of the most beautiful and pristine waters in America

The kind of waters that trout require—clean, cold, and flowing, with lots of nutrients—depend greatly on the surrounding landscape. Trees play a major role in trout health by shading streams from the sun and by retaining the soil and runoff. In other words, locations of good trout waters are also quality environments—places worth going for that alone, to watch for animals and birds, and also to fish. You find places like this in the Catskills of New York, in the Smoky and Blue Ridge Mountains through North Carolina into Georgia, and across Montana, Wyoming, Idaho, and northern California.

Many quality trout waters, however, run through farmland or ranchland, both of which often abut wilderness lands or

Upper Delaware River

- The Upper Delaware is a tailwater fishery, arising in two branches from reservoirs, and the fishing depends on steady water releases.

- The East and West Branches meet to form the main river at Junction Pool at Hancock, New York.

- Brown, brook, and rainbow trout can be found in the river branches and south to Callicoon, New York.

- Anglers can experience a variety of insect hatches, lots of grasshoppers in summer, and very good access along most of the river.

Au Sable River

- The Au Sable flows across the northeast portion of the lower peninsula of Michigan, and offers 180 miles of blue-ribbon trout water.

- Stretching from Frederic to Lake Huron, the Au Sable calls for a good drift boat and enough time to float its best sections.

- The river holds mostly brown trout, some reaching trophy size, with a number of rainbow and brook trout in places.

- There is a 9-mile fly-fishing-only section of the Au Sable, called the "Holy Water."

forest. Stream health is an issue in such places, as runoff from crops and livestock can cause problems.

Then there is the "tailwater"—water that is released through a dam from a reservoir. Such releases are often cold, fast-flowing, and make for deep water, thus creating trout habitats where one might not naturally occur to such an extent. This often results in quality trout fishing across a significant length of river. Tailwaters are found all around the country, and in some cases are stocked with hatchery-raised trout.

White and Little Red Rivers

- The White River and the Little Red River are tailwaters that produce year-round trout fishing in northern Arkansas.

- Both rivers have produced many big brown trout, and also hold numerous big rainbows, brook, and cutthroat trout.

- This part of the Ozarks is a major fishing center, and guide services and angler lodging are abundant.

- The White River has about 100 miles of trout water, and flows along the Ozark National Forest.

Upper Klamath Lake

- Oregon's Upper Klamath Lake is well-known for its very big rainbow trout, with fish averaging 5 pounds and easily reaching 12 or 15 pounds.

- The large redbands here eat a variety of forage fish, the high-protein diet giving the fish their size.

- In the spring, work the marshy edges, bays, and channels of this lake using dark nymphs, from sizes 6 to 10.

- Plugs and spoons also take big rainbows lingering in the mouths of tributaries.

THE FRESHWATER BARRACUDA

Few gamefish can match muskie, pike, and pickerel for aggressive predation and fighting

The members of the pike family look like they were designed to cause trouble. Their elongated, torpedo-shaped bodies end in a sharp, flat snout, and their greenish sides often bear a military-like camouflage pattern. Then there's the gaping mouth full of teeth that can grab and swallow sizable prey.

Pike and pickerel, where abundant, are often very willing

quarry. Pike can be very curious fish and will often follow a lure a distance before striking. Other times, both pickerel and pike make sudden, slashing strikes at lures. Muskies, or muskellunge (a Native American word meaning "ugly pike"), are a good bit more difficult to catch, especially larger, smart, old fish, but a muskie will often follow a lure all the way to the

Chain Pickerel

- Chain pickerel have dark horizontal markings like a series of chains down their olive sides.

- A black vertical patch under each eye is a key identifier, although pickerel are usually a good deal smaller than pike.

- Most chain pickerel are around 2 pounds and not much more than 25 or 30 inches long; the world record is a 9-pound, 6-ounce Georgia fish.

- Two smaller subspecies, the grass pickerel and redfin pickerel, have dark vertical markings on their sides.

Northern Pike

- Pike have strong green-colored sides marked with white, horizontal, bean-shaped spots, and often have orange-tinted, heavily marked fins.

- The pike's fin arrangement is the standard for this fish family, with its single dorsal fin close to the tail.

- A color variation occasionally results in a bright-bodied fish called the "silver pike," but it's the same species.

- Most pike don't exceed 28 inches or 10 pounds; the American record is a 46-pound, 2-ounce New York pike.

boat, where the angler must work the lure in an overlapping pattern to keep it in the water and get the muskie to grab it.

Pickerel are found all through the Northeast to Florida and up from Louisiana to the Midwest and into Canada. Pike inhabit cold waters across the Northeast and upper Midwest, in the Great Lake states, and across the Northwest and much of Canada. Muskies are native to the Great Lakes and upper Mississippi drainages, as far west as Iowa, and occurring in the southern Appalachians.

ZOOM

Pike have scales on their entire cheeks and top half of their gills, but muskies have visible scales only on half of their cheeks and the top halves of their gills. On the bottom edge of their jaw, pike have five pores or less, and muskies have six or more pores.

Muskie

- The muskie is the largest member of the pike family and occurs solely in North America, whereas other species in the pike family also occur in Europe and Asia.

- Most muskies don't break 40 inches, but can go much larger; the American record is a 69-pound Wisconsin fish.

- Muskies have light-green sides with vertical striations, unlike the horizontal markings of pike and pickerel.

- Variations include muskies with spotted sides, or sides that are plain olive or green, with little marking at all.

Tiger Muskie

- The tiger muskie is a sterile hybrid of a pike and muskie, occurring infrequently in nature but often in hatcheries for stocking purposes.

- Tiger muskies are named for their highly contrasted markings of wavy, vertical dark stripes against a lighter background.

- Originally prized as a rare and beautiful fish, tigers are a major quarry due to their muskie-like fighting strength and pike-like aggression.

- Most tigers range from 8 to 16 pounds, with the record fish reaching 51 pounds, 3 ounces.

CASTING INTO THE TEETH
Pickerel and pike often strike eagerly, making for fast, tough action

When they're hungry, pickerel and pike will chew up plugs and other lures like junkyard dogs. Pickerel will repeatedly slash at a lure half its size before finally chomping on it and thrashing wildly. They'll also trail a lure, something that in clear water is as exciting as sight-casting to trout. Pike will also follow lures, and other times will simply explode out of the weeds and grab what they see.

Pickerel and pike habitat overlaps a good deal across their range, and both species take to similar environments. But pickerel will often be closer to shore, in the most shallow weed and lily pad sections, and like somewhat warmer water than pike. Weedy structure in 5 or 6 feet of water to depths of 12 feet or more are pike's preferred place, with water temperatures from the mid-50s into the 60s (Fahrenheit). A water

Fishing for Pickerel

- Increasingly warm spring weather makes for better pickerel fishing as weeds grow, offering cover for ambush.

- Bright, flashy spoons, spinnerbaits, plugs, and in-line spinners are go-to lures, but weedless lures are a plus.

- Live-rigged baitfish, mainly shiners, minnows, or small suckers, are an ideal bait, hooked through the base of the dorsal fin.

- In colder weather, focus on fallen trees and submerged brush, and slow down your retrieve of small crankbaits or soft-plastic jerkbaits.

Fishing for Pike

- Pike in lakes seek thick, vegetative cover around structures like drop-offs, inlet mouths, and deeper coves and bays.

- In rivers, pike occupy slower and slack water in current seams, below points and islands, and below docks and dams.

- Get into an "ambush mentality"—where would a bigger, somewhat lazy predator want to hide, suspended, and watch for prey?

- In cold weather, let pike warm up a bit before fishing shallows; in warm weather, try dawn, dusk, and night fishing.

column with a mix of pickerel, perch, and largemouth bass in the upper reaches and pike deeper is common.

Any good largemouth bass outfit is enough to tussle with a pickerel, though if you target them specifically, use a leader heavier than the line. Pike outfits consist of a 6- or 7-foot, fast-action casting rod, with a spinning or baitcasting/conventional reel, that can handle a lure from 2 to 6 ounces. Load the reel with 12- to 15-pound test.

Fishing for Pike, Continued

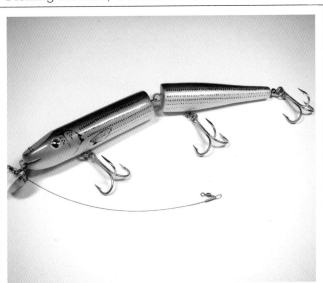

- Combinations of bright colors, metallic flash, wobble or spin, and noise make for successful pike lures.

- Fish shallow-running plugs and crankbaits over weeds, diving plugs along drop-offs, and spinnerbaits around brush and logs.

- Try spoons and in-line spinners fished along weed beds, or work white or silver jigs and swimbaits along the deepest weedy points.

- To guard against pike teeth, try a 20-pound-test monofilament or light, nylon-coated wire leader; big pike call for heavier braided-wire leaders.

Fly Fishing for Pike

- Fly fishing for pike can be excellent in weedy shallows where wading or casting from a boat is possible.

- Tippets should be rated to at least 12 pounds, and use 15 inches of 30-pound nylon-coated wire as a bite guard.

- A fly rod for pike should be at least an 8-weight, possibly a 10-weight.

- Cast divers and poppers on a floating line to shallow pike, or big streamers on slow-sinking lines.

THE GREAT FISH

Muskies are elusive, but their size, fight, and sheer magnificence are prized

Around the Great Lakes states and Canadian provinces there are small, dedicated groups of muskie anglers who go after their quarry like having a second job. In many places, the fish has a celebrity status, and individual catches are remembered (and revered) for years, along with highly successful fishing guides. There are magazines, conferences, and clubs dedicated

to muskie and muskie fishing. Custom, handmade muskie lures, often carved from wood, become collector's items.

Two things that muskie fishing immediately demands are a boat and lots of lure storage, because very little effective muskie fishing can be done from shore, and muskie lures are as big as what muskies eat—smaller gamefish, including

Muskie Habitat

- Muskies will range from shallow to deep water, and rove along at depths of 30 feet or more, especially in summer.

- Tributary mouths, seams of current, and drop-offs to deep water behind islands and rocks are muskie hangouts.

- Muskies will set up ambushes in patches of timber, submerged channels, or over bars and shoals on the bottom.

- Weeds at the edge of deep water or drop-offs, and floating weeds or vegetation are preferred muskie hideouts.

Fishing for Muskie

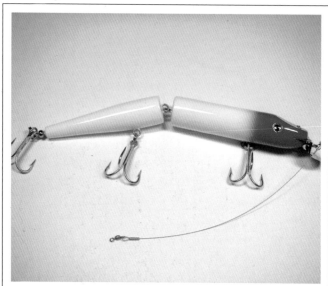

- In good conditions, start out shallow with jerkbaits or spinnerbaits, and if nothing happens, start working down with crankbaits.

- Experiment with bucktails of different sizes and colors, with different blade shapes, not just shallow, but at mid-depth and deep.

- Fish high-contrast-patterned diving plugs over and into deep vegetation and along drop-offs.

- Always work your lure in a figure-eight pattern at the boat if you see or suspect a muskie is following, or use an oval pattern for big fish.

other muskies and pike. Some commercially produced lures reach 12 or 14 inches in length, and include large, bucktail spinners, swimbaits, and soft plastics. Much like pike, muskies are attracted to brightness, flash, and high-contrast patterns.

Stout, 6- to 8-foot baitcasting rods capable of throwing heavy lures and quick, hard hook-sets are necessary. Muskie anglers almost always use conventional reels loaded with at least 20-pound test, monofilament or braided. Seven-strand wire leaders from 80- to 100-pound test that can stand up to muskie teeth are standard.

Night Fishing for Muskie

- For live bait, rig a 10-inch live sucker through the lips with a 7/0 heavy-gauge hook and drift it.

- Where legal, trolling with deep-running crankbaits or jerkbaits can cover a lot of water when muskies leave the shallows.

- Night fishing can be very productive in the summer or on very clear lakes that have a lot of daytime boat traffic.

- At night, cast noisy surface lures over weed-submerged sections, or work crankbaits along the edges of weed patches.

Fly Fishing for Muskie

- Few people fly fish for muskie, but it can be done with 10- or 11-weight, fast-action rods, and 10- to 15-inch flies.

- Target post-spawn muskies with flies in creek mouths, weedy coves, and shallow bays.

- Use snake-like, rabbit-fur flies (divers, usually) in color combination of white, green, chartreuse, black, and pink.

- Retrieve the fly with a continuous, quick hand-strip; if there are no strikes, change flies, or put on a sink-tip line and go deeper.

THE PIKE PERCH

Abundant walleye and sauger, both significant food fish, provide year-round fisheries

Inhabiting clear lakes and slower rivers throughout the Great Lakes states, walleyes draw fleets of anglers in boats much the same way the largemouth does in the South. Walleyes also inhabit numerous waters in the West and Northeast, and in limited places in the South. The species' name derives from a layer of light-gathering cells in its eyes; when fish are taken from the water, their eyes look similar to a deer's eyes reflecting car headlights. This appears similar to the human condition called "walleye"—having an opaque, white eyeball.

The walleye's older name, "walleyed pike," owes to its often being thought of as a member of the pike family, probably due to its significant teeth, sharp gill covers, and cold-water

Walleye

- Most walleyes are a gold-olive color, with a dark green dorsal surface and head and white belly.

- Specific identifiers for walleye are the reflective eye, a dark mark at the rear base of the first dorsal fin, and a white-tipped lower tail-fin lobe.

- Walleyes usually have elongated, paddle-shaped bodies, with a high, sharp, spine-tipped first dorsal fin.

- In general, walleyes reach upwards of 20 inches and 3 pounds; the all-tackle record is a 25-pound Tennessee fish.

Walleye Habitat

- Walleyes prefer mostly clear waters with rocky, sandy, or gravel bottoms in the open sections of reservoirs or lakes.

- Often walleyes can be found congregating near reefs and shoals, or over rock piles or along weedy sections.

- Water temperatures from the mid-60s Fahrenheit to the upper 70s are best for walleye activity.

- Walleyes are frequently found in schools of large size, especially during the late spring or early summer spawn.

habits. The walleye, however, is the largest member of the perch family in North America. A comparison of body shape and fin arrangement to the yellow perch will quickly show the walleye's lineage. Both the walleye and pike have elongated bodies, but their head shape and fin arrangement are entirely different. Oddly, in many places in Canada, walleyes are called "pickerel."

The sauger is the walleye's smaller but very similar cousin, sometimes called "sand pike." These fish are even better eating than walleye, and are often an ice-fishing quarry.

Sauger

Sauger Habitat

- Looking like a small walleye, saugers have black spots on their first dorsal fin, lack the white-tipped tail lobe, and have scaled cheeks.

- Saugers vary from brownish olive to a gray-brown with yellowish highlights and a white belly.

- The main sauger range goes through the Great Lakes states, south through the Appalachians to Tennessee, and west to Montana.

- Most saugers don't break 14 inches, with larger fish hitting 20 inches; the all-tackle record is an 8-pound, 12-ounce North Dakota fish.

- Saugers will tolerate water much more turbid than walleyes, and have been introduced farther south than walleyes.

- Shallow lakes and slow rivers with silty or turbid water ranging in temperature from the low 60s to mid-70s are the preferred sauger habitat.

- Saugers spend more time on the bottom than walleyes, and stay deeper more often.

- Most saugers are caught through the ice in their northern range, or incidentally by anglers pursuing walleyes.

PIKE & THE LIKE

161

THE WALLEYE BITE

Pursuit of these toothy perch involves every kind of technique, especially trolling

Wherever the baitfish go is where the walleye go. Sometimes that place is a slower section of a river, or it can be the big, open water of a deep lake. If walleyes aren't chasing baitfish, they're hanging around structure anticipating the baitfish. They do so in schools, and that's to the angler's advantage, because where you catch one walleye, there should be many

more. Casting and retrieving, drift-fishing, and trolling various baits and lures are all productive.

Walleyes, however, do not have a very strong strike, and often give several taps on a natural bait or seem to bump into a lure during the retrieve and then start pulling. Adult walleyes usually eat shiners, shad, minnows, perch, alewives

Trolling for Walleye

- When walleyes are deep, probing with sonar or trolling lures at differing depths are the main ways to locate them.

- Most walleye trolling is done at around 2 miles per hour or less, but enough speed is needed to create proper lure action.

- Spoons, plugs, and beaded in-line spinner-blade harnesses for worms or minnows work for trolling.

- In the summer, the largest walleyes often patrol the open waters of big lakes, chasing baitfish, which is a good situation for trolling.

Using Lures and Baits

- Cast diving crankbaits, jerkbaits and minnows, blade baits, spoons, spinnerbaits, and tube baits to walleye hangouts.

- In the fall, walleyes in lakes congregate on structure, where they can be targeted with cast-and-retrieve lures.

- Walleyes in rivers most often hug the deepest water they can find along cuts and structure, and bottom-seeking lures work best.

- A live minnow or small jig with a grub or worm can drift below a slip float through easy river current or over lake structure.

(a baitfish similar to shad), and crayfish, and this diet dictates lure and bait choices. Saugers tend to like to eat the same sort of things, but strike favored baits more aggressively than walleyes.

Spinning and baitcasting outfits are the main walleye tackle. Either of these can be used for trolling, though baitcasting or conventional reels are easier to use that way on big, deep water. Rod length varies from 6 to 7 feet and doesn't need to be longer except, again, when trolling deep. Monofilament or superlines work fine, in 6- to 12-pound test.

Using Lindy Rigs

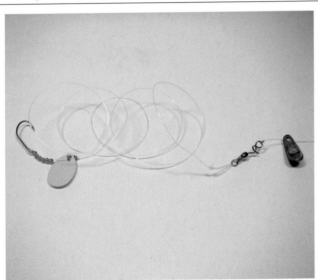

- Lindy Rigs baited with minnows, worms, or leeches can be still-fished, drifted, or slow-trolled.

- The sliding-sinker configuration on most Lindy Rigs lets walleye take the bait without feeling much resistance from the sinker.

- Bait Lindy Rigs by hooking a minnow through the lips, a night crawler through the nose or collar, or a leech behind its mouth.

- For shallow slow-trolling, keep the rig a bit behind the boat; for still-fishing, use a slip float to keep the sinker just off the bottom.

Using Jigs

- Saugers nail jigs, but keeping the jig vertical and on the bottom (enough weight) are key.

- Hair jigs or grub-tailed jigs from ¼ ounce to ½ ounce with round lead heads are good choices; go with light colors in clear water, and orange in silty waters.

- When jigs fail, use a round pink or green jig head to get a live minnow on the bottom.

- Target deep spots along riprap, below wing dams, and in the tailwaters immediately below main dams.

PIKE & THE LIKE

WATERS FOR WATER WOLVES

The toothy species pop up everywhere, but the northern tier holds the biggest promise

The hunt for trophy walleyes and members of the pike family, sometimes called "water wolves" for their toothy aggression, often takes anglers to the waterways of the Great Lakes and Canada. But given that the world-record 1961 chain pickerel was caught in Georgia (and the record redfin pickerel comes from South Carolina), this particular species obviously thrives wherever there's enough to eat in livable water, and trophy chain pickerel (any fish over 5 pounds) could lurk in thousands of waterways. Any healthy lake in Minnesota, Wisconsin, or the Dakotas could produce a trophy pickerel.

Walleye angling has benefited from extensive stocking programs, putting good walleye numbers and size within reach

Lake Erie

- Within easy reach of millions of anglers, Lake Erie has both large numbers of walleyes and many walleyes of significant size.

- As walleyes finish their spring spawning run, there will be large numbers in the Maumee and Sandusky river tributaries and inlets.

- During summer, as walleye move to deeper, cooler water, anglers often troll spoons and stickbaits.

- In the fall, vertically jig with a minnow bait, lightly hopping the jig up and down off the bottom.

Lake Champlain

- With numerous coves and conducive habitat across its 435 square miles of water, Lake Champlain could produce a record pickerel for New York or Vermont.

- A lot of pickerel ice fishing occurs on Champlain, but ice-out and summer also see steady quality fish.

- The Champlain record pickerel was a 5-pound, 8-ounce fish taken in March 2005.

- Pickerel in Lake Champlain are known to crossbreed with pike, creating a sizable, feisty hybrid.

of anglers in Montana, Idaho, and Washington. The Columbia River, famous for king salmon, is also a significant walleye destination. Impoundments in Tennessee and Missouri, such as Truman Lake and Norfork Lake (shared with Arkansas), could also offer up walleyes that would make national trophy-fish lists. Dam pools of the Mississippi River from Missouri northward produce some serious wintertime saugers.

An entire geographic region that might otherwise have the name Pike Land is the area comprised of Ontario, Manitoba, and Saskatchewan. So many lakes with major pike (30-inch fish or better) can be found scattered across this wide expanse. Plenty of waters qualify.

State-sponsored muskie stocking and conservation programs have created significant fisheries in a number of places. Missouri's Fellows, Hazel Creek, Henry Sever, Lake 35, and Pomme de Terre lakes are all managed for muskie. Pennsylvania anglers have a number of very good muskie-stocked lakes, including thousands of tiger muskies in waters such as East Branch Reservoir. Idaho's Hauser Lake and Utah's Pineview Reservoir are also tiger muskie hot spots.

Prime Pike Lakes

- Ontario's Lake Kesagami offers numerous trophy pike not too far from the major American cities of the Northeast.

- In far northern Saskatchewan, Wollaston Lake probably holds some of the largest pike in North America.

- Wisconsin's Lake Mendota, with its 40-inch minimum size limit, is one of the state's most popular trophy-pike lakes.

- New York's Lake Sacandaga, in the Adirondacks, is the source of the American record and still consistently produces big pike.

Lake of the Woods

- The huge amount of quality forage fish in Lake of the Woods, Minnesota, makes for multitudes of big muskies.

- More 50-inch-plus muskies are caught here than any other American water, despite the limited fishing pressure.

- The vast acreage of the Lake of the Woods is perfect muskie habitat, letting numerous fish to grow big and old.

- The key to muskie fishing here is to locate baitfish schools, then work lures at that depth along drop-offs and weed beds.

THE LEAPER: ATLANTIC SALMON

This great-fighting, beautiful fish might one day come back in numbers

Atlantic salmon are still a major quarry in eastern Canadian waters, as well as in waters in Scandinavia, northern Europe, Scotland, Ireland, and Russia. They were once hugely prolific in coastal rivers from Maine to Connecticut, but dams and other effects of industry killed off most of America's runs. A number of attempts to restore the Atlantic salmon in Ameri-

ca are under way in Maine.

This salmon, however, is definitely worth knowing—both as an international quarry and for the sake of understanding the kind of fishery that could return to American waters with enough effort. Much of the British fly-fishing arsenal, including many named fly patterns and big rods, were developed

Atlantic Salmon

- The Atlantic salmon and the brown trout are very closely related.

- In spawning colors, the Atlantic salmon often looks like a big, bullish brown trout.

- At sea, Atlantic salmon have a bluish back and silvery

sides with small black splotches, and adults have a squared-off tail fin.

- On the spawning run, the salmon take on a buttery yellow or caramel color with numerous reddish and black splotches on their sides, with the males developing a hooked jaw, or "kype."

More on Atlantic Salmon

- Atlantic salmon used to thrive in twenty-eight New England rivers, but are now found mostly in Quebec, Newfoundland, New Brunswick, and Nova Scotia.

- Most Atlantic salmon run from 10 to 20 pounds, but older fish—up to eight years old—can get large.

- The all-tackle world-record Atlantic salmon was a 79-pound, 2-ounce fish, caught in 1928 in the Tana River in Norway.

- The North American record Atlantic salmon was a 55-pound Quebec fish.

for the pursuit of Atlantic salmon. Two-handed fly rods called "Spey rods," named after the River Spey in Scotland, were created so that anglers could launch flies a good distance over deep, big rivers.

Just like Pacific salmon, the Atlantic salmon is pursued on its spawning run, but this salmon can be difficult to catch: They pass on fly after fly; make endless, speedy runs when hooked; and often leap clear of the water several times, building slack in the line to throw the hook. Hooking then bringing an Atlantic salmon to the net is a significant angling achievement.

········· GREEN ● LIGHT ·············

Two good organizations that are greatly involved in Atlantic salmon restoration in America are the Downeast Salmon Federation, www.mainesalmonrivers.org, and the Atlantic Salmon Federation, www.asf.ca, both of which are very pro-fishing and want to conserve the species as a viable sport fishery throughout its current and potential range.

Spawning Atlantic Salmon

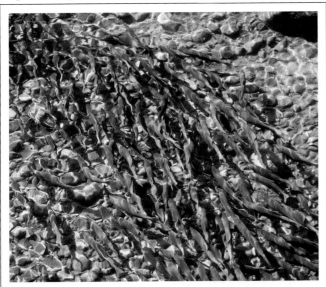

- Spawning Atlantic salmon enter rivers in the late spring and fall, but don't immediately move upriver.

- The spawn is not complete until late fall or early winter, and the fish can either then return to the sea or overwinter in the river.

- Atlantic salmon do not die after a first spawning, and can return to spawn two or three times.

- The biggest salmon usually return to freshwater the earliest, and are capable of multiple spawning runs over their lifetime.

Landlocked Salmon

- The landlocked salmon is a version of the Atlantic salmon that lives entirely in freshwater, in both lakes and rivers in New England and eastern Canada.

- Landlocked salmon dwell in the deeper sections of lakes, living on baitfish, and move up creeks to spawn.

- Landlocked salmon range from 3 to 8 pounds, with a 22-pound, 11-ounce Labrador fish standing as the all-tackle record.

- The landlocked salmon has been introduced to Lake Ontario and Lake Michigan, resulting in some big specimens.

SALMON

THE BIG RUNS: PACIFIC SALMON
These five oceangoing species are icons of the American Northwest

While they might require some travel for most anglers, the biggest species of Pacific salmon—chinook (king), coho (silver), and sockeye salmon—are worth the trek to the West Coast and Alaska. Strong, fierce, and determined fighters, these species offer great battles on medium to heavy tackle or fly tackle. Anglers sometimes specifically target the pink salmon when the three main species aren't around, while the chum salmon is almost always an incidental catch by the sport angler, although it is an important regional food fish.

In their sea-dwelling chrome-colored phase, Pacific salmon are excellent food fish. But once they begin to take on their spawning colors, their edibility drops quickly as they burn up

Chinook Salmon

- The chinook salmon is the largest of the Pacific species, easily reaching 50 pounds.

- Before spawning, chinooks have silvery bodies, with bluish backs and black spots above the lateral line, and lightly spotted fins.

- A key identifier of the chinook is its entirely black mouth, with black jaws and gums.

- The offical all-tackle record chinook is a 97-pound, 4-ounce Alaska fish caught in 1996.

Sockeye Salmon

- Sockeye salmon spawn only in coastal rivers that lead to a lake, where the sockeyes assemble for their final move upstream.

- At sea and early in the spawning run, sockeyes have greenish backs and silvery sides, with very few dark spots or speckles.

- Most sockeyes average 6 to 8 pounds, with a few breaking 10 pounds; the all-tackle record is a 15-pound, 3-ounce Alaska fish.

- A smaller, landlocked version of the sockeye, called the kokanee, dwell in numerous western lakes.

their own bodies for energy to make their run upstream. All Pacific species of salmon die after their single spawning run to their birth waters; in many places, salmon in full-spawn colors are off-limits to angling. Chinook, coho, kokanee sockeye, and pink salmon have been introduced to the Great Lakes.

The most well-known Pacific salmon by sight is the sockeye, often depicted in books in its brick-red spawning colors, its head a bright green. However, chinook salmon are often found in supermarkets, and are thus known for their edibility (the sockeye, with its high oil content, is probably the best eating of all).

Coho Salmon

- A bit larger than the sockeye, the coho is the most spectacular fighter of all Pacific species, often leaping clear of the water.

- Coho salmon in their prespawn phase have bluish-green backs, silver sides, and black spots over their backs.

- In spawning colors, cohos take on pinkish-red sides with black-green backs, heavily spotted backs, and greatly curved jaw kypes.

- Alaska cohos reach upwards of 16 pounds, but a 33-pound, 4-ounce New York (Great Lakes) fish is the all-tackle record.

Pink Salmon

- The pink salmon, the smallest Pacific species, lives for only two years, whereas other species live for four.

- Spawning males develop a humped back in front of the dorsal fin, resulting in the nickname "humpbacked salmon," or "humpie."

- At sea, pink salmon have a bluish back with black spots, and silver sides; spawning colors are brownish olive, and the males have a pink-red stripe.

- Most pink salmon don't surpass 5 pounds; the all-tackle record was a 13-pound, 1-ounce Ontario fish.

SALMON

ATLANTIC SALMON FISHING

In most places, fly fishing is the main Altantic salmon angling method, and it takes time

An Atlantic salmon might look at your fly on the first cast, lunge for it, miss, and never make a move toward it again. There is no explaining what will make this species strike at a fly once or more than once. Hence, dozens and dozens of fly patterns have been invented to induce the Atlantic salmon to grab and hold on. In some places in Canada and Europe, various metal lures are used, but in general, anglers fly-fish for Atlantic salmon coming in from the sea.

These fish frequently inhabit the deeper sections of large rivers and can sprint at high speed over significant distances, frequently going airborne at the end of such a run. So the fly fisher will need a 9- or 10-weight, 9- or 10-foot rod to make

Fishing for Atlantic Salmon

- Atlantic salmon anglers will see "early fish" that come in the spring and "late fish" that come upriver in the fall.

- The salmon will travel along the bottom in freshwater, hugging the gravel in both shallows and deep sections.

- Occasionally anglers will be able to sight-cast to resting Atlantic salmon, sometimes finding them along the edge of river.

- Most often, casting flies to long, deep pools and swinging flies through the current is the way to prospect for fish.

Using Flies

- Traditional salmon flies are intended to trigger a salmon's strike with their bright, flashy colors and high profile.

- The angler must get the fly to drift sideways to the current to present the full profile to the fish.

- Salmon often hit the fly on the "swing" as the fly comes around in the current at the end of a cast.

- Anglers work the tops, deep sections, and tails of pools where Atlantic salmon collect, swinging flies directly to them.

the necessary distance casts. Sinking and floating fly lines can both be deployed for Atlantic salmon fishing, depending on fly choice, but the reel should be loaded with as much backing as possible to handle long salmon runs. A standard fly rod with a fighting butt is a good idea. For those inclined, a two-handed Spey rod can help reach far sections of a big river, but the casting technique for these big sticks is an art all its own.

Using Flies, Continued

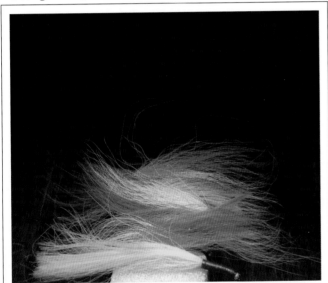

- Salmon flies were given proper names to identify the original, specific pattern.

- Atlantic salmon will also sometimes hit floating flies called Bombers—fat-bodied flies that seem to mimic an insect on the surface.

- Another Atlantic salmon dry fly is the Green Machine, which looks like a big, green nymph but doesn't mimic any actual insect.

- Atlantic salmon are not actually eating anything on their spawn run, but "react" to various flies out of instinctive reflex.

Fishing for Landlocked Salmon

- Fishing for landlocked (Atlantic) salmon often involves trolling flies through varying sections of deep lakes.

- Springtime trolling covers shallows after ice-out to mid-depths, and then the fish drop down to the coldest water in early summer.

- Fly-rod trolling setups involve 9-foot, 8- or 9-weight rods with 20-foot leaders on sinking lines; reels should have sufficient backing.

- Trolling flies for landlocked salmon are most often streamers that imitate smelt, which are silvery-amber, 4- to 7-inch-long baitfish.

SALMON

171

CATCHING PACIFIC SALMON

The best weather means hordes of anglers for western and Alaskan rivers

While the summer-through-fall spawning runs of Pacific salmon are the peak of the year, West Coast salmon fishing gets going on inshore waters in the wintertime. In the Great Lakes, the introduced populations of chinook and coho salmon can be chased by boat throughout the year, as these fish are actively feeding while in the main lakes.

Methods for taking Pacific species are more wide open than the tactics for Atlantic spawn-run salmon. From northern California to the Kenai Peninsula in Alaska, anglers head out to inshore waters, bays, and estuaries to catch chinook and coho salmon as they approach coastal rivers. Trolling and drifting natural baits and lures, jigging, back-trolling or

Fishing for Saltwater Salmon

- Deep-trolling whole rigged herring or herring strips is a standard approach for a lot of inshore chinook salmon fishing.

- Be careful not to get human or chemical scents on chinook baits, as the salmon can be scent-sensitive.

- "Black mouths," or immature king salmon, are a major target of inshore and pier fishing from winter into spring.

- Trolling just before tide changes is a key saltwater tactic for deeper chinooks and shallow cohos.

Fishing for Salmon in Freshwater

- Salmon–egg sacks drifted just off the bottom, with a float above the hook, nab chinooks in coastal rivers in summer.

- A variety of bright spoons and spinners cast from the bank will take cohos and sockeyes in rivers.

- Deep-running, crankbait-like lures, capable of fast wiggles or flutters, induce chinook strikes on numerous western and Alaska rivers.

- When bank fishing for chinooks, check the terrain downstream to be sure you can run after a hooked fish.

"mooching," and trolling Pacific-style salmon flies are all employed in western coastal waters and rivers. Anglers using downriggers nab the big kings in Puget Sound just as they do on Lake Ontario.

Runs of Pacific salmon in specific rivers have experienced periods of significant downturn, especially in California, Oregon, and Washington waters. In various West Coast watersheds, restoration efforts are under way to raise wild salmon populations. Dams, development, changing climate, and commercial harvests in Pacific waters continue to threaten salmon stocks.

Great Lakes Salmon

- The better man-made Great Lakes coho fisheries are in Lake Michigan and Lake Superior.

- Great Lakes chinooks and cohos moving up tributaries are best pursued close to the lake, as their strike reflex fades the farther they go upstream.

- Trolling for Great Lakes coho runs from late winter through fall, and chinook from summer through fall.

- Many of the same spoons, plugs, and baits used on the West Coast can also be successful in the Great Lakes.

Tackle Salmon

- Chinook salmon are often color-selective, and will strike a lure of a specific color more than any other on a given day.

- On the Great Lakes, a go-to trolling-lure color is bright green, but baitfish silver is also effective.

- Chinook call for heavy spinning tackle or conventional tackle, with line rated to 40 pounds.

- Sockeyes and cohos can be taken with medium-weight spinning or conventional tackle with a good drag system and a minimum of 15-pound-test line.

SALMON

PACIFIC SALMON ON FLIES

Fly casting takes lots of big silver fish, but is a lot different than Atlantic salmon fly fishing

The two main Pacific salmon species that are taken on the fly rod are the coho and sockeye, but a fly caster who puts the right fly in front of a river-running fish could take any Pacific salmon. Cohos are targeted specifically for their excellent fighting ability; like the Atlantic salmon, they leap high and often when in freshwater. Sockeyes are excellent gamefish

on medium-weight rods, such as 8-weights. They are often shallow enough for sight-casting, and strike as readily as cohos. Pink and chum salmon can also be taken on the fly, usually incidentally when anglers aim for coho and sockeye. Chinook salmon sometimes take flies, but are such big fish that they call for 10- or 11-weight rods. Anglers casting flies

Using Flies, Tippets, and Tackle

- In some western rivers, cohos overlap with spawning steelhead, and they strike flies cast for the steelhead.

- Cohos will sometimes chase flies, while at other times they will be sluggish and take only those flies that drift right to them.

- Tippets for salmon need to be strong without being a distraction to the fish—anywhere from 3X to 20-pound fluorocarbon.

- Sockeyes can make long, spirited runs on medium-weight fly tackle, but don't do as much leaping as cohos.

Pacific Salmon Patterns

- Attractor patterns do not specifically imitate natural bait but grab a salmon's attention with a variety of bright colors.

- Marabou flies are Pacific salmon flies tied specifically with puffy marabou feathers that swim and swirl in the water.

- Various patterns in pink, silver, white, bright orange, and green, bead head or not, will bring strikes from cohos and sockeyes.

- Chinook salmon can be taken on flies that combine bright or fluorescent pink, green, and red combined with black or purple.

to cohos often tangle with chinooks.

Flies for sockeye and coho can be as simple as a piece of green or hot-pink yarn on a red 2/0 hook. "Chromers," or salmon early from the ocean or lake, will still strike actively at bright, bothersome targets. The more a salmon takes on color, the less it will accurately strike, and thus many fish caught "in color" are foul-hooked. An unethical practice called "lifting"— attempting to intentionally foul-hook a salmon with a fly—is sometimes employed on some Great Lakes rivers.

···········   RED ● LIGHT   ·············

When the salmon show up on Alaska's rivers and streams, so do the brown bears. While most bears couldn't care less about anglers, they can be territorial, intensely protective of their young, and greatly irked when surprised. Make a good bit of noise as you move around a stream, and give any visible bear all the room in the world.

Bead Heads and Epoxy Flies

- Epoxy flies tied with dumb-bell heads and bead-head flies have enough weight to get down in shallow water if cast with floating line.

- Day-Glo egg, roe, and egg-sucking leech patterns can produce for Pacific salmon as well as Alaska rainbow trout and steelhead.

- Bead-head "comet" flies look like big dry flies but come in Day-Glo and metallic colors.

- Depending upon water depth and current, anglers should use a sink-tip fly line that sinks medium-fast or rapidly.

Fly Tactics for Pacific Salmon

- Fly presentations to Pacific salmon are almost always done on or just above the bottom.

- When sight-casting to salmon, cast upstream and drift the fly horizontally to the current and into the noses of the salmon.

- Similar to swinging a fly to (unseen) Atlantic salmon, Pacific species will often grab a fly on the end of its drift.

- Fly casting with baitfish-im-itating tube flies in shallow salt water close to shore can be highly productive for coho.

SALMON

GREAT RIVERS: TOP SALMON WATERS

Salmon are accessible in many places, but call for a good bit of dedication

Major Alaskan salmon waters include the Little Susitna, Deshka, and Talkeetna Rivers. A number of waterways in the Matanuksa-Susitna ("Mat-Su") Valley also can hold lots of good fish. In southwestern Alaska, the Goodnews River and the Golsovia River at Norton Sound and upstream are highly productive.

Southward along the British Columbia coast, Kelsey Bay and the Salmon River are major salmon destinations. Kumdis Bay and the Kumdis River hold many good salmon, and very good fishing can also be found around Vancouver Island. The Skeena River, in west-central British Columbia, produced the largest chinook caught on rod and reel, a 99.15-pound fish.

Tillamook Bay, in Oregon, and the waters off Astoria, Or-

The Great Lakes

- Anglers pursue good populations of chinook and coho in all the Great Lakes and in numerous lake tributaries.

- With charter services based in all the states bordering the lakes, the novice salmon angler can easily find expertise on the water.

- Attempts to stock land-locked Atlantic salmon in the Great Lakes have met with mixed success, with the best populations in Lake Michigan.

- Due to various chemical contaminants, anglers should limit how much Great Lakes salmon they eat per month.

Columbia River

- Finding the travel route of the fish in various sections of the Columbia and positioning the boat is the key.

- Spring-run chinooks in the Columbia are still feeding and will actively strike a lure.

- Fall-run Columbia chinooks are not eating actively, but will still strike a lure out of reflex.

- Troll cut herring or big salmon plugs or spinners on an incoming tide, then anchor the boat and cast big plugs or wobblers on an outgoing tide.

egon, and Ilwaco, Washington, are excellent salmon-fishing centers, and Buoy 10 at the mouth of the Columbia River has been known as a salmon hot spot. Also in the Northwest, the Willamette, Snake, Cowlitz, and Rogue Rivers all offer major salmon fishing.

In the Great Lakes, chinook and coho can be found in all the big lakes, and have big populations in Lake Michigan and Lake Ontario. Lake Michigan and Lake Superior tributaries across Wisconsin provide great spawn-run action, as do a number of Lake Ontario tributaries across central and western New York.

Miramichi River

- Summer and fall runs of Atlantic salmon on New Brunswick's Miramichi River bring thousands of 20-pound-class fish.

- Almost half of the fly-rod-caught salmon in North America come out of the Miramichi.

- Spring fishing for holdover Atlantic salmon begins here in April and goes to the end of May, with anglers sometimes managing to hook up to ten fish per day.

- Summer-run fish start in mid-June, with some of the largest fish arriving in September and October.

Kenai River

- Accessibility by main road makes Alaska's Kenai a very popular river, but given the size and duration of chinook, coho, and sockeye runs, there's plenty of opportunity.

- Chinook salmon arrive by June, sockeye in July, and coho in September through October.

- Trophy chinooks are taken mostly in the lower river, not far from Cook Inlet.

- The Kenai also offers big rainbow trout and very good Dolly Varden trout fishing (see page 172), along with numerous angling regulations.

SALMON

EAST COAST: FAMOUS NAMES

Millions of anglers have pursued and celebrated four major gamefish species

Gamefish along the bays, shores, and inlets of the eastern seaboard have long grabbed anglers' imaginations. The roster of species is more than enough to keep people excited. Obviously, saltwater gamefish have a lot more room to roam, and their behavior is greatly connected to the tides and the movement of baitfish.

The four species discussed here—striped bass, bluefish, black sea bass, and fluke—are marquee species in the Northeast, from Virginia northward. Striper, black sea bass, and fluke are all terrific eating; the bluefish is a bit oily, but an excellent fighter and most often the novice angler's first inshore saltwater catch, as they'll nail anything bright, flashy, and mov-

Striped Bass

- Marked by horizontal dark stripes on a green body, striped bass can be taken from the beach, along jetties, in bays, and in coastal rivers.

- Top-water and mid-depth plugs, big soft plastics, and bucktail jigs are frequent lure choices.

- A surf or fish-finder rig baited with clams or cut or whole (dead) bunker are go-to baits, as is a live-lined bunker.

- Most stripers run 10 to 30 pounds; the all-tackle record is a 78-pound, 8-ounce New Jersey fish.

Bluefish

- A member of the jack family, bluefish usually have bright silvery sides with a bluish back that gets dark green on bigger specimens.

- Key identifiers are the pointed, deeply forked tail and dark spot at the base of the pectoral fin.

- Bluefish take bright, flashy, moving lures, like spoons and jigs, and often travel in fast-moving, bait-devouring groups.

- Small "snappers" run up to 16 inches; adult fish can reach 12 pounds, and the record is a 31-pound, 12-ounce fish.

ing. Striped bass have been exported to West Coast inshore waters and stocked in numerous southern and southwestern freshwater reservoirs. Black sea bass are in no way related to freshwater black bass and appear nothing like them, with their big-heads and tapered bodies. Bluefish are renowned for their ferocious eating habits that frequently leave slicks of baitfish parts and fish oil on the water's surface. The fluke, one of the larger Atlantic coast flatfish and closely related to the flounder, is not a great fighter, but is fun to pursue and very good eating.

Black Sea Bass

- Inhabiting rough bottoms, the black sea bass has a dark gray, grayish-black, or bluish-black humpbacked body.

- Other identifiers are the white hash marks on the dorsal fins and the long top spine of the tail fin.

- Jigs and shrimp, squid, and worm baits drift-fished over deep structure up to 100 feet are often effective.

- Most black sea bass range from 1 to 8 pounds; a 9-pound, 8-ounce fish is the all-tackle record.

Fluke

- Also called summer flounder, flukes are left-eyed fish (left side up), and have a dusky brown-olive left side with brown spots.

- In warmer months, flukes inhabit sandy and muddy bottoms around structure in 8 to 16 feet of water.

- Fishing involves drifting or jigging hooks baited with live baitfish, squid, or shrimp.

- Most flukes range from 12 inches to 5 pounds, with a 22-pound, 7-ounce Montauk, New York, fish taking the all-tackle record.

WEST COAST: SUPER VARIETY
There are significant standouts in an endless roster of great Pacific coast gamefish

From the numerous salmon-fishing opportunities in the north (described in the previous chapter) to the yellowtail in warmer waters in southern California, anglers can find year-round action on the West Coast. With its long coastline, California presents a great variety of saltwater gamefish for a single state, including those of the landlocked Salton Sea.

Yellowtail are a premier gamefish in western seas, and are terrific fighters. Sometimes called kingfish, or specifically "California yellowtail" (to differentiate them from South Pacific and Asian subspecies), yellowtail frequently form schools that often cruise coastlines in search of baitfish. Over a dozen varieties of rockfish swim coastal waters from Alaska to south-

Yellowtail

- Related to the amberjack, the yellowtail is torpedo-shaped, with a long, blue-backed body and a silver-white underside.

- The main yellowtail identifiers are the fish's pointed, solid yellow, deeply forked tail fin and a brassy-yellow lateral stripe.

- Fishing with cut or whole bait or casting baitfish-imitating lures in the surf or inshore is effective for yellowtail.

- Most California yellowtail range from 5 to 20 pounds; the all-tackle record is an Australian fish of 114 pounds.

Yellow-eye Rockfish

- Yellow-eye rockfish are frequently called "red snapper" on the West Coast, but are in no way related to true snappers.

- Rockfish anglers must fish on the bottom, often in deep water, dropping heavy jigs with 16-ounce sinkers.

- Yellow-eye rockfish are usually a strong, solid orange in color and heavy-bodied, shaped a bit like a freshwater bass.

- Most yellow-eye rockfish are big, easily reaching 20 pounds or more; the all-tackle record was a 33-pound, 3-ounce Alaska fish.

ern California; of these, the yellow-eye rockfish is the most widespread and is an excellent food fish. These fish are deep dwellers over rocky bottom structure.

The white sea bass is not a true bass but a member of the weakfish family, and is often called "corvina." As hotly pursued as yellowtail, the white sea bass has suffered from overharvest. The California halibut and the Pacific halibut are the top Pacific coast flatfish in terms of angler hours. The California species ranges up to British Columbia, while the massive Pacific species swims from Oregon to Alaska.

White Sea Bass

- The bass's elongated body is bluish gray, with silvery sides and a white underside.

- A distinguishing feature is the thin ridge of flesh along the bass's underside from its midsection to pelvic fin.

- Cut baitfish of various sizes and live or dead squid are the main baits, but sea bass will sometimes take spoons or trolled soft-plastic squid.

- A wintertime fish, most sea bass are 10 to 20 pounds, with the all-tackle fish weighing 83 pounds, 3 ounces.

Halibut

- Left- or right-eyed, California halibut are dark brown and spotted on the top side, and range from 10 to 20 pounds.

- Take California halibut by drifting rigged baitfish or bouncing soft-plastic tailed jigs in deep structure.

- The Pacific halibut is usually right-eyed (both eyes on the right side of the body), and a dark grayish brown with white flecks and dark spots; it can easily reach 100 pounds.

- Deep-jig for Pacific halibut with heavy metal jigs baited with herring, bounced off the bottom.

181

SEA TROUT, REDFISH, TUNNY

These drum and tuna family members are excellent sport on medium to heavy tackle

Various members of the drum and croaker family are mainstays of coastal angling from the mid-Atlantic states through the Gulf of Mexico. Fish in this group can range from perch-size species to 60 pounds plus. Three major saltwater species are the weakfish, spotted sea trout, and red drum (also known as "redfish," "spot" or "channel bass").

Weakfish and spotted sea trout seem almost identical, visually, with both having long, tapered, silvery bodies and black dorsal spots. Both have papery mouths that give up fish hooks easily, hence the "weakfish" name, and both species fight well. While their ranges overlap, spotted sea trout are the more southerly species, occurring mostly in the Gulf

Weakfish

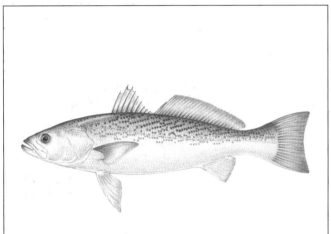

- Key identifiers of the weakfish are two large canine teeth and small, black dorsal spots that don't extend to the tail fin.

- Weakfish generally range from 12 to 24 inches and are easily taken on light tackle; the all-tackle record is 19 pounds, 2 ounces.

- Drifting bait (squid, shrimp, or cut fish) or casting small plugs, jigs, and spoons will take weakfish.

- In the summer, weakfish move into shallow water in bays and estuaries, over sandy or weedy bottoms.

Spotted Sea Trout

- To identify a spotted sea trout, look for bean-shaped black spots on its back, second dorsal find, and tail fin.

- Most spotted sea trout range up to 24 inches and 4 pounds; the all-tackle record is a 17-pound, 7-ounce fish.

- Spotted sea trout feed at all depths and can be taken with live and cut bait, jigs, and small plugs on medium tackle.

- Smaller sea trout form schools, while larger specimens are found in small groups, in deeper water.

of Mexico and upwards to North Carolina. Weakfish range from New England to Florida. The red drum, or redfish, is also a mostly southern fish, with the best populations seen from North Carolina to Louisiana. Though sometimes called "channel bass," the red drum is not a bass. Like other drums, it can make a thrumming noise using its air bladder.

The little tunny, or false albacore, is a true tuna, just much smaller than many of its cousins. Found from New England to the Caribbean, this small fish fights just as hard as a huge bluefin tuna, pound for pound.

ZOOM

Drum and croaker are so named because of noises they make by flexing a muscle against their swim bladder. The swim bladder, a gas-filled sac usually located in a fish's upper body, helps the fish control its buoyancy and rise or drop in the water column without having to use energy to swim.

Little Tunny (False Albacore)

- Shaped like larger tuna, little tunnies don't get much bigger than 24 inches; a 35-pound, 2-ounce fish is the all-tackle record.

- The little tunny is best identified by a bar of dark, tiger-stripe markings along its back and smudge-like spots behind the pectoral fin.

- Little tunnies often appear just under the surface, chasing herring, baitfish, and squid.

- Casting spoons, plugs, and flies on medium tackle often results in a vigorous fight with long, very fast runs.

Red Drum

- With a reddish-bronze back and silver-white lower sides, the red drum often reaches 12 pounds.

- Anglers can identify red drum by its circular black "eye spot" at the base of the tail fin; sometimes there are two or three such spots.

- As drums move in shallows, feeding off the bottom, anglers can sight-cast lures or flies to individual fish.

- Big red drum can be caught in the surf; a 94-pound, 2-ounce North Carolina fish is the all-tackle record.

FLORIDA SALT: A GRAND SLAM
Extraordinarily powerful and difficult fish await in the mangroves

As if Florida didn't have enough going for it as a major large-mouth bass destination (as well as peacock bass and big catfish), the inshore waters around the most southerly state are full of excellent gamefish. The premier species of this long list are the tarpon, bonefish, permit, and snook.

As big as tarpon get—up to 7 feet and 243 pounds (Florida record)—they're most closely related to members of the herring family. Their smashing strikes and leaping fight have made them into superstars. Bonefish, often referred to as "silver fox," are capable of astounding bursts of speed, no matter how small or big. Permits also exhibit bursts of speed and a strong, pulling fight. The difficulty the angler faces in catching these spooky, finicky fish is half the battle. Snook, which occur in warmer waters from Florida to South America, are

Bonefish

- Bonefish often feed head-down into sand or mud, eating crabs and shrimp, and the tip of their tail will break the surface.

- Most anglers catch bonefish in relatively shallow water along mangroves in tidal flats and channels.

- In general, bonefish reach 5 pounds, but can often reach 10; the all-tackle record is 19 pounds.

- Bright silver sides and head, a single dorsal fin, deeply forked tail, and pointed snout and sucker mouth identify the bonefish.

Tarpon

- Key identifiers of the tarpon, aside from size, are its heavy, upturned lower jaw, large silver scales, and a single dorsal fin with the last spine greatly elongated.

- Tarpon will range as far north as New Jersey, but are found in mostly in subtropical and tropical waters.

- The Florida tarpon fishery is almost entirely catch-and-release, and tarpon are little desired as food fish.

- Anglers frequently sight-cast to tarpon, using plugs, flies, or live mullet.

long, strong, silvery-white fish that strike readily and fight hard.

All four of these species are frequent fly-fishing quarry, and a catch of a tarpon, bonefish, and permit all in one day has long been called a "Grand Slam." Adding a snook to that daily list produces a "Super Slam." On medium to heavy spinning tackle, all four of these fish are excellent quarry.

Permit

- A member of the jack family, the permit has an oval-shaped, silvery-white body that seems compressed when viewed head-on.

- Key identifiers are the very similar second dorsal and anal fins, with a long second spine, and long, deeply forked tail fin.

- Live crabs or crab-imitating flies are frequent choices and are cast to visible, feeding fish in shallow waters.

- Many permits reach 25 pounds and 36 inches; the all-tackle record is a 53-pound, 4-ounce Florida fish.

Snook

- Most snook are caught and released in warm, inshore Florida waters, and are not a major food fish among sport anglers.

- A protruding lower jaw, strong black-colored lateral line, long pike-like head, and elongated body identify the snook.

- The average snook weighs 8 pounds, with some reaching 20 or more pounds; the all-tackle record is a 53-pound, 10-ounce Costa Rica fish.

- Casting live bait (mullet) or mid-depth plugs to mangrove cover on changing tides is a key tactic.

BLUE WATER: STRONG FISH
Offshore species can give anglers a serious run for their money, and wear them out

Away from the coastline, the angler will run into a large number of big, hard-fighting saltwater gamefish. Many of these species are "pelagic," meaning that they migrate long distances, following massive ocean currents along continental shelves. The species discussed here—the dolphin, wahoo, and two kinds of tuna—are highly popular fish that are found

in significant numbers. They call for dedicated pursuit using strong tackle and oceangoing boats.

Dolphins, also called "dorado," and "mahi mahi" in the Pacific, can range from a short distance offshore to far water. They inhabit both the Pacific and Atlantic Oceans. The wahoo, related to the mackerel, seems to have a good bit of barracuda

Dolphin

- The dolphin has a long, tapered, green-gold body; a deeply forked tail; and a single, long, blue dorsal fin atop a green back.

- Male dolphins (shown in the photograph) have a rising, blocky forehead; females have a rounded, flatter head.

- A strong leaper when hooked, dolphins are taken by trolling rigged baits or by casting surface plugs and flies to visible fish.

- Dolphins range up to 50 inches and 15 pounds; the all-tackle record is an 87-pound Costa Rican fish.

Wahoo

- Identifying features of the wahoo include vertical blue stripes along its entire length, a knife-like forked tail, moveable upper jaw, and multiple sharp teeth.

- Wahoos will collect in small groups around deep structure but also will hover underneath floating debris.

- Fast-trolling with rigged baits or deep-running plugs is the usual approach, with reels fully loaded with line to handle wahoo runs.

- Most wahoos reach 4 feet and 20 pounds; the all-tackle record is a 158-pound, 8-ounce Mexican fish.

thrown in. Also found in both oceans, it is thought to be one of the fastest gamefish in the world and will make a mind-blowing first run when hooked.

The bluefin and yellowfin tuna are both major sport and commercial species. The great bluefin suffers serious declines due to overfishing, mainly due to commercial efforts, but anglers must also play a role in recovering this species. Yellowfin are a major quarry for Californian anglers in the winter. Two other major sportfishing tuna species are the blackfin tuna in the Atlantic, and the big-eye tuna in the Atlantic and Pacific Oceans.

ZOOM

For years, anglers battled big fish while seated in a "fighting chair." But innovations in tackle have allowed for "stand-up" fighting: The rod butt is fit into a socket in a belt worn by the angler, sometimes with suspenders, and the angler can countersink his or her body weight against the pull of the fish, with proper drag adjustment.

Yellowfin Tuna

- Yellowfin tuna occur mostly in warmer Atlantic and Pacific waters, and will follow warm currents inshore.

- The yellowish second dorsal and anal fins grow long and pointed on yellowfin; often, a yellow or bluish color runs the length of the body.

- Yellowfin usually range in size from 20 to 80 pounds; the all-tackle record fish from Mexico weighed 388 pounds, 12 ounces.

- Casting live baitfish or trolling rigged baitfish or fish strips are effective methods for yellowfin.

Bluefin Tuna

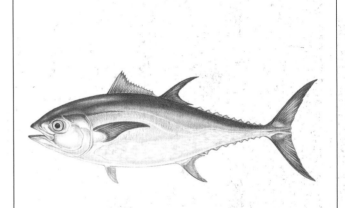

- Often forming large, long-distance traveling schools, the bluefin is one of the largest bony fish in the world.

- Bluefin tuna have a dark blue back, and their silvery sides have pale white spots in rows along the bottom.

- Bluefin can regularly reach 6 feet and upwards of 400 pounds; the all-tackle record from Nova Scotia weighed 1,496 pounds.

- Trolling or drift-fishing rigged baitfish, or trolling big spoons and plugs, will take bluefin from 50 to 120 feet deep.

TEETH & BILLS: MAJOR BIG GAME
Sharks and billfish are the ultimate saltwater fishing challenge

The combination of power, beauty, and danger that sharks and billfish offer has led to premier status as gamefish. It has also led, unfortunately, to much overfishing. Swordfish are showing some signs of recovery after serious declines, but are still at risk. Mako shark numbers continue to dwindle, and great white sharks are verging on becoming an endangered species, although the impact of sportfishing on these species versus the

impact of commercial fishing practices (usually the incidental "bycatch" of sharks) is not entirely known. But other shark and billfish species are abundant enough to be pursued actively by rod and reel, though catch-and-release practices are essential for these stocks to remain at fishable levels.

The leopard shark, blue shark, thresher shark, and the porbeagle shark (known in Alaska as the "salmon shark") are all

Lemon Shark

- Lemon sharks range from Delaware through the Florida Keys, and are good quarry on medium tackle.

- Most lemon sharks run from 4 to 7 feet long, and don't get much over 100 pounds.

- The largest fly-rodcaught lemon shark was a

- 385-pound Florida fish, the heaviest fish ever caught on fly tackle.

- On medium-weight spinning gear, lemon sharks take cut bait or whole, rigged baitfish; big streamers and shark flies work for fly casters.

Atlantic & Pacific Sailfish

- Atlantic and Pacific sailfish are thought to be the same species, although Pacific sailfish grow larger.

- The key sailfish identifier is its high, comb-like dorsal fin, often colored dark blue with black spots, which can be folded down.

- Pacific sailfish to 100 pounds are common, while Atlantic fish normally reach 60 pounds; the largest Pacific sailfish recorded was 221 pounds.

- Anglers troll rigged baitfish in spreads of teasers or drift live bait to take sailfish, usually close to the surface.

demanding, worthwhile quarry. The lemon shark is one of the most exciting inshore species, easily found in its range along the southern portion of the Atlantic coast.

From Florida to Central America, and from southern Californian waters to Hawaii, sailfish and striped and blue marlin stocks are still highly viable. These billfish, known for spectacular leaps and "tailwalking," are the premier species, and as such are always at risk for overfishing. They are prized as food fish internationally, but increasing catch-and-release regulations for sportfishing are in effect.

Striped Marlin

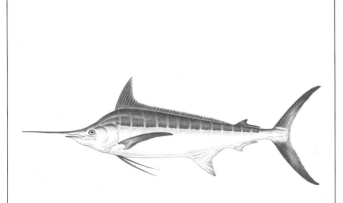

- Most American striped marlin fishing occurs on the southern California coast, summer through early fall.

- Striped marlins are a dark blue up top, with pale silver flanks and pale blue vertical bands; fins are spotted, and the bill is rounded.

- Generally ranging between 80 and 160 pounds, the American-record striped marlin is a 339-pound California fish.

- Trolling rigged baitfish and skirted teasers with rigged bait is the main approach, but anglers can cast baits to fish on the surface.

Blue Marlin

- Blue marlins range through the Pacific and Atlantic Oceans, with the largest American catch, 1,376 pounds, coming from Hawaii.

- The blue marlin is the largest of the marlins, although the male blue doesn't grow much larger than 300 pounds.

- The species has a dark blue back, an amber midline, and silver-white belly, with light blue vertical bands down its length.

- Most often, anglers catch blue marlin by trolling various rigged whole baitfish or baitfish strips.

CONCLUDING THE BATTLE

Angling talent isn't complete without knowing how to handle a spent fish

Often, as you fish along rivers or in lakes, you'll see an angler who has done everything right—picked the right lure and played a fish well—only to have the fish flopping all over the place on the bank or in the shallows. It's a sloppy way to end a good fight, and possibly can cause injury to the fish. The chances of losing a good fish are also very high when an an-gler makes improper or lazy attempts at landing the quarry.

Whether you want a fish for a quick photo and then release it, or you're angling to put fillets on the grill, getting the fish quickly and smoothly in hand is the finishing touch to the effort. Many freshwater fish are small enough to be managed by hand, and there are proper ways to do this. Nets and cra-

Landing a Fish on a Boat

- Keep the rod bent when bringing a fish to a boat, keeping the fish in the water.

- Maintain a workable length of line between the tip of the bent rod and the hook.

- If a fish goes under the boat, partially immerse the rod, keeping it bent and keeping the line off the boat bottom.

- Be close enough to the bow or stern so that you can clear the line around either if the fish circles the boat.

Landing a Fish on a Bank

- Use current to steer a tiring fish into slack water or a pool where you can finish the fight.

- Sometimes you can pull a big fish onto shallow gravel, with just its back out of the water, to be able to approach it.

- A big, athletic fish might bolt as you approach it; keep the rod bent but don't yank as it runs.

- Don't overtire a big, hard-fighting fish; have strong enough tackle to end the fight decisively.

dles are probably the easiest way to go, and most effective at securing the fish as well as limiting injury due to thrashing. Big fish definitely call for a landing device, unless you've got some experience and can get a salmon or pike in hand comfortably and also unhook it. Having a fishing partner when you're out for larger species is a big help.

YELLOW LIGHT

If you're fishing alone from a kayak or canoe, you're probably better off securing a big fish in the water alongside the hull and not trying to get it into the boat. Leaning over to pull a big fish—anything over 10 pounds—into the craft might result in a sudden swim.

Landing a Fish Safely

- Always wet your hands before handling a fish to preserve its mucous coating.

- Put your hand under the fish to cradle it in the water or press it lightly against your waders, but don't lift clear of the water if not necessary.

- Grasp trout and salmon of sufficient size by the tail, keeping them in the water.

- Bass and other non-toothy fish can be grasped by the lower jaw and held in the water or raised vertically.

Landing a Fish with a Net

- For small fish meant for release, use a shallow-bag net made of a nonabrasive material.

- Larger fish call for a net with a sufficiently deep bag and wide enough hoop for quick capture.

- Net fish head first; put the net in the water, draw the fish in close, then swiftly scoop the fish with the net.

- Boat nets should have a handle of at least 3 feet, and up to 5 feet if the boat has high sides.

SHARP STUFF: DEALING WITH TEETH

With larger, toothy fish, proper landing and unhooking prevents angler injury

Trout have teeth, called "volmerine" teeth, which are found on the tongue, and sunfish and bass have teeth, too. But none of these fish possess chompers that could break the skin. A lot of other fish do, however, especially a number of saltwater gamefish.

There is a very simple ground rule for dealing with toothy fish: Don't put your fingers in or near their mouths. Sounds pretty basic, but you'd be surprised at the number of people who take risks with such fish. Fish that can bite and break the skin call for various tools, detailed here.

In addition to teeth, anglers also need to be aware of fish spines, like those on catfish. Any dorsal spine on a fish, even

Retrieving the Lure

- Use leather or rubber gloves and long needle-nose pliers with a jaw spreader to get hooks removed.

- Match a jaw spreader to the size of the fish; too big a jaw spreader can injure a smaller fish.

- If a hook is too deep or takes too long to remove, have heavy-gauge wire cutters on hand to cut the lure free.

- Keep fingers and pliers clear when removing jaw spreaders, as some fish will immediately snap their jaws shut.

Landing a Muskie

- Play muskies (or pike) enough to tire them, but not to exhaustion, before trying to secure them in a cradle.

- Bring a muskie into a cradle head first, and keep the cradle in the water while removing the hook.

- Bring the two cradle rods together and hoist the cradle into the boat to measure the fish or take photos.

- Use a "lip grip," or a thickly gloved hand, to secure a muskie's head while holding it horizontally for a photograph.

a small fish, can puncture the skin if the fish leaps or thrashes at just the wrong moment, and given the general amount of bacteria in any fishing environment or on a fish's body (we're talking millions of bacteria), a spine poke might lead to a mild infection.

Additionally, a number of fish have very sharp gill covers—namely snook, walleye, and yellow perch—and northern pike have sharp gill rakers. These hard edges can slice through fingers. An easy way to avoid handling fish by their gills altogether is to rely on proper landing equipment.

Landing Toothy Fish

- Unhooking barracuda, big mackerel, and other non-shark species calls for a "lip grip" to secure the fish.

- Use "big-game" gloves with such species; wet these before touching the fish, and handle the fish minimally.

- Strong needle-nose pliers are essential for removing hooks from toothy mouths; stuck hooks can be cut with wire cutters.

- Don't get your fingers near or in gills, as gill rakers are knife sharp and a quick thrash of the fish's head could trap your fingers.

Landing a Shark

- Secure a shark at boat-side using a "tailer gaff" or rope around the base of its tail fin.

- Slide a short gaff hook over the lure or fly hook to yank it loose; cut the leader if a hook is stuck.

- Always wear big-game gloves around sharks of any size, as their fins and skin are abrasive and sharp.

- Be wary of picking up small sharks for photos—they can easily form a circle, mouth to tail, and bite.

193

FISH BAG: KEEPING YOUR CATCH
The old saying "Limit your kill, don't kill your limit" still holds true

The nutritional value of fish is not in dispute—fish is good for you, and has been a major part of the human diet for thousands of years. You can love fish and fishing, be an ardent conservationist, and still keep and eat a few fish now and then without questioning yourself. Leave the anti-meat and anti-fishing debate to those who seem to get the most charge out of making such noise.

But if you are going to keep fish for the grill, you have a few ethical responsibilities to uphold without fail. There is sport in pursuing and fighting fish, but not in killing them. When the time comes, you must dispatch fish quickly and immediately. They are not to be left flapping in buckets or sacks. Live fish can be secured temporarily in wells on boats, in buckets, or on stringers as long as they are able to breathe and suspend

Dispatching Fish

- Dispatching most freshwater game-fish involves a sharp rap on the head between the eyes.

- Use a "priest"—a small, lead-cored wooden bat—or some other kind of short club that is weighty enough to deliver a killing blow.

- Bleed oily-fleshed food species after a knockout blow to the head by making a deep cut right behind the gills.

- Large fish might require several head blows, delivered quickly; avoid using firearms.

Live-Wells

- Be sure your live-well aeration system is working sufficiently to keep fish alive until you return to the dock, and that the water is clean.

- Don't pack fish into live-wells; they should have enough room to turn around and maneuver slightly.

- Use live-wells to select the fish you wish to keep; release those you know you won't eat.

- Live-wells often transport invasive or exotic species (like snails or weeds), so clean wells thoroughly before fishing elsewhere.

properly in sufficiently deep water. Also, not taking the full bag limit every time and obeying slot limits—rules allowing anglers to keep fish in a specific size range to preserve brood stock—are essential to conserving fisheries.

The ethics surrounding the taking of trophy fish are in a bit more of a gray area. Many anglers avoid altogether the taking of a big fish that is not to be eaten, preferring instead to photograph the fish and rely on replica mounts. This is a nice way to go, as it returns a breeding fish to the water and also provides work for a fishing artist, of which there are many.

But taking a few true trophy fish in one's lifetime is wholly reasonable if the basic criterion is met: the fish is an exceptional specimen of a species that exists in sufficient breeding numbers in the water from which it comes.

Using a Gaff

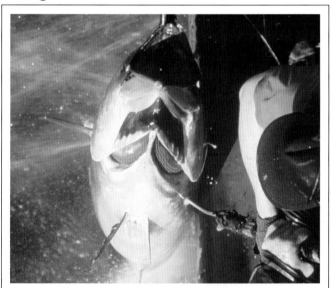

- Vigorous saltwater fish to be kept can be secured with a gaff—a sharp steel hook on the end of a handle.

- Gaff a fish through the shoulders or back; gaffing the tail will be ineffective and chaotic.

- Fish with wide mouths can be gaffed in the lower jaw, either from the underside or through the mouth.

- A flying gaff—a rope-connected gaff hook that detaches from a long handle—helps with big fish.

After the Fish Is Landed . . .

- Gutting fish helps the quality of the meat, but be sure not to cut open any viscera.

- Killing fish to be kept means they stay put; many an angler has lost a live fish that leapt out of an opened cooler.

- Put kept fish out of the sun covered with wet branches, wet sand, or newspaper if you don't have a cooler.

- Most anglers don't use creels anymore, but if you put gutted trout in one, line it with wet fern fronds or spruce branches.

195

SAFE RETURN: PUTTING FISH BACK

Catch-and-release fishing hinges on handling fish in ways to minimize stress

Catch-and-release angling has become a standard at all levels of fishing, from the smallest trout streams to blue-water big-game fishing. Conserving fisheries has all kinds of benefits. First, putting a significant number of fish back in the water, especially breeding-age fish, ensures that sportfishing and fish for the grill will be available next year, the year after

that, and so on. Second, given the millions of angler dollars that flow into small towns, tackle shops, and guide services, keeping fisheries viable is an essential part of regional economies. In many places, especially "blue ribbon" trout streams, catch-and-release is standard practice, and local guides tightly enforce the rule.

Hook Removal

- Use barbless J-hooks, and strike fish quickly so they don't swallow the hook, or use circle hooks.

- Keep fish in the water, without touching them, and remove hooks with pliers or forceps.

- Don't jerk or shake a hook

to remove it—grasp it as close to the point as possible and smoothly twist and pull.

- For smaller saltwater fish, use a "hook puller," a blunt hook that wraps around and removes the fishhook, partly raising the fish out of the water.

Equipment for Successful Release of Fish

- Use sufficiently strong tackle that can defeat a fish and bring it to hand or boat-side without exhausting it.

- If netting a fish while wading, keep the mesh in the water after securing the fish.

- Secure a larger fish boat-side using a lip grip, or a small gaff that hooks the lower lip of big, strong species.

- Cradles aren't just for pike and muskie—any longer fish, such as steelhead or striper, benefit from proper cradle use.

The main issue of catch-and-release fishing is keeping the fish in the water at the time of unhooking, not touching the fish but using tools to remove the hook. A fish properly played and not overstressed by the fight will revive more quickly if not taken completely from the water or handled.

Making catch-and-release work involves a number of technical issues, from hook selection to the way you play fish. You'll fish just a little differently to make this happen, but it won't affect your enjoyment of the sport.

Reviving a Fish

- To revive a fish, point its head into the current, cradling its body and grasping its tail, and gently move it back and forth.

- Hang on to it until it attempts to swim out of your grasp.

- Don't simply toss back a fish; tend to it until it swims on its own.

- If it turns belly-up after you tried to revive it, grab its tail, right it, and continue to move it so water flows over its gills.

YELLOW ● LIGHT

Some fish with swollen swim bladders can slowly release the pressure out their mouths and revive completely. But with other fish that arrive with a swollen bladder, the practice of puncturing the bladder to relieve pressure is questionable at best. When taking deep fish injured by pressure change, consider having a fish fry.

Dealing with Fish Injury

- Embedded hooks should be cut, at the leader or through the shank, if they cannot be removed.

- Fish that are bleeding steadily from the gills are too injured to release; keep and kill these.

- Fish taken deep, usually over 30 feet, should be raised as slowly as possible to allow for pressure adjustment.

- Those fish that arrive with severely distended swim bladders (due to depth and pressure change) are not good candidates for catch-and-release.

BIG SMILE: FISH PHOTOS

Fishing memories often rely heavily on photographs, so take care to get them right

Cameras are everywhere these days, from cell phone cameras, to point-and-shoots, to digital SLRs (single-lens reflex cameras). For most people, the fishing photo has to do two essential things: show the angler clearly, and show the fish clearly. To that end, there are a couple crucial issues: composition and lighting. Composition is what's in the photo and the angle at which that subject is shown. With lighting, the trick is to have enough, as shaded areas seen clearly by the naked eye turn into dark patches in photos. But you can get too much light from direct sun, or a lot of sun reflected off the water's surface.

Two other important photography issues are the self-timer

Avoiding a Bad Photo

- Bad photos are obvious—faces in shadow, fish squirming or long dead, and/or no thought given to the background.

- Have a fishing partner get the camera out and start framing the photo before landing the fish.

- Unhook fish to be released, ready the camera, pose with the fish, quickly take two shots, and then release the fish.

- Use a lip-grip to secure larger fish as you pose for photographs, cradling the fish with your other hand.

Framing the Shot

- Fill the field of view with the fish; focus on the face and upper body of the angler.

- The fish should be held across the angler's body, angling the fish's body toward the camera.

- Take advantage of a camera's "macro" setting (often depicted with a flower symbol) to fill the frame with an angler and fish.

- Focus on the fish's eyes; shoot bright or silvery fish at an angle to the light so their markings are clearer.

and your partner. Many times, you'll find yourself fishing alone. If you happen to catch a great fish and have a camera, knowing how to very quickly set up the self-timer is essential. Also have a net in which you can secure the fish in the water while you swiftly tend to setting up the shot. When fishing with friends, be sure they know how to operate your camera to be able to take a photo of you. Provide this instruction before you start fishing, if you've got anything more complicated than a point-and-shoot. Cell phone camera shots work in a pinch, but their quality is usually limited.

ZOOM

Whether you keep fish or not, photograph them while they're alive and just taken from the water after the fight. Dead fish very quickly loose their brilliance, and don't look like their true selves in photos. Fish that have been kept properly in a live-well or on a stringer should photograph sufficiently.

Using the Flash

- Under overcast skies, or in shade, use your flash ("fill flash") to illuminate details.

- If the sun is bright, position the subject and photographer so the sun is off to their side, not directly in line.

- A fill-flash shot will brighten dawn and dusk photography; shooting at night calls for a lens filter that can reduce flash glare.

- If you have a digital camera, experiment with manual settings before a fish is caught to get a good exposure.

Photographing a Trophy Fish

- With a trophy fish to be released, take a full, clear body shot for the sake of an artificial mount.

- Use a tripod whenever possible, especially when shooting at slower speeds, to steady the exposure.

- Consider both the back-ground and foreground—remove clutter (like bait boxes), or look for good vistas like mountains or bridges.

- Flowing water can be blurred with a longer exposure, but this brightens the shot, so a lens filter is needed.

SELF-HOOKED: FINESSING BARBS
When you catch yourself instead of the fish, there's an effective first aid

There isn't an angler in the world who hasn't hooked him- or herself. It comes with the sport. Most of the time, people hook their fingers, and removal isn't too hard, especially if a fishing partner knows how to do it. But casting-related injuries—treble hooks embedded in shoulders, or flies popped through ear lobes—can be tougher and quite painful. A single hook that passes all the way through, with the point exposed (like the streamer fly through the ear lobe), simply calls for pushing the point through past the barb, cutting the bend below the barb, and pulling the shank out. An embedded multi-hook situation might require a trip to the emergency room if basic removal techniques and wire cutters don't work.

Assessing Hook Injury

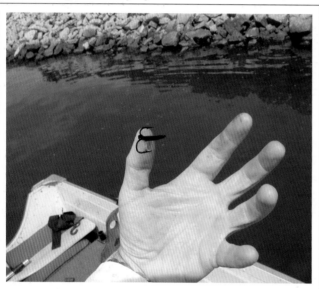

- Single hooks or one point of a treble hook can usually be easily removed, if they are movable while embedded.

- Hooks that don't flex or turn, or cause sharp pain, are too deep into the flesh for basic removal techniques.

- Cut the hook free of the leader or lure to work on it from any angle.

- If the point is close to the skin surface and there's little pain, push this out past the barb and cut the shank.

Removing Hooks Using Line, Part One

- With a hook that is not too deep and is in relatively soft tissue, the whole hook can be pulled free with fishing line.

- Take a 40-inch section of 18- or 20-pound-test line and double this, forming a 20-inch section.

- Wrap the doubled section of line around the hook bend and secure the line tightly in one hand.

- Have enough line from the hook to your hand that you can give the hook a quick tug.

Two very important items to remember: 1) clean puncture wounds, and 2) get up-to-date tetanus shots. Hook points drive dirt and bacteria down into the wound, so first thoroughly bleed a hook puncture, as the spilling blood will carry debris and bacteria out, and then wash and flush the hole completely. Watch the site for infection. And a tetanus booster isn't a bad idea if some time has passed since your last one, because a fishhook can have all kinds of nasty stuff on it, and now some of that might be in your bloodstream.

ZOOM

Irrigating puncture wounds is key to cleaning them. In your first-aid kit, have a small squirt bottle with a very narrow, pointed nozzle that you can use to shoot soapy water into the wound. Warm water and soap are the best for cleaning wounds, with a swab of iodine over the skin surface when done. Don't use rubbing alcohol or peroxide.

Removing Hooks Using Line, Part Two

- Press a thumb into the top of the hook shank, over the eye and part of the shank.

- The pressure of your thumb on the top of the shank should disengage the barb in the tissue just under the skin.

- The barb should now be aligned with the path that the hook point made through the soft tissue.

- While applying thumb pressure, give a quick, strong jerk on the fishing line to pull the hook free.

An Embedded Hook

- The hook point and barb should come free with just one clean pull of the line.

- If the hook doesn't come free, the barb is seriously embedded; don't try pulling the hook again.

- If not too painful, and if the hook point is not too deep, see if the point can be pushed forward and popped through the skin.

- In case neither approach works, or the hook isn't flexible in the skin, head for the emergency room.

MORE ICE: PRESERVING FRESH FISH
Ensuring the quality of your dinner starts as soon as you catch a fish

In general, the sooner a fish is eaten, the better; properly frozen fish are usually just fine, but fish eaten on the day of the catch, or within hours, are always best. The biggest problems facing the would-be cook are the spoilage of fish and the drying out of the meat. "Spoilage" means that the meat has been contaminated by matter from inside the fish's viscera that was accidentally released by a knife cut, or the meat has

begun to break down and become inedible due to excessive heat or significant change in temperature. A number of measures can be taken to prevent these two problems when the fish are killed or taken from live-wells or stringers at the end of the day.

Keeping dead fish well chilled is the main issue. Fish that have been bled and/or gutted should be put in crushed ice

Handling Panfish

- Dispatch live panfish with a quick rap on the head, and then quickly gut them.

- Gutting panfish requires a short cut to the anal fin and removal of a small amount of entrails.

- Larger panfish can be filleted, but they can also be frozen whole with skin and fins intact.

- Pat dry a whole panfish with a paper towel, then double-layer plastic cling-wrap over it before freezing.

Handling Bigger Fish

- Big fish take up to twenty minutes to bleed out; place the fish head-down in a bucket, or secure it head-down on the deck.

- Periodically rinse the fish with cold water to keep blood from clotting at the site of the cut.

- Wait until a big fish stops bleeding before gutting it.

- Fish killed with a billy club won't bleed out completely, so knock out and immobilize big fish and then bleed it, which will kill it.

in a cooler. This is a temporary method of storage, to be used while you continue fishing. You can keep fresh, dead fish on ice for maybe twelve hours without much worry, as long as you add new ice as necessary. While the ice in the cooler slowly melts, keep the cooler drain-hole open so that the cold water running out also carries with it any fluids emanating from the fish, as this also will help preserve freshness.

Gutting a Fish

- Clean your knife with water and wipe it down between each fish that you gut.

- A bloody knife can transfer contaminants from one gutted fish to the next if you accidentally cut into viscera in the first fish.

- Surfaces where fish are gutted should be flushed clean with water between each fish.

- Don't cut into the meat any deeper than necessary to remove entrails; filleting or steaking will come later.

Preserving Fish to Eat

- Fish meant to be eaten soon should be kept on ice in coolers or on ice in the refrigerator.

- Wrap fresh fish in plastic wrap before putting them on ice in the refrigerator.

- Oily fish, small fish, and fish with delicate flesh can be kept on ice no more than half a day before they must be frozen.

- Whole, gutted fish of good size and lean (non-oily), thick flesh can be kept on ice in a proper cooler up to forty-eight hours.

CUTTING BOARD: PREPARING FISH

Your specific recipe for each meal determines how you cut and section a fish

With fish (and all game meats, in fact), the more you cut into the meat, the more surface area you expose, and the sooner it'll become dry. If you have a whole fish on your hands, one that has been properly gutted and iced, and can't use it right away, keep it whole and on ice or freeze it.

When you've got a fish dressed and ready to be cut into fillets or steaks, be sure that the body cavity has been completely cleaned and all bits of viscera removed. Also, many fish have a dark "blood line" running along the underside of the spine. Cut into the tissue securing this and remove it.

If you fillet fish, remove the skin, and thus the scales. But with fish meant for steaking or other cuts, remove the scales. Scal-

Dressing a Fish

- A fully dressed fish is without head, entrails, fins, and scales, and is ready for steaking or whole cooking.

- To "pan dress" small fish (panfish), scale them, then make a shallow cut along the dorsal fin and pull out the fin.

- Complete pan dressing by slicing alongside the anal fin and pulling it out, then cut off the head and slice the belly and remove the entrails.

- Cut the tail fin off a pan-dressed fish if desired.

Filleting a Fish

- Leave the head intact for fish that will be filleted, but be sure to remove the scales.

- With a filleting knife, make an angled cut behind the gills, cutting down to the backbone.

- Torque the knife blade toward the tail and make a single, smooth cut to remove an entire side of the fish.

- Don't cut through the skin at the base of the tail; fit the blade between the up-turned skin and meat, and cut the skin free.

ing is easily accomplished: Run a knife blade at a 40-degree angle against the scale edges, from tail to head, or use a scaler tool in the same way. Doing so while the head and tail fin are still intact makes for easier work, as you have better points to grasp and better leverage for working with the fish.

Small catfish, including bullheads, can be dressed easily: Cut through the skin completely around the head, and then make a shallow cut along the back on one side from head to tail fin. Grab the edge of skin at the head with pliers and pull the entire side of skin off in a sheet. Repeat this on the other side, and then pull down on the head until you break the spine, and keep pulling the head away, bringing the entrails with it. Pull out the dorsal fin and cut off the tail, and you have a completely dressed out catfish.

Butterfly Fillets

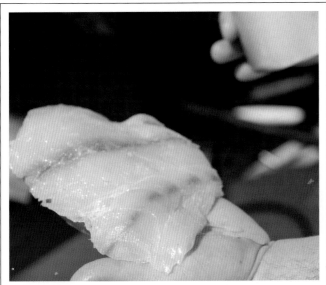

- To create joined (butterfly) fillets, first remove the scales and then cut off the fish's head.

- Cut along the backbone, slicing the ribs, across the body and through the tail section, but don't cut the belly skin.

- Turn the fish over and repeat, slicing the length of the fish's side, through the ribs and tail, but don't cut the underside.

- Pull away the backbone and entrails, and cut away any ribs in the fillets.

Steaked Fish

- With a stout-bladed knife, cut a whole, dressed fish across its body, side to side through the spine, to create several cross-sections, or steaks.

- Fish steaks contain whole ribs and vertebrae that should pull away from cooked flesh.

- Rib sections in standard fillets can be cut away once the fillet is skinned.

- Pike and muskie fillets have central "Y-bones" that must be removed with two lengthwise cuts that create a wedge of flesh; these species often eat better steaked.

205

SHORE MEALS: COOKING IN CAMP

Great meals don't require a full kitchen—just some know-how and fresh fish

Depending upon how much you like to "rough it," cooking fish in camp can involve anything from just a bonfire and some tinfoil to a full-size deep fryer. Modern portable camp stoves and gas grills are usually very lightweight and small, but powerful enough; a number of camp stoves are small enough for backpacking.

If there's an inherent problem to cooking with a campfire, it's regulating the heat—you can't dial a campfire to 350 degrees. This requires a few adaptations: setting the grill at the correct height over the fire, or putting tinfoil pouches close enough to the coals and estimating a cooking time based on the size of the fish.

KNACK FISHING FOR EVERYONE

Grilling Fillets and Steaks

- Don't grill over coals burning with a high flame; wait until the coals are starting to turn gray along the edges.

- Grill fish over medium-hot coals, because high heat will cook them too quickly and burn fillets or steaks.

- Coat a clean grill surface with a light oil so the fillets or steaks don't stick to the metal during cooking.

- Turn fillets and steaks over just once, halfway through grilling, because turning them more can break them apart.

Marinating Fish

- Delicate-fleshed fish, especially when fresh, don't require much more seasoning than salt and pepper.

- If marinating, put fish in the marinade for thirty to sixty minutes before cooking.

- Before using a marinade as a cooking sauce, bring it to

a near boil for five minutes first, to kill any bacteria that might have come off the fish.

- Keep thicker fillets or steaks moist while on the grill by brushing on a thin coating of light oil.

How do you know when the fish is ready? First, you should cook fish for ten minutes at 350 degrees Fahrenheit for every inch of thickness. Thus, half-inch-thick fillets take around five minutes; you can turn the fillets over halfway through as long as doing so doesn't cause the meat to break apart. Thoroughly cooked fish changes from its translucent raw appearance to a solid color (usually white), and it will be flaky when prodded with a fork. If you have a meat thermometer, the interior of a thoroughly cooked piece of fish should reach almost 150 degrees.

Fish at the Campfire

- To make a "hobo-pack," put oil, salt, pepper, and greens on two layers of tinfoil, and place a small whole fish (trout) on top.

- Add seasonings or sauces, then cover the fish with a tinfoil sheet and roll up the edges.

- Put the pack on top of another foil sheet and fold up all four sides of the sheet over the pack.

- Tuck the pack against hot campfire coals for about ten minutes, then check; or put on a grill over the heat.

Making a Campfire

- Don't use river rocks (round, water-smoothed rocks) to build a campfire site, as these can contain pockets of water that might burst in heat.

- Use dry pieces of hardwoods for campfires; avoid fresh wood and wood from conifers.

- Once the kindling is burning, add the firewood; cut the firewood pieces the same size to moderate the heat.

- Add more or less wood to different sections of the site to create areas of medium to high heat.

HOT OIL: FRYING FISH

Breaded-and-fried fish is a standard dish, but there are ways to spice it up

When you get right down to it, frying is simply cooking in fat. Butter, bacon fat, and fatback have been central to this endeavor for hundreds of years. But vegetable oils, such as safflower oil, corn oil, and peanut oil, can also be used, and at times are better both health-wise and because they can be heated to higher temperatures without smoking.

As in all fish cooking, getting the heat correct is essential, because frying at too high a temperature will burn the outside of the fish (which is usually breaded) but not cook the inside. Under-frying will deliver an oil- or fat-soggy fillet.

Most frying—whether done in a skillet, on a greased baking sheet in the oven, or in a deep-fat fryer—first calls for cover-

KNACK FISHING FOR EVERYONE

Making a Fish Batter

- Before coating fillets with crumbs or fry batter, pat them dry.

- A deep-fry batter can be a simple mix of flour, salt, dill, vinegar, baking soda, and water; beer is sometimes used instead of water and vinegar.

- Eggs and milk, which hold together breadcrumb coatings, can also thicken fry batters.

- Deep-fry batter should be the consistency of pancake mix when fillets are dipped and coated; let prepared batter stand, cool, for a while before using.

Sautéed Fish

- Fillets, steaks, and whole, dressed small fish can be sautéed, or pan-fried, using a large iron skillet.

- Heat butter or oil until it starts to bubble, then add the fish and cook until lightly browned and flaky.

- Be sure your skillet (either

iron or other material) is wide enough to evenly space all the fillets with no crowding.

- Do not cover a skillet while frying fish, as the heat of the cooking must be allowed to escape for proper frying.

ing fillets in a breadcrumb or batter coating. There are many special recipes for this, but the basic form is a mix of eggs, milk, and breadcrumbs, or a batter of water, salt, and flour, in which the fillets are drenched. Lean-fleshed fish—such as trout, largemouth bass, crappie, sea trout, and fluke—work best for frying. Oily-fleshed fish, like salmon, mackerel, and tuna, do not readily lend themselves to frying and are better grilled, broiled, or baked.

COOKING YOUR CATCH

Deep-Fried Fish

- Add one or two fillets to the hot oil at a time, then let the oil return to full temperature before adding more.

- Keep fish chilled before putting them in the oil, as the temperature difference helps seal the bread coating.

- Some catfish-frying recipes for whole fish call for a low oil temperature, around 325 degrees Fahrenheit, which means longer cooking.

- Have just enough oil in the fryer to cover all the fish that you put in the fry basket.

Oven-Fried Fish

- To "oven-fry" fillets or steaks, place breaded pieces on a greased baking pan, spacing them evenly.

- Pour a thin layer of melted butter or oil over the fillets and bake at 500 degrees Fahrenheit.

- Oven-frying isn't true frying, but the fillets don't have to be turned and are ready in twelve to fifteen minutes.

- Putting fried fillets on paper towels or strips of brown paper bag after cooking helps soak up excess oil.

FISH DINNER: COOKING VARIETIES

Getting the timing and heat just right are essential to good fish meals

Cooking fish has some basic objectives: to break down the connective tissues of the flesh; to make fish proteins more easily digestible; and to bring out the best flavors of a given kind of fish. The greatest risk in this is overcooking. Fish also can't be turned or flipped a lot during the cooking process, especially toward the end, when often a leaner-fleshed fish gets flaky and cooking has lessened the connectivity of the flesh.

Baking can work for just about any cut of fish, but broiling, which involves a direct heat source (as opposed to the more ambient heat of baking), often calls for thicker cuts. Broiled fish also comes out of the heat quite hot, and is served this

Baked Fish

- Briefly preheat the oven, and then bake fillets, steaks, or whole fish at 350 degrees Fahrenheit.

- Keep an eye on baking fish, making sure it doesn't cook too hot or quickly.

- Fish that are not baked in a coating or sauce should be basted with oil or melted butter several times during the baking process.

- Whole, dressed fish filled with bread stuffing or other kinds of stuffing require longer baking, up to forty-five minutes at 350 degrees.

Broiled and Grilled Fish

- Be sure to brush the broiler-pan ribbing or grill with oil so the fish won't stick to it while cooking.

- Fillets that still have skin attached should be broiled skin-side down.

- For thawed fish, set the broiler pan roughly 4 to 6 inches away from the heat source; grill fish 5 to 6 inches above the coals.

- Don't start grilling fish until the charcoal briquettes have become edged in white and give off steady, even heat.

210

way. Grilling is basically a form of broiling, with the heat coming from below rather than above, and calls for frequent marinating during the cooking process to keep the fish moist.

Plank-cooking fish in a baking oven is a good approach for thicker cuts or oily fish, but also works for a number of dishes that benefit from the slower cooking of planking. Poaching is cooking by simmering fish in liquid, usually some kind of prepared sauce. Steamed fish is exactly that: fish cooked using steam from heated water, a method that works well with thicker cuts of lean-fleshed fish.

MAKE IT EASY

Planked-fish recipe: 2 pounds fish steaks (lean-fleshed fish), 2 tablespoons oil (olive, peanut, or safflower), 2 tablespoons lemon juice, 1 teaspoon salt, ½ teaspoon paprika, pepper to taste. Oil a cedar-wood plank (roughly 20 by 25 inches) and preheat it for three minutes at 350 degrees Fahrenheit. Brush the plank with oil and add the fish steaks, spacing them evenly. Brush the fish with oil and sauces that work well with the flavor of the fish. Bake at 350 degrees for twenty minutes or until the flesh flakes.

Planked Fish

- Soak a cooking plank, submerged, in freshwater for about an hour prior to use (to prevent burning while cooking).

- Most any cut works on a plank—fillet, steak, or whole fish—but the cooking time takes 50 percent longer than direct heat.

- Brush the plank with oil to prevent the fish from sticking; cook fillets skin-side down if skin is intact.

- Watch the plank to be sure it doesn't ignite or drop ash into a gas grill.

Poached Fish

- Fillets and small whole, dressed fish can be poached by simmering the fish in a large saucepan.

- Place the fish in a simmering sauce deep enough to cover the sides of the fish but not the top of the fillet.

- The simmering sauce can be salted and seasoned water, milk, or broth, or white wine and water.

- Cover the saucepan and simmer the fish on medium heat until the fish turns opaque and flakes easily.

FISH & FLAVOR: GETTING IT RIGHT

The taste of various fishes differs widely, so matching seasonings and sauces is crucial

Before seasoning or coating a fish in a sauce, consider how the fish tastes. Is it light and sweet, such as walleye or crappie, which can be overpowered by strong flavors? Or is the fish strong-tasting and oily, like a mackerel or bluefish? Most fish benefit from minimal seasoning: salts, peppers, citruses, vegetables, and herbs. Little else is necessary when not us-

ing a breadcrumb coating or batter. Salts, peppers, and herbs can be lightly rubbed onto a fillet or steak, and fish can be sautéed, poached, or broiled with the vegetables and citrus fruits.

Most marinades and sauces make use of lighter flavors—milk or cream, soy sauce, white wine, sherry, and even honey.

Making a Rub

- For a Caribbean dish, soak lean-fleshed saltwater fish in water and lime juice for twenty minutes.

- Rinse the lime juice and season the fish with garlic, chive, onion, thyme, salt, and pepper, working the seasoning into the seams in the flesh.

- Dredge the fish in flour, dip it in a beaten egg, and then coat it with breadcrumbs.

- Pan-fry the fish in hot oil for five minutes on each side, turning once, until browned.

Creating Woodsmoke Flavor

- Precook ten 12-inch whole trout, covering each with a slice of bacon, baking at 200 degrees Fahrenheit for fifteen minutes.

- Layer foil over a charcoal grill; add rosemary, dill, thyme, basil, lemon slices, and oil; poke holes in the foil; and ignite the charcoal.

- Place the precooked trout on the foil, without the bacon, on top of the seasonings.

- Add damp hickory chips to grayed charcoal briquettes and cook for twenty minutes (close the grill hood if it has one).

The marinade can be reduced into a sauce served with the fish. Shallots, fennel, and mushrooms can be added to sauces as they reduce. Sliced garlic works well with several fish dishes, including salmon. Tuna is strong enough to stand up to the strength of wasabi tempered with guacamole. Black beans are flavorful but mild enough to be mashed into a sauce, with garlic, to season catfish dishes. The recipes included here are intended to address a basic issue related to lean-fleshed fish: creating enjoyable flavors that don't overpower the fish with citrus, herbs, wood flavors, and sauces.

As for picking wines, the adage that white wine goes with fish works when a white is paired with lean, delicate-fleshed fish such as sole or trout. A red wine's flavor can overpower such fish, and the chemical nature of it can react unpleasantly with that of the fish. But with stronger-flavored fish—either an oily fish, such as mackerel, or a dish with spices—lighter red wines and stronger-flavored whites can work fine. The key is that the wine should compliment but not overtake the taste of the dish. The same goes for beer.

Making a Wine Sauce

- Cover fillets of one large walleye in flour, then season with salt, pepper, and rosemary.

- Pan-fry the fillet in olive oil until the fish becomes a golden brown and starts to flake; remove the fillet.

- Deglaze the pan with white wine, adding juice of half a lemon and finely chopped parsley and dill.

- Sauté the herbs for a minute, remove the pan from the heat, swirl in 2 tablespoons of butter, and pour the sauce over the fillets.

Pairing Fish with Drink

- Fried fish pair swell with crisp, high-acid white wines such as Pinot Grigio, Sauvignon Blanc, or Muscadet.

- Fish dishes prepared with stronger spices can stand up to red Burgundy, a Pinot Noir, or a drier French Gewürztraminer.

- Pair higher-acid wines, such as a white Burgundy or red Anjou, with fatty, richer fish such as salmon or tuna.

- Medium-bodied beers (lagers) work well with lighter freshwater fish such as crappie, largemouth bass, and catfish.

213

THE IMPROVED CLINCH

This is the first really useful knot that most anglers learn to tie to lures and hooks

The improved clinch knot is a highly common knot in fishing today, and works fine with monofilament line up to 20-pound test. It's not the best knot to tie with braided lines. The breaking strength of this knot, when tied properly, is close to 95 percent.

This knot locks against the hook eye or split ring. That's all

right for some lures, but for those lures that need a lot of swimming action, or bass bugs and larger streamer flies and crab patterns, the improved clinch can prove too restricting. Connect the leader or tippet with the non-slip loop knot in such instances (see page 218–19). The improved clinch works well for very small flies tied to 6X or 7X tippets, but be

Clinch Knot: Step 1

- Use the clinch knot for attaching line and leader to swivels, sinkers, or terminal tackle (lures, flies).

- The number of times you wrap the tag end around the standing line depends on the monofilament's thickness and flexibility.

- The heavier the monofilament, the less easily the wraps will wind, stack, and cinch together as the knot is finished.

- The popularity of this knot among anglers has led to its other common name, the "fisherman's knot."

Clinch Knot: Step 2

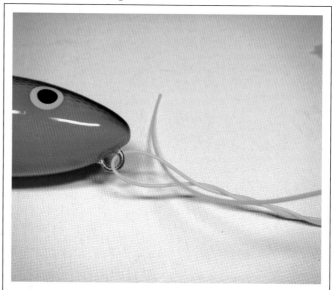

- The knot starts by passing the tag end through the split ring of the lure, or swivel ring, and bringing it back up along the standing line.

- You can also make two passes through the split ring with thinner, lighter lines.

- Very thin "microfilaments"

sometimes don't lend themselves to making this knot, as the wraps sometimes don't space evenly at tightening.

- On heavier lines, over 20-pound test, just make one pass (though the bottom loop), not two, and tighten the knot.

careful that the knot's rigidity doesn't put small dry flies at an odd angle.

Vary the number of wraps depending upon the diameter or test rating of the monofilament. For lines rated from 4- to 8-pound test, six wraps work fine. Five wraps suffice for lines rated from 8- to 16-pound test. Above 20-pound test, wrap the tag end three or four times around the standing line. Always make sure the wraps tighten evenly, without overlapping, and stack evenly and that the tag end is secured tightly against the split ring under the wraps.

The "tag end" is the forward, cut end of the line that leads the line though hook eyes or split rings. The "standing line" is the main body of the line. A "wrap" is one complete revolution of the tag end around the standing line. A "bight" is a loop formed by doubling the tag end.

Clinch Knot: Step 3

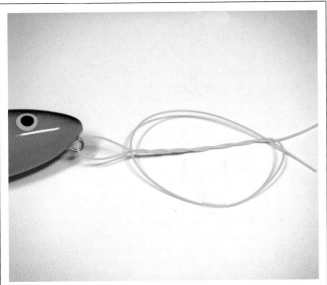

- Make four to six wraps around the standing line with the tag end; space these evenly and don't try to make them tightly.

- Pass the tag end through the loop between the split ring and the first wrap.

- Pass the tag end through

the loop just created by the descending tag end and the standing line.

- Pull and hold on to the tag end, and then pull on the standing line, pulling away from the lure.

Clinch Knot: Step 4

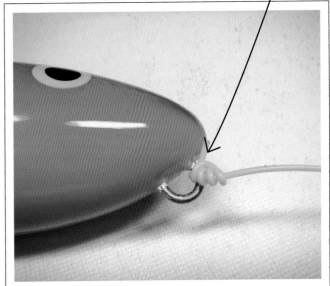

- Tighten the knot by pulling on both the standing line and tag end; the wraps should stack up and cinch.

- Pull steadily on the lure or fly and the standing line, and then pull again on the tag end; press down on the wraps to even them if need be.

- Clip the tag end very close to the knot.

- A variation for light lines is the double-improved clinch knot, which is tied using a doubled line.

THE PALOMAR KNOT

This very strong knot has the added plus of being quite easy to tie

The Palomar knot is the alternative to the improved clinch knot (see page 214–15) for securing terminal tackle, and unlike the improved clinch, this is a knot that works well with braided lines or microfilament lines. It is also especially good for tying tippets to flies that need a lot of action because the finished Palomar knot is smaller than the improved clinch and thus affects the fly's movement less.

This knot works well with monofilament up to 20-pound test, but not much beyond. The thickness and stiffness of heavier monofilament often won't allow the knot to cinch tightly and evenly against the split ring, and most likely the knot will come loose. But if you're using such heavy monofilament, when chasing big fish in fresh or salt water, you can opt for the basic clinch knot.

Palomar Knot: Step 1

- In this knot, the bight formed by the tag end creates the entire body of the knot.

- With thin or microfilament lines, you can pass the doubled loop twice through the split ring of the lure or the hook eye.

- The doubled line distributes stress throughout the knot evenly, making this a highly consistent knot when tied correctly.

- Making a bight longer than you think won't hurt—you're going to pull it tight in the end.

Palomar Knot: Step 2

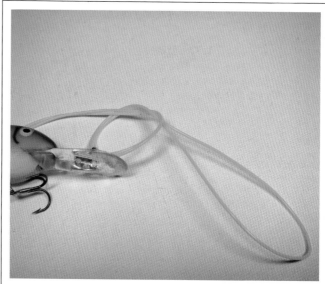

- Pass the bight through the hook eye so that you have 6 to 8 inches on the other side.

- Bend the bight back around, crossing the standing line, and make a single overhand knot with the bight and line.

- Making the knot should form a circle of doubled line in front of the lure.

- If you pass the bight through the split ring twice, forming a small interim loop, tie the overhand knot above this.

216

The basic Palomar knots provides 90 to 95 percent breaking strength with monofilament. There is also a triple Palomar knot, detailed below. This is a useful terminal knot for the increasingly popular superlines, or for tying a stronger Palomar in regular monofilament. It's just slightly more difficult than the standard Palomar, but operates on the same idea of using a doubled line to form the knot.

Palomar Knot: Step 3

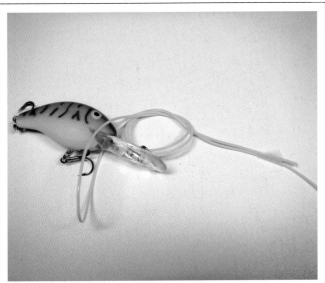

- Tie the overhand knot so that you have a significant length of bight extending away from the knot.

- Open up this length of bight so that you have a lasso-like loop.

- Pass the body of the lure or fly through this loop; the bight section needs to be long enough to accommodate the whole lure.

- Get the lure through the loop, and then just let it hang again from the line.

Palomar Knot: Step 4

- With the lure through the loop, moisten the knot, and pull on the standing line and on the bight end.

- Cinch the knot into a small fist shape and cut the bight end closely (both strands).

- In the triple Palomar variation, for light lines, pass a long bight through the split ring four times, making three small loops.

- With the bight, tie a single half knot over the standing line, over the loops, and then fit the lure through the bite and cinch.

THE NON-SLIP LOOP KNOT
Similar to the improved clinch, this knot is only slightly trickier

The non-slip loop knot creates a small, fixed loop that doesn't cinch against the hook eye or split ring, and therefore puts zero direct tension on the lure. This helps maximize the lure's darting, wiggling, or swimming action in the water. This knot is also a very good choice for weighted flies as it lets them fall freely through the water, putting full emphasis on the wavy, life-like effect of various types of fly materials and feathers.

Sometimes referred to as the "non-slip mono knot," the non-slip loop knot is something of a variation of the improved clinch knot, and can easily be tied with monofilament line from 4- to 60-pound test. This isn't a knot that works very well with braided line, though an experienced knot tier could probably make it work with a new monofilament "superline." Just as with the improved clinch knot, the barrel wraps on

Non-slip Loop Knot: Step 1

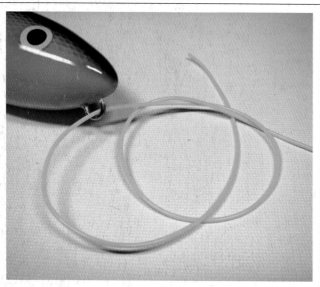

- This knot is a good way to attach sinkers, too, given that sinkers have specific performance characteristics, just like lures.

- The free play of this knot lets a sinker descend and anchor itself the way it was designed to do.

- Whenever a non-slip loop is needed, in camping or outdoors, this knot can work, depending upon the tying material.

- It can be tough to tie with very light lines, such as some of the very lightest fly tippets.

Non-slip Loop Knot: Step 2

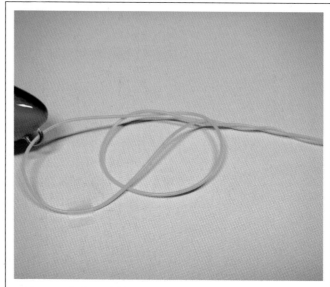

- Tie a single, loose overhand knot in the standing line, and then pass the tag end through the lure's split ring.

- How far up the standing line you make the overhand knot controls the loop size.

- Lighter lines make small loops easily; heavier lines

- are stiffer and more difficult to get into very small loops.

- Pass the tag end through the main loop of the overhand knot, but don't tighten.

218

the standing line need to stack up evenly, something that rarely works out well with braided line.

The main objective while tying this knot is to get the loop right. A loop that's a bit bigger than it should be isn't a major problem, but no loop in any test line should be wider than half the lure width, otherwise it can act as a baffle in front of the lure, affecting the performance. Loops in front of flies can be pretty small, as long as they let the fly swim freely.

Use this knot with plugs and jerkbaits, and lures that need to wobble, like certain kinds of spoons. It's also right for big flies like bass bugs and bulky streamers for trout, pike, and stripers. It has about a 70 percent breaking strength when tied correctly, but as you fish with it, check the terminal loop now and then to make sure it hasn't been nicked or abraded.

Non-slip Loop Knot: Step 3

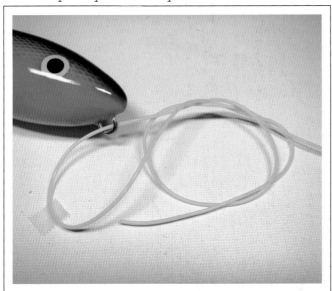

- Wrap the tag end around the standing line, just like in a clinch knot (see pages 214–15).

- The test-line strength determines how many wraps you make around the standing line above the knot.

- For monofilament including 10-pound test, make seven wraps; for 10- to 14-pound test, make five wraps.

- Four wraps will suffice for monofilament from 16- to 40-pound test. Over 40-pound test, make three wraps.

Non-slip Loop Knot: Step 4

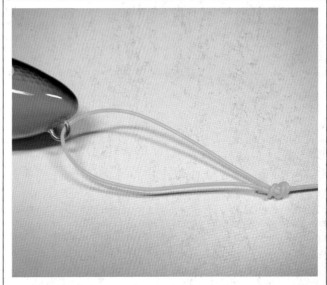

- Complete the wraps, and slip the tag end through the overhand knot, going in the opposite direction that it came through.

- Pull a short length of the tag end through the overhand knot loop toward the lure.

- Pull evenly on the standing line and the tag end to close the overhand knot and snug up the wraps, cinching the tag end.

- To finish the knot, pull on the loop and the tag end, seating the wraps tightly and securing the whole knot.

IMPROVED FIGURE-EIGHT KNOT

This is a deceptively simple knot to tie but offers a good amount of strength

The improved figure-eight knot is an effective knot for tying lures and flies directly to the leader or tippet, respectively, when you're not using some kind of heavy bite-proof section or shock tippet. When tied correctly, this knot is reasonably small. This knot is also called the Orvis knot, which came about after an angler won a contest held by the Orvis Company to see who could develop the strongest line-to-hook knot that was also simple and reliable.

In light monofilament test weights, 6 pounds and less, this knot is as strong as and possibly stronger than the Palomar and Trilene knots. And it will tie effectively with heavier monofilaments up to 16-pound test.

Improved Figure-Eight Knot: Step 1

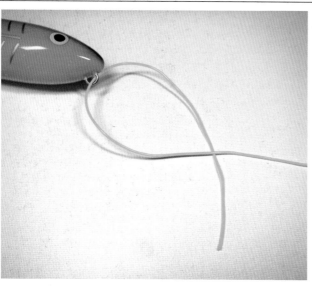

- The improved figure-eight, Palomar, and Trilene knots all compete as the strongest terminal knot for fly fishing.

- Depending upon what size tippet with which these three knots are tied, one can perform better than the other.

- The improved figure-eight is a good go-to knot for smaller flies, despite its tendency to tighten off-center.

- Light and medium braided lines can work with this knot, provided the wraps are made evenly and the knot tightened smoothly.

Improved Figure-Eight Knot: Step 2

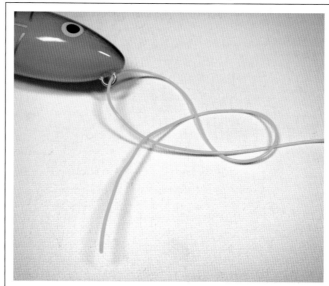

- Pull the tag end through the split ring, then bring it back and wrap it under the standing line.

- Bring the tag end over the standing line. Turn it back down toward the lure, putting the tag end into the bottom loop.

- These two turns of the tag end create a loose figure eight, with an upper and bottom loop.

- Start the knot with a tag end long enough to make the figure eight and then several wraps afterward.

If there is one issue about this knot, it's that it tends to dip at an angle when tightened in the final step. So when finished, you might need to push the knot into a proper alignment, directly with the line and hook shaft or lure body. This really isn't much of a problem unless you use this knot with small flies, as the knot might get cockeyed again as you cast. With lures and larger flies, upwards of size 4, the weight of the lure or fly will keep the knot straight.

Improved Figure-Eight Knot: Step 3

- Pull the tag end through and over the bottom loop and again double back toward the standing line.

- Wrap the tag end two or three times through the upper figure-eight loop.

- Snug the wraps a bit, and then pull on the tag end in one hand, and hold the lure in your other hand.

- Don't leave the finished knot with any small loop—cinch it closed all the way.

Improved Figure 8 Knot: Step 4

- This is an effective knot for small plugs, in-line spinners, and crankbaits, and attaching sinkers up to 1 ounce.

- Monofilaments beyond 16-pound test won't form neatly or cinch exactly with this knot.

- Some very thin superlines might slide in this knot; it won't work very well with braided lines as the wraps and knot won't come together smoothly.

- This is not an effective line-to-line connection.

FISHING KNOTS

221

THE UNI-SNELL KNOT

When snelling your own hooks, this is the easiest leader-to-hook connector

A "snell" traditionally is a knot that secures a hook with an up- or down-turned eye to a leader. This gives the line the advantage of a direct pull on the hook, thus resulting in better hook-setting, and better chances of catching fish. Its best application is for fishing with bait.

Yet a snell knot isn't one that many anglers know how to tie

because hooks have come pre-snelled in packages for years. But when tied correctly, it is strong and very practical, and definitely a knot worth knowing, especially if you need to rig specialized bait hooks intended for specific kinds of bait aimed at particular species of fish.

The uni-snell knot is a variation on the conventional snell,

Uni-Snell Knot: Step 1

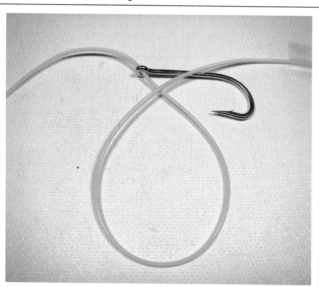

- Usually, your hook and line will match, with lighter lines paired to lighter hooks.

- Some small hooks, however, are used for larger species, and line size will be determined by the fish.

- Pull 6 to 8 inches through the hook eye and down the

shank in preparation for making the knot.

- Create a sizable loop of line below the shank and pinch it with your thumb and finger to hold it in place.

Uni-Snell Knot: Step 2

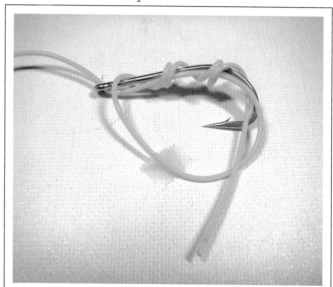

- Wrap the tag end around the shank and come through the loop, making the wraps even and snug.

- The maximum number of wraps is seven; no need to go higher, no matter how light the line might be.

- The heavier the line, the

fewer wraps you'll make through the loop.

- Pinch the wraps with your thumb and index finger as you go, keeping them snug against the shank.

and is worth knowing because it can work well with both nylon monofilament and some superlines. It also tends to be a bit quicker to tie than a regular snell, and has a very good strength-to-size ratio. The uni-snell can be tied effectively with light- and medium-diameter lines, and some heavier lines, upwards of 20-pound test. Some very heavy or stiff monofilament lines won't work with this knot—the line will simply be too stiff to wrap tightly against the hook shank. Snells are limited to applications with hooks, because they require a shank or shaft around which to wrap.

Uni-Snell Knot: Step 3

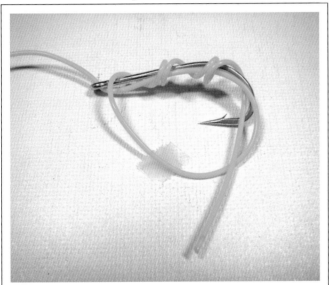

- Bring the tag end through the loop after the last wrap and pull it down past the bend.

- If you intend to keep the loop for holding bait, tighten the knot in the middle of the shank; otherwise, close the knot near the eye of the hook.

- Tighten the knot by pulling simultaneously and evenly on the tag end and standing line.

- Cut the tag end just under the last wrap; the wraps should stack evenly in a barrel shape.

Adding a Bait Loop

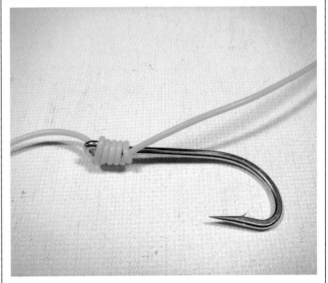

- To make a bait loop, complete the knot in the middle of the shank, and tighten so the wraps will slide along the shank.

- Push the standing line into the hook, through the eye; a loop should emerge from the bottom of the knot.

- Make this loop big enough for a salmon egg, piece of shrimp, or another smaller bait.

- Pull the loop closed snugly, around the bit and pull on the tag end to tighten the wraps against the shank.

FISHING KNOTS

MAKING THE HAYWIRE TWIST
When the fish are going to munch on your leader, reach for the steel

Single-strand wire tied in this twist is mainly used in saltwater fishing, when casting lures and baits to toothy or rough-mouthed inshore species—such as big bluefish, certain mackerels, barracuda, sharks, and sometimes striped bass—around riprap and jetties where a fish could drag the leader against rough surfaces. This isn't a terminal connection that you can use for heavy-duty, offshore big-game fishing; for

that, you'll need much heavier, coated wire and cable (multi-strand wire). But the haywire twist also affords a good bit of security when fishing for pike, muskie, and big lake trout.

This kind of wire, which is called "piano wire" in some tackle shops, is pretty easy to work with for the sake of making the haywire twist; you can't really make any kind of knot out of this material, except for a basic figure-eight knot. This twist

Haywire Twist: Step 1

Haywire Twist: Step 2

- Single-strand wire ranges from 20- to 80-pound strength.

- The strength of single-strand wire leader should match or better the strength of the standing line.

- Single-strand wire is unfinished and uncoated, while heavier-duty wire is often nylon- or titanium-coated and resistant to kinking.

- You can easily coil single-strand wire leaders in storage for later use.

- The finished leader should be from 12 to 28 inches, depending on the size of the fish and lure.

- The standard five twists and five wraps are plenty—making more will just bunch up the wire.

- The "twist" is a shallow crossover of the tag end over the standing line; the wrap is a tight 90 degrees to the standing line.

- Put loops in both ends of the leader, each a little less than the diameter of a dime.

is designed so that the wraps won't come loose under the heavy pressure that big, fast, strong fish can put on your tackle.

Single-strand wire does kink easily. Small kinks can be straightened, but a bad kink means it's time to tie the jig or plug with new wire. However, single-strand is also quite inexpensive, and resists abrasion terrifically.

FISHING KNOTS

Haywire Twist: Step 3

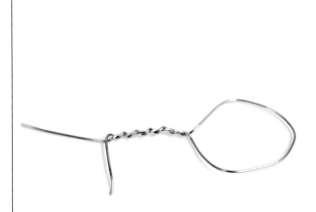

- Pass the tag end through the lure's ring eye, double back, and make four twists over the standing line (wire).

- Above the last twist make three or four wraps of the tag end around the standing line, at 90 degrees to the line.

- Bend the tag end into a crank shape, and turn it until the wire separates.

- Next, make a loop in the butt end of the wire leader (for attachment to the main line).

Haywire Twist: Step 4

- Don't cut away the tag end—this will make a sharp edge that will cut your fingers.

- Tie the tag end of the line from the reel to a snap-swivel; connect the snap to the leader butt-end loop.

- One drawback: You can't quickly change lures or flies in this setup.

- You can make a reusable haywire twist with no wraps by covering the twists with plastic tubing.

THE SURGEON'S KNOT
This is an easy way to join lighter monofilaments of similar diameter

The surgeon's knot has been around for a long time, but it's a basic design that works very well in a variety of situations. Tying it in cold weather, with stiff fingers and stiffened line, isn't too hard, for example.

This knot incorporates three tucks (putting the tag end through a loop), and this helps a good deal with thinner lines, or lines that are a bit slick. It's a very workable knot with

monofilament or fluorocarbon, and also works with braided lines, although when tied with braided line, it has to be carefully tightened to make sure the tucks bind and seat evenly. You can attach monofilament to braid with a variation of this knot, but it's a bit tough to tie, and such lines might be better linked using a small swivel.

The surgeon's knot is popular among fly fishers because it

Surgeon's Knot: Step 1

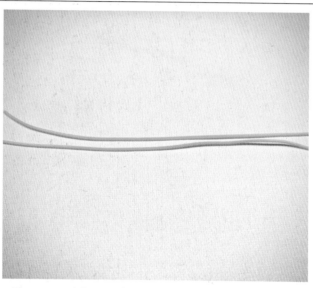

- The surgeon's knot tied correctly should be as strong or stronger than a blood knot (see page 228–29).

- This knot can't be tied using doubled lengths of line, as can be done with the blood knot and line-to-line uni-knot.

- Bring together and overlap 6 or 8 inches of each line to be joined, pinching them in place.

- These overlapping lines should be reasonably close in diameter and strength; one shouldn't be significantly thicker than the other.

Surgeon's Knot: Step 2

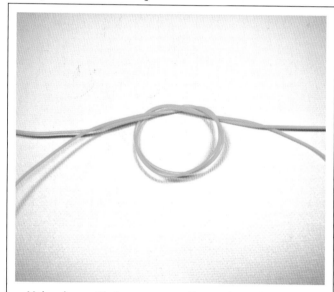

- Make a loop with the overlapping sections, pinch it, and then tuck one tag end and the entire length of the other line through.

- Bringing the entire smaller-diameter line, or the entire tippet, through the loop might be easiest.

- Repeat the tuck, again bringing one tag end and the entire length of the other line through the loop.

- Be sure to keep the loop and first tuck pinched together and don't let them slip as you make the second tuck.

serves well as a connection between the leader to the tippet. In a pinch, it can also be used to make fly leaders, connecting the various sections of a fly-line leader, but blood knots usually make that connection. Tied properly, the surgeon's knot has breaking strength in the 95 percent range. It works best with lines up to 12-pound test.

Surgeon's Knot: Step 3

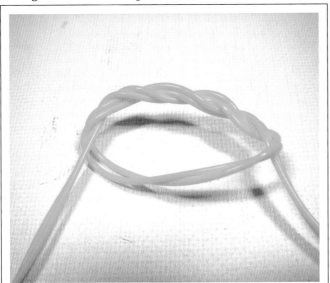

- Keep the loop evenly shaped as you go; don't let it get lopsided or you'll have to even it up as you tighten the knot.

- Make a third and final tuck with the one tag end and the other entire line or with the whole tippet.

- Don't make the tucks too tightly as you go.

- You should have what amounts to a triple overhand knot, ready to be tightened, with the loop made by both strands still slightly open.

Surgeon's Knot: Step 4

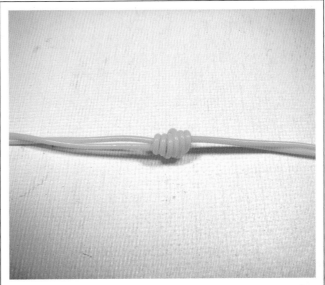

- Hold both lines and both tag ends in either hand (a tag end and a standing line in either hand) and pull evenly to tighten.

- Make sure the tucks stack into a neat bundle, and clip the tag ends very closely.

- For connecting braided line to mono this way, first overlap and twist both sections of line around each other twenty times.

- Wet the lines and tie, making four tucks instead of three.

FISHING KNOTS

LOW PROFILE: THE BLOOD KNOT
Creating this neat stack of barrel wraps is easier than it seems

The blood knot supposedly got its name from its usage in the British Navy as a knot tied in the strands of a whip used for flogging disobedient sailors. It has long since come into very practical, peaceable usage.

Fly fishers frequently use blood knots to construct tapered leaders, and to link descending sections of monofilament from the butt section to the tippet. The ensuing series of

blood knots create a leader that unfurls naturally, without kinking or being misshaped (assuming the knots were tied correctly). Blood knots are also useful in constructing rigs or connecting leaders to the main line.

This knot is best used for tying together strands of monofilament that are the same or close in diameter (hence its use in creating a leader with a tapering diameter). The blood

Blood Knot: Step 1

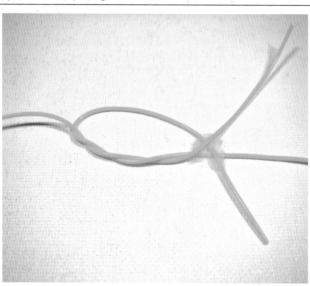

- Overlap 5 to 6 inches of the two lines to get the knot started.

- Too much overlapping line will be clumsy.

- You'll need one hand to hold the lines together and the other hand to make the wraps with the tag end.

- Don't twirl together the tag end and the line around which you're wrapping it— that will create unwanted twists. Wrap the first tag end in even turns around the other line without twisting that standing line.

Blood Knot: Step 2

- With 2- to 12-pound-test line, make five wraps with each tag end around each standing line.

- With line up to 20-pound test, make three or four wraps.

- With the first set of wraps completed, bring the

tag end back and down between the two lines, pinching it in place.

- Wrap the other tag end around the opposite standing line, and bring tag end through the center loop in the opposite direction of the first tag end.

knot isn't a knot that works well with most braided lines, or to join monofilament to braided line. Some of the slick, coated superbraids—lines that might not yet have come on the market at the time of the writing of this book—might take a blood knot fine, in the hands of a good knot tier. A better knot for attaching braid to braid is the double-uni knot (see pages 230–31).

Blood Knot: Step 3

- Pull on both tag ends—one going up, one going down—to bring the wraps together and seat them snugly.

- Use each hand to hold each standing line, using the fingers of each hand to pull on the tag ends.

- With the wraps seated, pull smoothly on the standing lines to close and cinch the knot completely.

- You should have an even, barrel-shaped knot with the tag ends above and below; trim the tag ends even with the wraps.

Adding a Dropper Fly

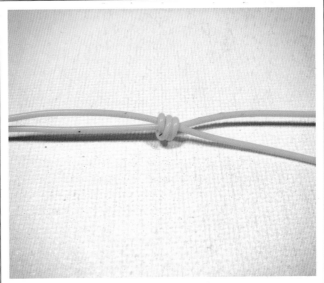

- For fly fishing, you can extend a length of line from a blood knot for tying on a second, or "dropper," fly close to the bottom of the leader.

- Employ up to 12 inches of one line instead of the usual 5 or 6 inches of overlapping line in Step 1.

- As you finish the wraps, draw this extra-long tag-end length through the center loop.

- When you close the knot, this dropper extension will come directly from the knot center.

THE DOUBLE UNI-KNOT

This alternative to the blood knot has a slightly wider application

The double, or "line-to-line," uni-knot is also a very good knot for joining lines together. It's a pretty simple incorporation of two uni ("universal") knots tied on either standing line. Some anglers find this knot easier and faster to tie than the blood knot. The double uni-knot has equivalent strength to the blood knot, and it works quite well for joining monofilament lines, and mono to braided lines. In fact, it's a better go-to knot for this application than the blood knot, either for connecting mono to braid, or braid to braid. Making this knot with braided line calls for three wraps at the most.

The circumstances surrounding the connection of monofilament to braided line often involve connecting a main (braided) line to a monofilament leader. While this can be made using a barrel swivel as the connector of the leader

Double Uni-Knot: Step 1

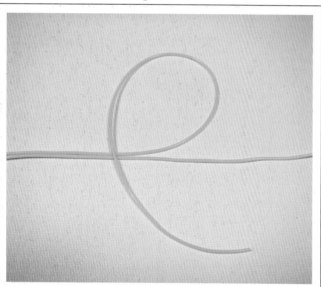

- Overlap 6 to 8 inches of the two lines to be joined, and pinch them in the middle.

- Take one tag end and make a small loop, laying this loop below the adjacent standing line.

- The lower half of the loop as it lies along the standing line forms a section of doubled line.

- Wrap the tag end around this double-strand section, making five wraps and pulling the tag end out the top of the loop.

Double Uni-Knot: Step 2

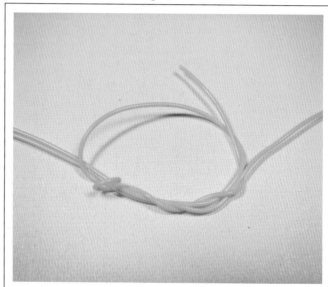

- Still pinching together the two overlapped lines, pull the tag end out from the loop, closing the wraps.

- Cinch the tag-end wraps snugly around the standing line, forming an even barrel of wraps similar to half a completed blood knot.

- Don't tighten the wraps so much that they bend or kink the standing line.

- The standing line should be able to slide through the wraps if pulled; don't cut the tag end yet.

230

and line, a well-tied double uni-knot might be better when using lighter lines, or when casting smaller lures.

One particular advantage of tying the double uni-knot over tying the blood knot is that you secure each set of wraps as you make it, rather than having a knot that is a series of loose wraps that has to be held together and not let unravel, as you get to the moment when you tighten everything. Once you've tied half of the double uni, you can leave it alone to make the other half.

Moistening this knot is important because of the way each half comes together. The cinched barrel of wraps must be able to slide along the standing line so each barrel meets, forming a single unit. If tied correctly, the knot shouldn't slip while fishing or fighting a fish. Many anglers have noted that the double uni-knot has a slimmer profile than the blood knot.

Double Uni-Knot: Step 3

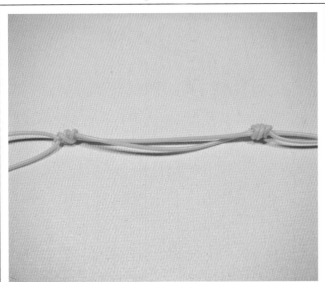

- Repeat this wrapping-the-loop process with the other tag end.

- Make the same number of wraps if joining lines of the same diameter.

- You don't need to pinch the lines together as you make the second knot, but have enough length of tag end that you don't pull that line through the first knot.

- When completed, the two knots (barrel wraps) should be about the same size and roughly an inch apart.

Double Uni-Knot: Step 4

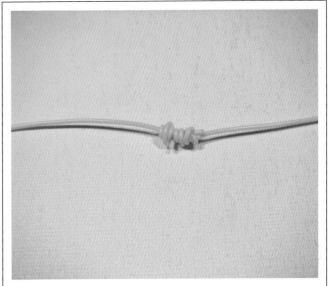

- After wetting the whole assembly, pull the two standing lines in opposite directions, sliding the knots together.

- Seat the knots snugly against each other and tug on the tag ends to cinch the wraps completely, then cut the tag ends.

- Five wraps of the tag end work for lines up to 12-pound test; with lines 12- to 20-pound test, make four wraps.

- If joining lines of differing diameters, make one fewer wrap with the tag end of the heavier line.

TIGHT GRIP: THE TUBE KNOT

Once you know the blood knot and double uni-knot, the nail knot will be easy

Most people shake their heads when they first see the tube knot, or nail knot, because they see a bunch of coils and some kind of implement—a nail, drinking straw, or stick—alongside the knot, and they're often confused about the tying procedure. But actually, it's easy to tie and is a great knot to know, especially for fly fishers who need a strong knot with

which to attach a leader butt end to the end of the main fly line, and to attach backing to the end of the fly line.

The tube knot is useful in affixing a smaller-diameter line to a larger-diameter line, especially a smaller line that can really cinch tightly against the larger line. Monofilament, backing line, and braided line affixed to a fly line all do just that: cinch

KNACK FISHING FOR EVERYONE

Tube Knot: Step 1

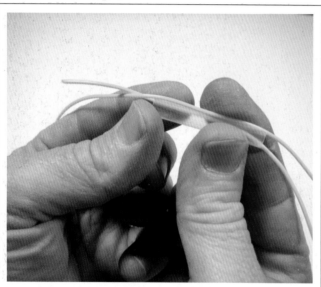

- Overlap the thin and thick lines, with the thinner line coming from the left (for right-handers).

- Place the section of tube against both lines, and pinch the thin and thick lines and the tube together with your left hand.

- Wrap the tag end of the thin line around both lines and the tube, moving from right to left.

- Create a series of five or six wraps around both lines and the tube, holding them in place with your left fingers.

Tube Knot: Step 2

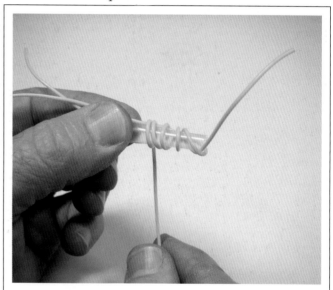

- After the final wrap, insert the tag end of the thin line into the tube and bring it out the other open end.

- Pinch the wraps lightly with your left thumb and forefinger, and with your right hand slip the tube out from under your left fingers and the wraps.

- Pull the tube completely off the thin line.

- Hold the assembly of wraps lightly in your fingers, and pull steadily on the tag end of the thin line.

really tightly. You can tie this knot with a section of a plastic drinking straw, the body of a ballpoint pen, a knitting needle, or a nail—anything that helps make a tunnel of wrapped line—but a hollow cylinder makes for the easiest approach.

This knot in its doubled form (two tube knots back to back, like the double uni-knot—see pages 228–31) can work with monofilament; a single nail knot between strands of monofilament can slide and give way. When the wraps close evenly, this knot can tightly secure a braided line to another braided line.

Tube Knot: Step 3

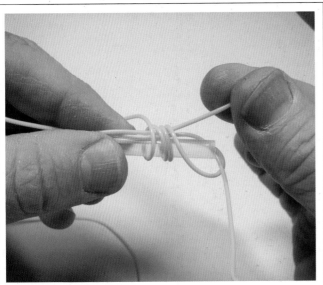

- Pulling the tag end will cinch the wraps around the two lines; do this slowly, watching to be sure each wrap tightens evenly.

- Pull on the main section of thin line and the tag end, and then pull on the thin line and thick line simultaneously.

- The wraps should sit in a solid, fist-shaped, even-sided knot with the thin line extending without any kinks out the bottom.

- Trim the tag ends close enough to the knot that they don't stick out.

Double Tube Knot

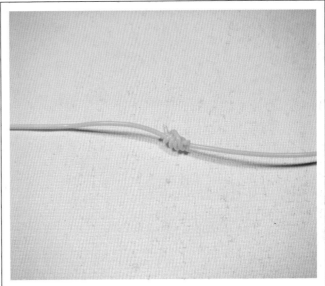

- A double tube knot can be used to secure two lines of the same or similar diameter.

- Overlap a significant length of the two lines, and then tie but don't tighten one tube knot with one tag end.

- Tie a second tube knot with the other tag end on the other standing line, and don't tighten it.

- Pull the standing lines to unite the knots, and then pull on the tag ends and standing lines to cinch them completely.

FISHING KNOTS

EASY LOOP: THE SPIDER HITCH

This knot makes a good connection point for lighter, freshwater leaders

A "hitch" is a knot that forms a loop or noose in a line for the sake of attaching a second line or connecting the line to an object. That's exactly what this knot is for—creating a loop to which you can secure a main line to a leader, or a doubled leader section in a hook rig. Properly tied, it should have upwards of 90 percent breaking strength, but it isn't a good loop

knot for really heavy big-game applications in salt water. It is, however, a very effective knot when working with heavier line, over 20-pound test, and can be tied easily enough with braided line. It's also a very useful knot for fly fishers or anyone using light leaders and lines in freshwater.

Sometimes called the "five-times around" knot, the name

Spider Hitch: Step 1

- Take a length of line a bit longer than the leader you need (to compensate for the line used in the knot), and make a bight in one end.

- If using a tapered section of monofilament, make the bight in the thicker end.

- Pinch the doubled line together with the fingers of one hand, and make the knot with your free hand.

- Overlap the bight to make a small loop, not much wider than a quarter (coin).

Spider Hitch: Step 2

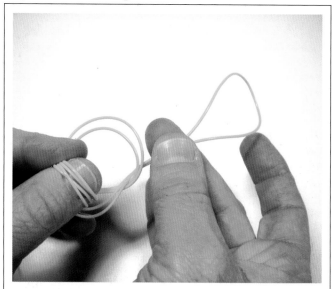

- Pinch the small loop at its base, between your thumb and forefinger, holding it upright.

- Take the length of the bight and wrap it five times evenly but not tightly across your thumbnail (going between your thumb and forefinger).

- Stack each wrap on top of the previous one, with the first wrap across the base of your thumbnail.

- After the fifth wrap, tuck the length of bight through the small loop of doubled line.

"Spider" does not make a reference to web-tying by a spider, but is a proper nickname, deriving from a man named Ed "Spider" Andresen, a fishing writer and magazine editor. In the early 1960s, or so the story goes, Andresen learned this knot from a Cuban fishing guide. He then showed the knot to a line-making company, and his name became attached to it. Originally intended for saltwater use, the knot's applicability surpassed that purpose.

Spider Hitch: Step 3

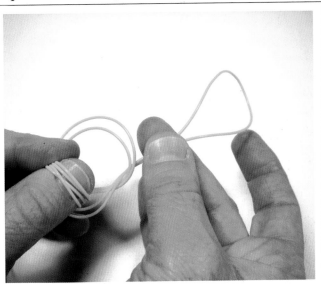

- Pull the bight through the small loop and begin pulling the top wrap on your thumb.

- Unwind the wraps off your thumb evenly, one by one, pulling their slack through the loop.

- Steadily draw the last wrap through the loop and then snug the knot by pulling on the bight and tag end.

- Hold the tag end and standing line in one hand and the bight in the other, and pull in opposite directions to cinch the knot.

Spider Hitch: Step 4

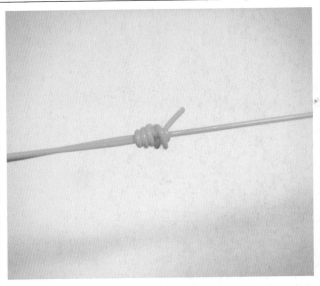

- Cut the tag end close to the knot, and you'll have a leader section with a looped end.

- An effective heavy-duty bait rig, especially for big catfish, uses the Spider hitch to create a double snell.

- Snell the bight end to a circle or J-hook, giving you a double snell and a section of double leader above it to the knot.

- Put a big bead against the hitch knot, and then add a sliding egg sinker on top of this.

FISHING KNOTS

RESOURCE DIRECTORY

Fishing Resources: Print and Web Sites

Take a look at the list of books and Web sites here for up-to-date angling techniques for various gamefish species, tackle selection, stories and narrative explanations of the why's of fishing, and forums and real-time fishing reports. This is by no means an exhaustive list, but can serve as a starting point, with a good mix of the practical and the entertaining.

How-to Books

1. Ristori, Al. *The Complete Book of Surf Fishing*. Skyhorse Publishing, 2008.
Everything you need to know to get started in the surf, with species-specific strategies.

2. Dance, Bill. *IGFA's 101 Freshwater Fishing Tips & Tricks*. Skyhorse Publishing, 2007.
A practical how-to guide from one of the all-time American professionals, endorsed by the International Game Fish Association.

3. Wulff, Joan. *Joan Wulff's Fly Casting Accuracy.* The Lyons Press, 1997.
Essential casting instruction from one of the most talented fly casters in the history of the sport in North America.

4. Talleur, Dick; Lord, Macauley; Whitlock, Dave. *L.L. Bean Fly-Tying Handbook, Revised and Updated*. The Lyons Press, 2006.
An easy-to-follow introduction to tying highly useful flies, written by one of the masters of the craft.

5. Rosenbauer, Tom. *The Orvis Fly Fishing Guide, Revised and Updated).* The Lyons Press, 2007.
The bible of fly-fishing how-to books, updated with excellent color illustrations and photos.

6. Mitchell, Rickey Noel. *The Orvis Guide to Personal Fishing Craft.* The Lyons Press, 2005.
Provides thorough instruction in evaluating, selecting, and fishing from inflatables, pontoon boats, kayaks, canoes, and johnboats.

7. Kreh, Lefty and Sosin, Mark. *Practical Fishing Knots*. The Lyons Press, 1991
Highly illustrated, step-by-step instructions for all the knots the angler should know.

8. **Pro Tactics** Series, The Lyons Press (various authors)
Species-specific how-to books on walleye (Mark Martin), muskie (Jack Burns and Rob Kimm), panfish (Jason Durham), bass (Karen Savik), pike (Jack Penny), catfish (Keith Sutton), ice fishing (Jason Durham), and steelhead and salmon (W. H. Gross); with other books in the series on tackle repair, cooking fish, and outfitting boats.

9. Martin, Roland. *Roland Martin's 101 Bass-Catching Secrets*. Skyhorse Publishing, 2008.
Roland Martin's bass-fishing teachings are the gold standard, and his instruction here covers a wide range of angling situations.

10. Pollizotto, Martin. *Saltwater Fishing Made Easy.* International Marine/Ragged Mountain Press, 2006.

A very practical guide to the overall basics o catching a number of saltwater species in shore and offshore.

11. Kreh, Lefty. *Solving Fly-Casting Problems* The Lyons Press, 2000.
An indispensable guide from one of the greatest thinkers on fly-casting techniques.

12. Combs, Trey. *Steelhead Fly Fishing*. The Lyons Press, 1999.
This is the touchstone title on one of the most obsessive pursuits in all of American fishing: trying to take a steelhead on a fly.

13. van Vliet, John. *Trout: The Complete Guide to Catching Trout with Flies, Artificial Lures, and Live Bait* (Revised Edition). Creative Publishing International, 2008.
A brand-new, highly up-to-date guide to al the essential methods for catching trout.

Narrative and Storytelling Books

1. Lyons, Nick. *A Flyfisher's World*. Atlantic Monthly Press, 1998.
A deeply insightful, even spiritual, examination of the nature of fly fishing and why people fish at all.

2. Babb, James. *Fly-Fishin' Fool*. The Lyons Press, 1995.
With thirty-one humorous essays covering everything fly fishing, this is a must-have title from one of the greatest wits of American angling

3. Leeson, Ted. *The Habit of Rivers*. The Lyons Press, 2006
A collection of essays and stories about fly fishing Western rivers and streams from an award-winning writer.

4. Kaminsky, Peter. *The Moon Pulled Up an Acre of Bass*. Hyperion, 2002.
An enjoyable, stirring memoir of a season of saltwater fly fishing in one of the greatest places to cast a line: Montauk, New York.

5. DiBenedetto, David. *On the Run*. Harper Paperbacks, 2004.
Entertaining, true-life stories about the dedicated anglers who chase striped bass down the Atlantic coast, from New England to North Carolina.

6. Burke, Monte. *Sowbelly: The Obsessive Quest for the World-Record Largemouth Bass*. Plume, 2006.
This is the complete chronicle of the pursuit of the Holy Grail of American freshwater fishing.

Reference and Fish Identification Books

1. McClane, A. J. *McClane's Standard Fishing Encyclopedia*. Holt, Rinehart and Winston, 1972.
While not as up-to-date as other books listed here, this book, the original twentieth-century angling reference, is a must-have.

2. Ford, Flick. *Fish: 77 Great Fish of North America*. The Greenwich Workshop Press, 2006.

One of the best collections of fish art to come along in a while, from a lifelong angler and fish-painter.

3. Shultz, Ken. *Ken Schultz's Field Guide to Freshwater Fish* and *Ken Schultz's Field Guide to Saltwater Fish*. Wiley, 2003. *Ken Schultz's Fishing Encyclopedia.* IDG Books, 2000
Nicely illustrated, easy-to-use handbooks for identifying all major gamefish species and a great encyclopedia for the new century.

4. Behnke, Robert. *Trout and Salmon of North America*. Free Press, 2002.
Worth having for the illustrations alone, this book provides succinct biological information from one of the country's best authorities on trout and salmon.

5. Ross, John. *Trout Unlimited's Guide to America's 100 Best Trout Streams*. The Lyons Press, 2005.
A roster of essential and "blue-ribbon" streams for trout fishing, which can be supplemented with real-time Internet research.

6. Prosek, James. *Trout of the World*. Harry N. Abrams, 2003.
One of the most interesting books in recent times, with beautiful illustrations and detailed text that chronicle numerous trout unknown to most Western anglers.

Cooking and Fish Preparation

1. Watson, Lucia. *Cooking Freshwater Fish*. In-Fisherman, 2006.

Down-home recipes from the chef and owner of the famous Lucia's restaurant of Minneapolis.

2. Finamore, Roy and Mooen, Rick. *Fish Without a Doubt: The Cook's Essential Companion*. Houghton Mifflin, 2008.
For the cook with some advanced skills interested in creating flavorful fish dishes that work for freshwater and saltwater species.

Web Sites

www.americanangler.com
A good site for fly-fishing how-to from a premier angling magazine.

www.animatedknots.com
Look here for tying instructions that show the processes for a number of fishing knots.

www.asafishing.org/asa
Site of the sportfishing industry's trade group, full of angler- and consumer-oriented information.

www.asf.ca
Site of the Atlantic Salmon Federation, dedicated to Atlantic salmon angling and conservation.

www.carpanglersgroup.com
Written by and for carp anglers, with a lot of insight from British carp anglers who prize the species.

www.crappie.com
A good site for state-by-state crappie-fishing forums and discussion threads.

www.fedflyfishers.org
The Federation of Fly Fishers site, full of information for would-be members, conservation updates, and tips on gear.

www.fieldandstream.com
Jam-packed with useful online articles and enjoyable reader photos.

www.fishingclub.com
The site of North American Fisherman, with lots of gear and technique information.

www.floridasportsman.com
Videos and online articles from the magazine all about Florida saltwater fishing.

www.flyfisherman.com
Lots of regional reports, gear information, and technical how-to from the online version of the longest-running fly-fishing magazine.

www.flytyer.com
The place to go if you're tying your own flies for techniques, information on materials, and new patterns.

www.freshwater-fishing.org
The site of the National Fresh Water Fishing Hall of Fame and Museum.

http://grayssportingjournal.com
A good introduction to one of the more literary and art-driven outdoors magazines in America.

www.igfa.org
The site of the International Game Fish Association, the main record-keeping body of freshwater and saltwater fishing worldwide.

www.in-fisherman.com
A lot of online how-to content and videos connected to the extensive line of *In Fisherman* magazines.

www.fedflyfishers.org
The site of the Federation of Fly Fishers, a group dedicated to conservation and promoting the sport.

www.mainesalmonrivers.org
Information about efforts to restore Atlantic salmon in Maine.

www.midcurrent.com
A very good all-around online resource about fly-fishing tackle, techniques, news, and articles.

www.outdoorlife.com
An online cornucopia of how-to, gear tips, great photos, and columns from one of America's oldest outdoor magazines.

www.procats.com
A highly useful resource for catfishers pursuing big whiskers, with an active forum.

www.saltwatersportsman.com
A good source of fishing conditions along various coastlines and online gear reviews.

http://sports.espn.go.com/outdoors/bassmaster/index
This is the place to go to follow the BASS competition results for all your favorite pro anglers.

www.stripers247.com
The site for all things related to striped bass in fresh and salt water.

www.thisisfly.com
A slick, fun, irreverent online fly-fishing magazine.

www.troutnut.com
An excellent species-by-species guide for identifying aquatic insects.

www.tu.org
The site of Trout Unlimited, a major coldwater (trout and salmon) conservation group that also offers a lot of expertise and information to fly fishers.

http://water.usgs.gov
Get real-time stream-flow conditions from the U.S. Geological Survey.

www.walleyehunter.com
A useful site for current walleye fishing conditions for the upper Midwest.

www.westcoastangler.com
An all-around source for gear info, fishing reports, techniques, and tackle shopping for West Coast saltwater fishing.

www.wildsalmon.org
Site for a network of efforts to promote and monitor salmon restoration efforts in western American rivers.

www.wildsalmoncenter.org
Site for the Wild Salmon Center, which seeks to identify, understand, and protect the best wild salmon ecosystems of the Pacific Rim.

PHOTO CREDITS

INDEX

INDEX